Contemporary
Field Work Practices in
Rehabilitation

Publication Number 833

AMERICAN LECTURE SERIES®

A Publication in

The BANNERSTONE DIVISION *of*

AMERICAN LECTURES IN SOCIAL AND REHABILITATION PSYCHOLOGY

Consulting Editors

JOHN G. CULL, Ph.D.

Director, Regional Counselor Training Program

Department of Rehabilitation Counseling

Virginia Commonwealth University

Fishersville, Virginia

and

RICHARD E. HARDY, Ed.D.

Chairman, Department of Rehabilitation Counseling

Virginia Commonwealth University

Richmond, Virginia

The following books have appeared thus far in this Series: Vocational Rehabilitation: Profession and Process—John G. Cull, Jr. and Richard E. Hardy

The American Lecture Series in Social and Rehabilitation Psychology offers books which are concerned with man's role in his milieu. Emphasis is placed on how this role can be made more effective in a time of social conflict and a deteriorating physical environment. The books are oriented toward descriptions of what future roles should be and are not concerned exclusively with the delineation and definition of contemporary behavior. Contributors are concerned to a considerable extent with prediction through the use of a functional view of man as opposed to a descriptive anatomical point of view.

Books in this series are written mainly for the professional practitioner; however, academicians will find them of considerable value in both graduate and undergraduate courses in the helping services.

Contemporary Field Work Practices in Rehabilitation

By

JOHN G. CULL, JR., Ph.D.

*Director, Regional Counselor Training Program
Department of Rehabilitation Counseling
Virginia Commonwealth University
Fishersville, Virginia*

and

CRAIG R. COLVIN, M.Ed.

*Assistant Professor, Regional Counselor Training Program
Department of Rehabilitation Counseling
Virginia Commonwealth University
Fishersville, Virginia*

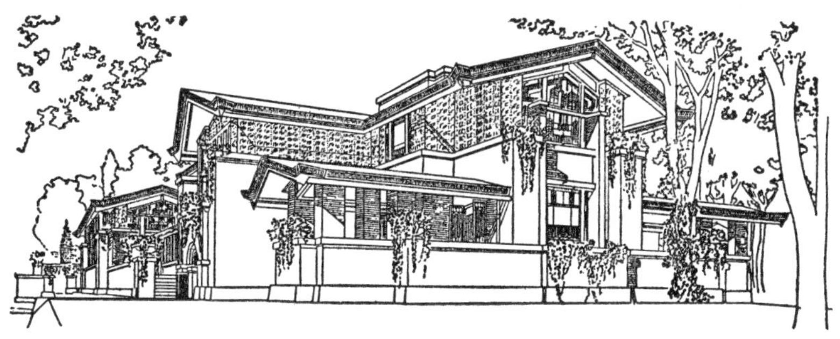

CHARLES C THOMAS • PUBLISHER
Springfield • Illinois • U.S.A.

Published and Distributed Throughout the World by
CHARLES C THOMAS • PUBLISHER
BANNERSTONE HOUSE
301-327 East Lawrence Avenue, Springfield, Illinois, U.S.A.
NATCHEZ PLANTATION HOUSE
735 North Atlantic Boulevard, Fort Lauderdale, Florida, U.S.A.

ISBN 0-398-02265-8

Library of Congress Catalog Card Number: 71-175070

Printed in the United States of America
EE-11

This book is dedicated to our children

David, Dana, and Rebecca

and

Ashley and Cristin

EDITORS' FOREWORD

At long last there is an answer to the often asked question: "How do we continue to train professional rehabilitation employees once they have left university and short-term training programs?" The authors have made a significant contribution to the professional literature in rehabilitation through their book, *Contemporary Field Work Practices in Rehabilitation*. The book fits well into the "Social and Rehabilitation Psychology Lecture Series," published by Charles C Thomas, in that it is a highly practical, realistic, and practitioner-oriented volume.

This book should be of great value to rehabilitation supervisors and in-service training officers nationwide as they attempt to help counselors and other rehabilitation personnel improve their work skills in the field. Also, this text should be used in university internship programs for rehabilitation counseling students, as well as employed counselors in in-service training projects and programs, and for other professionals normally considered "team members" within the helping professions.

Of particular value are the twenty-seven field work exercises, which cover various topics, including cooperative agency agreements, the initial interview, correctional rehabilitation, the selection of a vocation, the involvement of rehabilitation workers and a comprehensive rehabilitation facility, the development of a work sample, and many others. An extensive appendix section has been developed including such items as evaluation forms that supervisors may utilize in assessing counselor growth, a checksheet regarding caseload management, and a counselor's code of ethics.

It is obvious that this book is an outgrowth of years of work experience within the field of rehabilitation. The authors are sensitive to training needs, and the result of their work should greatly enhance the effectiveness of rehabilitation and social service workers in various rehabilitation disciplines for years to come.

JOHN G. CULL
RICHARD E. HARDY
Consulting Editors

PREFACE

A field work text is a necessity in order to provide the inexperienced vocational rehabilitation worker and university intern an up-to-date approach to his newly chosen profession. This book has been written to serve all state and private agencies utilizing the numerous university rehabilitation counseling internship programs as well as the ongoing in-service training programs offered by vocational rehabilitation. This publication should become a worthwhile teaching device for those actively involved in this dynamic and challenging profession throughout the country.

Contemporary Field Work Practices in Rehabilitation has been developed in such a manner that the district office supervisor or training coordinator as well as the university faculty member can adapt the assignments to the training requirements of his newly employed staff or the university intern without depending necessarily upon preceding academic work. After examining the text, one will see it sets guidelines for the planning, selection, assignment, training, and supervision of the worker in a field experience program; it deals with important management techniques and common problems related to coordination; it is an overall plan of what shall be covered and to whom the work shall be directed; and there is provision for flexibility despite the apparent structure and content.

Though some may feel this is an academic exercise solely for the benefit of a university, it must be pointed out that much effort has gone into making this publication meaningful to the counselor carrying a caseload and at the same time fulfilling the needs of the graduate student working on his internship with public and private vocational rehabilitation agencies. There has been concerted effort to achieve a balance of theoretical implications and practical work. As rehabilitation educators, we realize the counselor has a job to perform for the agency in addition to his educational obligations. The university also realizes newly employed rehabilitation workers come to the agency with various educational backgrounds and work experiences. Even so, there needs to be a vehicle by which these counselors will begin to function on a level with one another as quickly as practicable. This field work experience can be such a vehicle if it is approached with a conscientious, professional attitude.

The counselor and intern as "professionals" also have been taken into consideration in the development of this publication. The physician, dentist, lawyer, or engineer has had extensive academic study as well as practical experience directly related to his chosen vocation when he begins to practice in his profession. Yet when the neophyte vocational rehabilitation worker or university intern becomes an employee of the agency, he usually has had limited professional exposure directly related to his newly chosen profession. The first day on the job he is seen as a "professional" rehabilitation worker by his clients and by others traditionally regarded as members of the rehabilitation team. Therefore, it is essential that in a short period of time the trainee be given relevant assignments which, in turn, become the tools by which he can gain a better understanding of human behavior, individual client needs, case recording techniques and a multitude of other factors comprising the total rehabilitation process.

The purpose of this text is to develop a professional approach to rehabilitation, not a method whereby one receives a technician's approach. The university's objective, as well as the state vocational rehabilitation agency's objective, is to train professionals, not technicians.

Hopefully, the book will provide impetus for the counselor trainee and the intern to investigate the *total* rehabilitation process. In doing so, there must be a clear understanding that the completion of these exercises does not insure success on the job; completion will provide him with an awareness or an approach to rehabilitation which has been proven to be effective with outstanding counselors across the country. Consistent with the goals of both the university, state, and private agencies is the desire to furnish the individual necessary tools with which to become an outstanding counselor capable of self-motivation rather than an average or mediocre counselor requiring close supervision and instruction by his local supervisor.

The major charge as outlined in the Joint Liaison Committee's report *Guidelines for Supervised Clinical Practice* (1963) has been incorporated in this text.

The authors wish to thank the many who contributed to this book. Appreciation is extended to the other faculty members in the Department of Rehabilitation Counseling of Virginia Commonwealth University for their suggestions. Gratitude is expressed to the directors of university and college rehabilitation counselor training programs for sending us copies of their field work manuals for review along with helpful suggestions.

We also wish to express our gratitude to the following who have training responsibilities for their contributions and support: Wendell Taylor (Kentucky), Larry Freeman (West Virginia), Paul Bassett and Andrew McGlamery (Virginia), John Cobun (Maryland), and Joe Morrow and J. W. Smith (North Carolina). Probably the greatest thanks should be given to the supervisors throughout the Middle Atlantic and Southeast States who contributed their time and energy and especially to the counselors who, as graduate students in the Regional Counselor Training Program in Fishersville, Virginia, have participated in the development of this book.

Particular thanks must go to Marianne Cashatt, Marc Cooper, Garnet Hall, Leonard Miller, and Larry Kriloff for their contributions of actual work samples; this was accomplished in addition to their already overtaxed workload.

Lastly, Emmett Molloy deserves recognition for the initial efforts afforded this text; his ideas finally have reached fruition.

John Cull
Craig Colvin

INTRODUCTION

The supervised field work experience is a planned educational program to supplement the knowledge and skills acquired in the academic setting. It is a method of training characterized by "doing" under the guidance and supervision of rehabilitation specialists. One of the primary goals of this book is to integrate academic course work and field work. While students are attending training programs, they are exposed to theoretical principles which have practical applications. When they assume responsibilities in the field, these counselors must be able to put theoretical principles into practice.

The exercises contained herein and the guidance the trainee receives from his supervisor should enable him to work more effectively with clients. The ultimate goal of such a program as described in this book is the trainee's total involvement over the entire spectrum of the rehabilitation process. After working in this type of situation, the trainee should develop greater understanding of this process and, in turn, be able to serve clients in his area with increased professionalism.

J.C.
C.C.

CONTENTS

FIELD WORK EXERCISES

APPENDICES

Contemporary
Field Work Practices in
Rehabilitation

PURPOSE AND OBJECTIVES OF
SUPERVISED FIELD WORK

The purpose of supervised field work is to introduce the trainee to those germane activities which are fundamental to the *outstanding* vocational rehabilitation counselor's routine professional responsibilities. In addition, this book will establish guidelines, requirements, and responsibilities for the agency training supervisor, training coordinator, and faculty supervisor.

Field work emphasizes the importance of (1) working with actual cases and (2) training that is educational and, by agency standards, productive. Meaningful activity in which knowledgeable counselors normally are involved should become an integral part of the field training process. Ideally, caseloads should be assigned which are appropriate for a counselor trainee, and there should be case selection to promote better understanding of services, disabilities, and concepts. Realistically, this often is impossible since the counselor usually assumes some responsibility for a caseload immediately upon employment. Therefore, it is necessary for the counselor trainee and his supervisor to integrate training and caseload management as well as possible so that professional growth and development will occur along with production. These exercises ideally should follow a period of professional training in which the counselor trainee has had an opportunity to work closely with others in an academic setting; yet they have been designed so that previous educational involvement in rehabilitation is not mandatory.

In order for the counselor trainee to complete the field work assignments, there should be opportunity for involvement and participation in vocational diagnosis, counseling, caseload management, and job placement. There should be regularly scheduled weekly conferences between the counselor trainee and his training coordinator in which a thorough analysis is made of field work underway or completed. In those instances where a faculty supervisor is involved in field work practices, he should make scheduled on-site visits and participate in training and supervision of the counselor trainee.

The underlying rationale for the advocacy of supervised field work is that shared responsibility exists among the members of the rehabilitation training team although each has different but complimentary roles in relation to the counselor trainee. Through a united team effort the trainee is supported in becoming a disciplined professional worker.

The following major field work objectives have been formulated, substantiating the overall rationale for the field work experience.

1. Guide the trainee toward the development of general professional skills and technical knowledge relating to the total rehabilitation process.

2. Supplement the knowledge and skills gained by the trainee in the academic phase of training.

3. Provide an opportunity for the trainee to make practical application of classroom instruction.

4. Provide the new rehabilitation worker an opportunity to develop confidence in his ability to apply new techniques in various counseling situations.

5. Assist the trainee in developing those skills required to make more effective use of time and resources.

6. Assist the trainee in making a valid prediction of client potential and prognosis.

7. Enable the trainee to investigate various counseling approaches which in turn will enable him to help the client gain insight into his own interests and abilities subsequent to making his own decisions.

8. Help the trainee develop a harmonious working relationship with his supervisor, fellow workers, and other professional personnel in related organizations.

9. Furnish, in conjunction with the academic phase of training, impetus to encourage trainees to consider seriously supplementing their professional growth through additional study.

10. Bring together in a realistic setting the diverse problems encountered in actual life situations.

11. Enable the trainee to organize and consolidate his philosophy and attitudes.

12. Help the trainee acquire understanding of the realities of the counselor-client relationship and the part that knowledge plays in this relationship.

13. Introduce the trainee to the nature of his chosen profession by acquainting him with organizational structure, protocol, relationships, processes, and working conditions.

14. Help the trainee proceed to understand the relationship of rehabilitation counseling to the total teamwork process and work cooperatively within this framework.

15. Help the trainee, with assistance from his supervisor, to identify areas of specialization for which he may have particular interest or aptitude.

16. Reduce the period of time needed for on-the-job training in his profession.

17. Provide an opportunity for the trainee, his training coordinator, and the faculty supervisor to evaluate the strengths and weaknesses of the trainee as well as of the field work program itself.

18. Stimulate the formulation of an identification with a professional role.

19. Provide an awareness of the process of community organization in meeting the needs of his client.

20. Inculcate high standards of professional ethics and give the trainee experience in actual interpersonal relationships which involve ethical decisions and practice.

21. Encourage the trainee to seek out new and better ways to serve his client more effectively, not relying solely on past methods but developing new approaches and supporting ideas which increase quantity and promote quality in client services.

Before the trainee begins his field work, it is essential that everyone involved know the purpose of such an experience. Only through this type of understanding can one expect the assignment to be successful. Therefore, it is necessary to promote a free exchange of ideas and dialogue between the trainee, his supervisor, state office personnel, and the university faculty supervisor in order to increase the effectiveness of this endeavor. Such dialogue will allow the respective members of the training team to ask questions and make comments regarding ways in which they might better serve the counselor trainee. Additionally, appropriate feedback at the completion of the recommended assignments should provide vital information concerning methods which might be utilized for the improvement of the field work program in the future.

To communicate effectively, it is essential to define certain terms prior to the outset of the field work.

A. The *supervised field work experience* is a planned educational program to supplement the knowledge and skills learned in the academic setting. This work normally will take place in the trainee's local office or customary work station.

B. A *trainee* is the individual working within a rehabilitation setting. He may be either (1) a full-time graduate student involved in a university's master's degree program in rehabilitation counseling; (2) a rehabilitation counselor trainee participating in orientation training similar to that offered by Virginia Commonwealth University; or (3) a counselor involved in a public or private agency's in-service training conference. Usually he is considered a trainee until his supervisor has determined that he is capable of functioning on the professional level within the realm of his stated responsibilities (See Appendix K).

C. The *training coordinator* should be a counselor of senior rank, immediate supervisor, a training specialist, or an administrator designated by the rehabilitation agency to have responsibility for the training, supervision, and evaluation of the trainee during his period of supervised field work. The training coordinator should work closely with the agency training supervisor (and the faculty supervisor if there is university involvement) in all aspects of this training experience. The training coordinator probably has as much if not more responsibility for the training of this individual than the training supervisor or the faculty supervisor, since the coordinator has direct and continued contact with the trainee throughout his field work experience.

D. The *agency training supervisor* is the individual who has been designated by the rehabilitation agency to have responsibility for its indoctrination, orientation, staff development, and in-service and out-service training programs. This person is located ordinarily in a central office, whereas the trainee's coordinator is located in the local or district office. The agency training supervisor should work closely with the faculty supervisor and the training coordinator to make field assignments and to plan, initiate, and supervise the overall field experience.

E. The *faculty supervisor* is the director of a university rehabilitation counselor training program or his representative who has supervisory responsibility of the trainee's field work experience. In those instances where there is university involvement and the trainee is receiving graduate credit for the field work, the faculty supervisor has a responsible role in furnishing appropriate supervision and feedback. For those states adopting this text for their particular in-service training needs, there probably will not be a faculty supervisor involved; however, he probably will act as a consultant. In that case, the agency training supervisor should assume the major responsibility for directing this experience.

TRAINING CONTENT IN A PROGRAM OF SUPERVISED FIELD WORK EXPERIENCE

The development of this textbook has been directed toward three distinct groups:

1. The newly employed vocational rehabilitation counselor who will be attending an orientation program similar to that conducted by Virginia Commonwealth University at the Regional Counselor Training Program in Fishersville, Virginia.

2. The full-time graduate student involved in a university's master's degree program in rehabilitation counseling.

3. The participants in an ongoing in-service training program as offered by the majority of state vocational rehabilitation agencies and private organizations.

The supervised field work experience should be incorporated into the trainee's regular work assignment. It should be planned so as to contribute to the agency's goals and objectives. The individual training plan—developed jointly by the training coordinator, the agency training supervisor, and the trainee often working in conjunction with a faculty supervisor should be based upon the individual trainee's professional needs and focused on the total rehabilitation process. Prior to his participation in the field work program or internship, the training coordinator or faculty member should introduce the trainee to this book. After the trainee has had time to read over the material and discuss it with his coordinator, tentative assignments should be made.

Further discussion relative to finalizing the assignments of particular exercises should occur after meeting with the other members of the training team. As a suggestion, an interim period of predetermined length should be scheduled between the academic phase of training and the initiation of field work. This interim should provide the trainee time to become acquainted with his fellow workers and his work station, as well as other factors present in a new work situation.

During this interim, the coordinator and faculty supervisor should study the particular needs of the trainee in respect to the responsibilities and activities of his work assignment. Since the university faculty supervisor and the district office training coordinator have certain conceptions regarding the assignment of exercises, the faculty member should outline the exercises and possibly include additional assignments and explain their rationale to the counselor trainee for inclusion in his field work program.

Once the assignments have been finalized, a training plan should be completed within a specified length of time, approved by the training coordinator, and then mailed to the faculty supervisor with a copy going to the state training supervisor.

It is imperative that the counselor trainee as well as the training coordinator differentiate between the traditional type of practicum performed by a graduate student involved in the university setting and the field work as designed in this book. The objective of these exercises is to bridge the gap between the academic setting and the practical setting existing in the local vocational rehabilitation office situation. This training approach has been realistically oriented to counselor needs: It is neither an academic approach per se, nor is it necessary to give the newly employed worker philosophical descriptions in order to justify the primacy of a particular technique.

In the exercises which follow, it will be noticed that in addition to individual assignments there is a brief statement supporting the rationale for the inclusion of each exercise in the book. Additionally, actual samples of counselor trainee work have been included in an effort to help clarify and limit questions which might arise in the field. These examples have been chosen as typical responses made by superior counselors.

As stated previously, a large number of professionals in rehabilitation have been approached in an effort to single out professional activities of the outstanding counselor. Several studies have indicated that an agency can employ almost anyone and, in turn, train him in the rudiments of rehabilitation; but in most instances he never attains a high level of professionalism. These exercises were chosen specifically for the reason that the outstanding counselor performs the majority of these functions as a part of his daily routine professional activities.

There should be a clear understanding that the completion of these exercises does not necessarily insure success on the job. Education must continue during the entire professional career of those involved in a particular profession, especially those in vocational rehabilitation. The agency, therefore, has a prime responsibility for supplementing and extending the preparation attained in an academic setting. Certain kinds of information and knowledge can best be obtained only over an indefinite or extended period of time in a work setting. Skills such as working with other professionls in a team relationship can only be introduced and initiated in the formal educational program. Technical skills develop and become perfected only after extensive practice. Maturity and independence, while they are fostered in the training program, can develop with the passage of time and the accumulation of experience. Consequently, rehabilitation agencies must be reasonable in their expectations and avoid comparing young and inexperienced counselors with older, mature, and experienced staff members.

If the newly employed rehabilitation worker has not begun to adopt some of the techniques outlined in the following pages, it is the intent of these assignments to encourage him to do so. It is anticipated that the trainee will not "just complete the exercises in order to fulfill a requirement," but that he will continue using newly acquired approaches in his routine professional activities with the agency. Again, these exercises are developed with the intent of perpetuating outstanding professional behavior and characteristics in the counselor rather than insisting upon his completion of them simply to fulfill a state agency or university requirement.

SELECTION OF FIELD WORK EXERCISES

In the following table, one will find a grid which has the various types of rehabilitation position classifications listed in the left margin and numbers across the top. These numbers correspond to the various exercises in this text. Locate your job title and notice that certain blocks on the grid have been marked. These correspond to exercises which faculty members in university programs and the majority of state agency training supervisors feel are relevant to professional activities of a rehabilitation worker.

After the trainee has had several meetings with the faculty supervisor and the training coordinator, a specified number of checkmarks should be circled in the column corresponding to your job title. These represent exercises you will complete. If for any reason one of the chosen exercises does not approximate your professional duties in the field, discuss the possibilities of substituting another exercise with the training coordinator and then immediately contact the faculty supervisor for final approval. If a request for a substitution is not sent to the faculty supervisor in a reasonable length of time after the final assignments have been made, the trainee will not receive credit for that exercise.

Even though the ultimate responsibility for assigning a grade to the completed field work experience rests with the faculty supervisor, he will base part of his final decision upon the training coordinator's written narrative report (see Appendix E).

Prior to commencing work it is important that the trainee read *every* exercise carefully so that he can evaluate the appropriateness of the choices made by the faculty supervisor or his training coordinator.

JOB CLASSIFICATIONS OF PROFESSIONAL WORKERS EMPLOYED BY VOCATIONAL

REHABILITATION AND EXERCISES APPROPRIATE TO THEIR CASELOAD

	1	2	3	4	5	6	7	8	9	10	11	12	13	14	15	16	17	18	19	20	21	22	23	24	25	26	27
BLIND	X	X	X			X	X	X		X	X	X	X	X	X	X		X				X	X	X		X	X
CORRECTIONS	X		X	X	X	X	X	X	X	X	X	X	X	X	X	X	X	X	X	X		X	X	X			X
EVALUATION	X		X	X		X			X	X	X	X		X								X	X	X	X		X
GENERAL	X	X	X			X	X	X	X	X	X	X	X	X	X	X		X		X		X	X				X
MENTAL HEALTH	X		X	X	X	X	X	X		X	X	X	X	X	X	X		X				X	X	X			X
MENTAL RETARDATION	X	X	X		X	X	X	X		X	X	X	X	X	X	X		X				X	X	X			X
PLACEMENT	X		X	X		X		X		X	X	X	X	X		X		X				X	X				X
SCHOOL	X		X	X	X	X	X	X	X	X	X	X	X	X	X	X		X			X	X	X				X
WORKSHOP	X		X	X	X	X		X		X	X	X	X	X		X		X				X	X	X	X		X

PREPARATION AND FORMAT OF WRITTEN ASSIGNMENTS

One of the most effective methods of communicating the results of the supervised field work to the agency supervisor and the faculty supervisor is through the completion of written assignments by the trainee. These assignments will be examined by the faculty supervisor at the end of the training period as well as at periodic intervals. In the latter event it should be possible for both supervisors, representing the agency and the faculty, to evaluate the reports to see how well the supervised field work is meeting the trainee's needs and expectations and to determine the effectiveness of the trainee in writing reports. The obvious mark of a true professional is how well he communicates with others, not only verbally, but also in written communication.

A predetermined number of written assignments are to be completed. The faculty supervisor will assign several exercises to be completed by the trainee along with those that will be selected by the trainee's coordinator. All exercises are to be typed and double-spaced on standard typing paper. In order for the field work to be considered complete, there must be a table of contents listing the assigned exercises. Additionally, the work must be identified by a title page including name, work assignment, office address, the last date in which academic training began, as well as when the field work began.

All field work assignments are to be sent in before the date specified by the faculty supervisor or training coordinator. On this date, one copy of the completed report must be in the faculty member's office suitably bound in a manila folder, pressboard cover, or other binding. Using a binder in which the various assignments are not firmly attached, such as the clear covers with a sliding plastic strip securing the left-hand margins of the paper together, is not recommended. These have a tendency to separate and become disarranged or possibly lost.

There are several exercises which should be duplicated separately and kept in the local office for utilization by other counselors serving the territory. The reason for this is quite obvious: Even though the trainee is gathering pertinent information relative to his geographic area of responsibility, other professional counselors also have need for this type of material. As previously mentioned, the assignments are not oriented solely to fulfill university requirements, but are intended to create an awareness of the total rehabilitation process. Since these exercises are an intrinsic part of the routine activities of outstanding counselors, it logically is assumed other counselors should adopt these techniques.

The duplication of certain exercises has another fundamental purpose. As additional counselors accept the rationale and techniques utilized in these exercises, the local vocational rehabilitation office soon will begin to accumulate a vast amount of information relative to community resources, job placement possibilities, labor market trends, and innovative approaches to rehabilitation which might be effective in such a locale. As an example, many office supervisors now require their counselors to make at least one new business survey per month. This contact is written up on a form similar to the one found in this book. As months go by it is evident a significant amount of occupational information can be gathered which will benefit everyone in that office and, in turn, the client. With this in mind, a special note will be made regarding which exercises should be duplicated.

Before embarking on this field work assignment, it is highly recommended that you read Appendix L regarding rehabilitation ethics. Particular attention should be given to the section discussing confidentiality of information. Under no circumstances should the counselor or intern divulge his client's name in these exercises. If you feel compelled to use a name other than "Mr. X," "Miss Y," or "John Doe," let the reader know the name is purely fictitious.

OUTLINE OF TRAINEE RESPONSIBILITIES FOR THE FIELD WORK EXPERIENCE

Prior to commencing the field work, be sure you have reviewed the following checklist of items regarding the responsibilities for completing the assignments:

1. The *entire* book should be read.

2. The material should be discussed with your training coordinator. You and he then will select, tentatively, the appropriate exercises in relation to your caseload responsibilities.

3. The exercises selected by you and your training coordinator are to be discussed with the faculty supervisor. The faculty supervisor then will make several additional assignments that you will be responsible for completing.

4. A second meeting should be planned with your training coordinator to discuss the recommendations and assignments suggested by the faculty supervisor.

5. The training coordinator will then develop a plan regarding the final selection of exercises to be completed by the trainee. This plan (see example in Appendix A) should include the assignments which the trainee is responsible for completing. If a faculty supervisor is involved, he should have a copy of this plan before the trainee begins his field work.

6. The appropriate exercises should be completed on a schedule as determined by the training coordinator or faculty supervisor.

7. The finished report should include the appropriate forms and worksheets described in the appendices.

8. All reports are to be typed, doubled-spaced with standard margins. The final report is to be suitably bound with a title page (including name, work assignment, address, and class in which you participated) and a table of contents.

9. The distribution of copies should be as follows: one copy to the state training supervisor, one copy for your training coordinator and/or district office supervisor, and one copy for

your personal records. If a university is associated with the trainee's field work program, the faculty supervisor will require one copy.

10. Before putting the final exercises into the binder, duplicate those exercises which could be utilized by the other professional workers in your office or territory (e.g. the exercises on job placement, community resources, cooperative agreement, job surveys, labor market trends). These exercises should be placed in a separate file accessible to counselors in the local office.

11. Your training coordinator should select and complete an appropriate evaluation form (located in the appendices).

12. The trainee is to complete the Rehabilitation Field Work Questionnaire and Evaluation Form found in Appendix J. (The training coordinator's evaluation report and the trainee's evaluation report are to be included with the completed assignments when it is sent to the faculty supervisor.)

13. Difficulties experienced with the field work should be noted so that they may be discussed with the training coordinator and/or faculty supervisor during field visitations.

FIELD WORK EXERCISES
AND
STUDENT WORK

Exercise 1

FREQUENCY REPORTS: COMPUTER PRINT-OUT

RATIONALE

Every vocational rehabilitation counselor should be keenly aware of the clients who comprise his caseload. The majority of rehabilitation agencies have converted from a manual system to a computer print-out system to record and report data relative to the counselor's caseload. To initiate your professional responsibility, it is imperative you understand each component of this computer print-out (for those agencies still utilizing the manual method of case reporting, the counselor will follow the same steps as directed in this exercise). The counselor must become familiar with the various codes on his print-out as soon as possible so that he can gain a better understanding of his total caseload.

ASSIGNMENT

Prepare a facsimile of one page of your computer print-out (or manual procedure for reporting) and analyze the various components. Give the rationale for the inclusion of these elements and decide whether or not they are appropriate for your particular needs in your office setting. Discuss how this information can help you serve clients more efficiently.

STUDENT WORK: SAMPLE 1

Vocational Rehabilitation's Computer Print-out

As a new counselor with vocational rehabilitation I will attempt to analyze, interpret, and recommend improvements concerning the vocational rehabilitation master list (computer print-out), which we receive on a monthly basis.

By completing the above assignment it is my hope to achieve a greater understanding of, and the ability to use this master list. It is also my intention that what is said in this paper will

21

provide the impetus for others to probe into this document. The master list should be of special interest to all vocational rehabilitation personnel, and especially the counselor, as it represents a synopsis of his entire caseload. For the counselor, no other document in his possession reveals such a simple, yet extensive description of the clients being served. Therefore, it is especially this writer's hope that as counselors, you will want to make an analysis, interpretation, and recommendations concerning this valuable tool.

The history of the master list in our state proceeds from the most current, January 11, 1971, back to January 31, 1967. This date, January 31, 1967, represents the first computer print-out since the changeover from the manual procedure. Therefore, I infer that I have a computer print-out history of the clients that have been served since that time. This is good to know; however, what is more important is the current master list which contains the valuable information of those being served now.

To further define the master list, and according to our vocational rehabilitation manual dated 1970, it is a roster of all cases processed by the counselor. According to the manual, its purpose is to provide:

1. Each counselor with a roster of his cases, arranged alphabetically according to status.

2. Each supervisor with a copy of all the master lists in his district.

3. A means of recording status changes.

4. A means for transferring cases.

The above is true; however, the master list can be even more meaningful to the person who will use it diligently.

In order to proceed it is necessary to look at a facsimile of a master list. A facsimile of this counselor's master list is herewith attached for the purpose of study. As one will notice, the item REPORT VR050, which is located at the top left side of the page, is placed here to identify this particular vocational rehabilitation report (computer print-out). This can be helpful to the reader in eliminating the possibility of mistaking this compu-

REPORT VR050 VOCATIONAL REHABILITATION MASTER LIST 01/11/71 Page 1

DISTRICT GREESBORO   COUNSELOR 0610 HALL

ADDRESS		CO	AGE	R	ED	SEX	SS DL	DIS BIL	PA	TE	RS	R1 A-B-C	NO MOS	CURRENT STATUS	NAME OF CLIENT		VR NUMBER	NEW STATS	TRANSFER CASELOAD	CO
1804 Fox St	Greensboro	41	40			1		643	Y	1	50	70/11	1	00	Arrow	John E	100628	02		
Rt. 4 Box 742B	Burlington	01	49			2		30X	N	1	70	70/04	6	02	Blake	Jane C	100615			
2480 Green St	Greensboro	41	19	1	12	1		379	N	1	24	70/05	7	06	Howell	James M	100792			
Rt. 3	Summerfield	41	39	1	11	1	1	379	N	1	50	69/09	15	06	Ivan	Henry R	100534			
1028 White St	Reidsville	79	55	1	02	1	1	370	N	1	24	70/08	3	10	Lee	Archie C	100964	12		
1042 Red St	High Point	41	59	2	10	1	1	332	N	1	72	69/07		16	Mills	Robert N	100625			
1102 Orange St	Leakesville	79	24	1	13	1	1	670	N	1	50	69/10	14	18	Nance	Jackie P	100942	20		
Rt. 3	Greensboro	41	41	1	10	1	1	379	N	1	50	69/11	13	20	Oval	Arnold L	100739	22		
935 Purple St	Greensboro	41	25	2	13	1	1	394	N	1	79	64/08	8	22	Palmer	Michael R	100654			
Rt. 1	Burlington	01	43	1	06	1	1	643	N	1	24	68/12		24	Scatter	Harold R	100792	25	0704	37
343 Yellow St	Greensboro	41	40	2	06	2	1	379	N	1	50	70/11		26	Thomas	Myrtle M	100685			

ter print-out from those which serve other administrative and fiscal matters.

Reading from left to right the next item is GREENSBORO DISTRICT. This is an important item inasmuch as it relates to the district office where the clients are being served. (There are approximately 25 district offices within our state.)

The next item is COUNSELOR 0610 HALL. The number (0610) indicates the counselor caseload number, and the name (HALL) indicates the last name of the counselor who is charged with the caseload. This item is necessary on the master list because it identifies the counselor (by the last name) who is responsible for the particular caseload within the state.

Item 126 is the counselor's code number. This item is included because it identifies the respective counselors within the state. These code numbers have been assigned by the state office to facilitate statistical recording as well as providing a more accurate method of counselor identification. Since there may be more than one page comprising the master list, it is important to have the pages numbered as Page 1, etc.

The date (01/11/71) on the master list is important because it indicates how current this print-out is. Also, the counselor can use this date in determining the number of months clients have been in the various statuses, as well as in which month clients were placed in these statuses.

The first item to the extreme left side of the page, under REPORT VR050, is the *Address*. It is necessary to have each client's current address so that the state office has up-to-date records at all times. If a client's address has changed, the change should be recorded on the current master list (the original and each copy) by crossing out, in red pencil, the former address and above it print the current address. (The same procedure for correction applies to county code, age, race, education, sex, SSDI status, disability, public assistance, Trust Fund, referral source, and name.) It is not necessary to wait until the master list is received in order to make changes in data; an interoffice memorandum giving the client's VR number, name, caseload code, and the change to be made is sufficient.

The second item, from left to right, on the master list is the county, *CO*. A code number is used here instead of the county name because it occupies less space on the print-out, and it is more appropriate for computerization. (This is also the rationale for other numbers and letters being used in lieu of wording throughout the remainder of this paper.) The code number reveals the county in which the client resides. After looking at the facsimile of my print-out, it is easy to determine which counties have the largest and smallest representation of clients being served on this caseload. For instance, one can readily observe that county number 41 is well represented, though counties 01 and 79 are not represented as often. Theoretically, several reasons could be given for this, but perhaps the most obvious and appropriate is that counties 01 and 79 do not have as large a population as 41.

The next item on the master list is *AGE*. Client's ages are very important because of their relation to disabilities, education, and current status. Also, it seems appropriate to have this item on the master list in order for the counselor to consider the feasibility of short-term or long-term planning. Whereas long-term planning might be in order for a younger client, it might not be as feasible for an older client. Another reason for having this item on the master list would be that it affords the counselor an opportunity to review quickly the range of client ages in respect to one another; i.e. the distribution of ages. By doing this, the counselor can see whether or not he has an evenly distributed caseload as far as the age factor is concerned.

The next item on the master list is race, *R*. This item is not as important as some others. However, by having this item listed on the master list it affords the counselor an opportunity to review the different races being served on the particular caseload as well as the number of clients within each group. By making such a review it might bring to the attention of the counselor any partiality being shown by the counselor with regard to race. For instance, by observing the attached master list it can be noted that there are six whites (1's) and three Negroes (2's). Even though racial discrimination is not the policy of vocational rehabilitation, an unconscious, biased attitude on the part of the counselor as well as negligence of his caseload could produce a situation that might bear resemblance.

Furthermore, as you will note on the computer print-out, a client in the current status of 00 has no race code (number). The reason for this is that the initial referral from (Form R1-A) of our state division of vocational rehabilitation does not contain a place for race to be recorded. Only after the Form R1-B is submitted to the state office (after the client advances into extended evaluation, closed after evaluation, or plan development) will the master list reflect the race code. Only the Forms R1-B and R-4 (application) reflect the race code.

The next item is education, *ED*. This is important because it can be indicative of the client's level of intellectual ability. However, his lack of educational opportunities also may have been one of his problems and the counselor should take this into consideration. Therefore, it may be necessary for vocational rehabilitation to sponsor him for special training in an attempt to assist him in attaining his optimum level of intellectual functioning. As you will note on the master list, some clients' education years are not stated. The reason is the same as was for race; the R1-B had not been submitted to the state office.

Because of the confusion resulting from names of individuals, the next item, *SEX*, indicates whether the client is male or female. The total number of clients being served representative of each sex can be tabulated easily by adding males and females within this column.

The next item on the master list is titled Social Security Disability Insurance, *SSDI*. This is necessary due to the fact that it may be feasible to serve clients from Social Security Trust Funds if they are receiving SSDI benefits, rather than utilizing general program funds (section 2 funds). This could be especially practical if section 2 funds were near exhaustion or depleted. Again, code numbers are used and by noting the SSDI column on the sample master list, the counselor readily can see that most of these applicants were allowed benefits (Code 1).

Different code numbers represent the particular status of an applicant seeking SSDI benefits. The counselor can interpret these code numbers and see the current SSDI status of clients; this would help to determine what action needs to be taken by the counselor. A client that is receiving SSDI benefits has an advantage as far as maintenance for himself and his family is concerned (which is especially helpful while he is involved in some vocational rehabilitation program). This is another reason for reviewing this particular item on the master list. Further investigation of this list reveals that some clients' SSDI statuses are not shown. The reason is again the same as was for race and education, being that the R1-B had not been submitted to the state office.

The following item is disability, *DISBIL*. This is a very important item inasmuch as it should be considered strongly when contemplating a plan for the provision of services for the client. It should be pointed out that the code number under this column represents only the major disability of the client and may not give the counselor the total picture of the clients' overall condition. Therefore, the counselor should make a note on his copy of any secondary or other disabilities existing with specific clients. Additionally, this category is especially helpful in relation to client training and job placement. Furthermore, at the beginning of one's employment with vocational rehabilitation, it would behoove anyone working with his master list to familiarize himself especially with the different disability code numbers. Correct and expedient interpretation of the disabilities represented on one's caseload is imperative.

Another item on the master list is Public Assistance, *PA*. It is important to know what public assistance, if any, the client may be receiving while undergoing a vocational rehabilitation sponsored program. This information is now acquired on each referral and specified on the R1-A that is submitted to the state office. On the attached master list sample it should be noted that "Y" represents "Yes" (he is receiving public assistance) and "N" represents "No" (he is not receiving this assistance). If the counselor has this information available to him he is in a much better position to determine whether the client can maintain himself and his family on public assistance during his rehabilitation period, or if it will be necessary for vocational rehabilitation to intervene and supplement these funds.

The master list contains another column specifically designed for clients utilizing the Social Security Trust Fund program (*TF*). This is included because it is a financial resource for rehabilitating SSDI clients. Unlike the general program, which is operated with section 2 funds, a client receiving SSDI benefits does not need to meet certain financial eligibility requirements. Therefore, clients that are receiving SSDI benefits as the result of a disability may have their rehabilitation program financed by Social Security Trust Funds. After examining the attached master list it is noted (by the code number 1) that all clients are being provided services by means of the Social Security Trust Fund program. If the column under *TF* does not indicate any number then the clients are not being served under this program.

Still another item on the master list is the referral source, *RS*. This is a very important item because the counselor can review the print-out by reading and interpreting the code numbers and, in turn, determine where the referrals are originating. Also, this item can benefit the counselor because it provides an additional source of information regarding clients on the case-load as well as a possibility for future referrals.

The next item on the counselor's computer print-out relates to the referral forms (R1-A,B,C). This has been included because it specifies the date of the referral. By reviewing the master list, the counselor quickly can determine the number of months a client has been on the case-load (referral status). This is done in an effort to maintain a uniform and logical progression or flow of clients through the rehabilitation process. If there is an unusual delay in this flow, the counselor can attempt to rectify this problem, thereby keeping his caseload flowing smoothly and up-to-date.

The next item on the master list relates to the number of months clients have been in a particular status, *NO MOS*. This is extremely important since without it the counselor would not have any way of knowing the length of time a client had been in a particular status. If, by chance, the number of months specified under this column has not been provided, the counselor must go to the client's case folder to acquire this information. As an example one can see readily by the sample included that clients in the current status of 16 and 24 do not have the number of months recorded under the *NO MOS* column. This counselor feels that these months should be recorded on the master list because it is of necessity to know the length of time each client has been in status 16 (physical restoration) and status 24 (services interrupted) respectively. As for Status 26 (closed rehabilitated), this item only will show up once on the master list and that is at the successful termination of the client from the counselor's caseload.

The next item on the master list is *CURRENT STATUS*. This item is important because it reveals the client's current status during his rehabilitation program. The counselor can see by scanning this category that all statuses are not represented. He should consider this as an indication that there needs to be some action taken to put clients in status 12, 14, etc. By reviewing this item it can reveal quickly to the counselor all of his clients' statuses without resorting to the individual case folder.

The next item on the master list is *NAME OF CLIENT*. Needless to say this is the most important item of all. Without the name of the client, the other items on this master list would be meaningless. Numbers representing names here might be better for computer use; however, for the counselor it would be burdensome to associate numbers with names. Notice that it is important to have the client's full name listed: last name, first name, and middle initial. It is helpful to have the middle initial for the purpose of distinguishing between two clients that might have the same first and last name.

The next item is the *VR NUMBER*. It is the most exact method of identifying a person. In the event that two clients have the same first name, middle initial, and last name, the *VR NUMBER* would serve to distinguish between the two. The utilization of numbers is not intended to dehumanize clients; it is for the specific purpose of maintaining accurate records.

The next item on the list is new status, *NEW STAT*. The counselor can record the new or current status of clients in this column (the exception to this is on the original master list which must be returned to the state office). An update from status 02 to status 04, 06, or 10 is not acceptable on the original master list, as these statuses are reflected automatically when the form R1-B is submitted and, in turn, processed by the state office. Also, closed statuses (08, 26, 28, or 30) are not to be updated on the original master list; these statuses are keypunched from the form R1-C and automatically will appear when the data sheet has been processed. Nevertheless, the person using the copies of the master list can note under the *NEW STATS* column changes of clients' statuses. By doing this the person making the changes can keep abreast of the forthcoming computer print-out.

The next item on the master list, *TRANSFER CASELOAD*, is related obviously to the transference of cases to another counselor's caseload. This is a necessary print-out component; by reviewing and keeping this information current on the master list, the counselor can recall quickly what cases were transferred, to whom, and the approximate date of the transfer. Ample space in this column has been provided to record the caseload code number of the counselor accepting the transfer of the case. A code number is appropriate due to limited space for the counselor's full name.

The last item on the master list is related to the county where the case is being transferred, *CO*. This information is important inasmuch as it reveals the county in which the client now resides. A county code number is recorded in this column instead of a name due to space limitations.

Even though there is not a *REMARKS* column on this master list, this counselor feels that it would be helpful to have such an addition. This column could be used for recording pertinent client information for the counselor's use.

Most counselors could use this column when reviewing their print-outs each month and make tentative plans and other notes concerning each client. Also, this would be a good place to record the action taken on inactive authorizations that are outstanding. The ideal location for this *REMARKS* column would be on the extreme right-hand side of the page.

In conclusion, this counselor would like to acknowledge that he has acquired a better understanding of the computer print-out by attempting to analyze, interpret, and make recommendations concerning its use. Also, this exercise has stimulated my curiosity to the point of wanting to learn more about this useful tool and its integration for effective caseload management.

Exercise 2

FREQUENCY REPORTS: SOURCE OF REFERRALS

RATIONALE

As a newly employed rehabilitation worker, you can better understand a caseload by investigating from where and how the referrals have come to your attention. As an example, who in your community has been referring the majority of clients to you? It is important to identify trends occurring regarding the referral of clients to your agency. Through such an investigation, it may become apparent that the agency has not done a good public relations job or has not provided the services needed by the referral source.

ASSIGNMENT

Prepare a frequency distribution of your caseload by referral source. If your agency has standards and/or guidelines for evaluation of referral sources, use them. In the frequency distribution, list the name of organization referring clients to you and the number of referrals made. This can be procured by examining your active caseload. After all referral sources have been listed with the number of referrals from each, add them up; this should represent your total active caseload. In order for these figures to be more meaningful to you, place the number of referrals from each source in terms of a percentage. For example, if you have 100 total active cases and 13 clients were referred to you by the Social Security Administration, 13 percent of your caseload would be Social Security referral cases. Evaluate in detail this distribution and include suggestions for increasing and improving the quantity of referrals from the different sources.

STUDENT WORK: SAMPLE 1

In preparing a report of frequency distribution, I am taking into consideration only the cases which are in an active status on

	No. of Cases	Percentage of Caseload %
Physicians	38	25
Clinics	34	22
General hospitals	22	14
Elementary or high school	19	12
Colleges or universities	1	1
Department of Correction	1	1
Department of Social Services	18	12
Employment Security Commission	1	1
Self-referred	11	7
Other individuals	3	2
Other public organization or agency	3	2
Sanatorium	1	1
Total	152	100

my caseload. Cases which are in a referral status are not included in this report; however, I feel I should make some note of them in the overall evaluation of my caseload.

In January, 1970, a suboffice was established in this geographic area to provide vocational rehabilitation services on a full-time basis to the people of Halifax and Northampton counties. These two counties were served previously by a counselor from another office, and because he was limited in his visits to this area, his referrals were somewhat limited. In December, 1969, I accepted a transfer caseload from this counselor covering a two-county area. My first master list of January, 1970, showed a total caseload of 181 people. This figure included both those in a referral and an active status. My master list for July, 1970, shows a total caseload of 323 people. This figure represents 171 cases in referral status and 152 active cases. This shows an increase in my caseload of almost 100 percent. I feel that this increase is primarily due to the fact that for the first time since the beginning of vocational rehabilitation in North Carolina, Halifax and Northampton counties are being served by a full-time counselor located in a much more convenient location. More people and more agencies have become aware of our agency and the variety of services we can provide; therefore, I feel the number of referrals to vocational rehabilitation will continue to increase. By the time this field training exercise is submitted for review, my case-load will probably already have more cases in active and referral status; thus the figures presented in this exercise will already be obsolete.

My frequency distribution by referral source shows that the greatest number of referrals come from physicians and clinics. I feel that this is primarily because these sources are more familiar with vocational rehabilitation and the services we can provide. In the majority of cases referred by physicians, medical information is easily obtained or more readily available. The three orthopedic clinics and the county health departments refer the second largest number of referrals. Again, this is primarily because physical restoration services are involved.

Other referral sources refer people to vocational rehabilitation for a variety of services, most often for vocational training or assistance with job placement. Practically all referrals from educational institutions are for training purposes. It is expected that referrals from local high schools will increase now that my office is in a more convenient location. Many referrals now in a referral status come from referral sources other than those listed on the frequency report.

I should mention here that referrals from Departments of Social Services and the Department of Corrections have been somewhat lower than expected. Our central office in Raleigh has created positions for a state coordinator between those agencies and our agency. These state coordinators, working together with the two agencies, should promote better understanding and working relationships, thereby creating better services for clients. It is expected that with the use of the new referral feedback form now used by the Departments of Social Services and the Employment Security Commission, referrals from these two agencies will automatically increase. Counselor visits to county Departments of Social Services have been increased also.

I feel that even though the percentage of referrals from many sources is low that they will increase by virtue of the fact that our new office is located in a much more convenient place to provide services for the people of the area. I feel that in order to increase the number of referrals to vocational rehabilitation, it is my responsibility to inform people and other referral sources of the purpose, aims, and services offered by my agency.

Many people in my area of responsibility were unaware that vocational rehabilitation even existed, and those that had some knowledge of the agency did not know enough about it to really be of help to them. Many of the agencies in this area knew that vocational rehabilitation existed as an agency, but because of a lack of a close working relationship there was a lack of understanding about what services our agency could provide and eligibility criteria. I found it particularly difficult to explain the agency I worked for at first because I was just as "ignorant" as most other people about vocational rehabilitation.

Through actual work experience, the Regional Counselor Training Program at Fishersville, Virginia, and personal contact with clients, other agencies, and referral sources, I have gained numerous ideas as to how I can communicate the story of vocational rehabilitation to the communities I serve. I feel strongly about a counselor being interested in his work in order to do a good job in the field of communications. I first began my communications job by getting to know many of the referral sources, including the physicians of the area and other cooperating agencies, and most of all, by getting to know my clients. I, too, feel that a good public relations program has to be started in an area such as the one I am working in. In addition to being invited to speak before groups, I feel that utilizing radio and newspaper can be very helpful in communicating the story of vocational rehabilitation.

Being invited to staff meetings of other agencies to explain our agency is one of the most effective ways in which to build understanding and good relationships among agencies. I feel that much of the communications I have been involved in was that which we might label "intentional." I feel the most important way to communicate vocational rehabilitation is to show people that you are really and truly interested in them and their future. Often your behavior while away from work could have as much, if not more, reflection on your agency than what you do while at work.

Basically, I feel that in order to communicate vocational rehabilitation services to the communities I serve I must believe in my job and have an unselfish interest in it. I feel that I must make the time and efforts to let the community know about my agency and how I might serve not only a handicapped individual but how my agency might better serve the community. This can be done only if I take the initiative and interest in the people whose money I spend.

STUDENT WORK: SAMPLE 2

Prepare a frequency distribution of your caseload by referral source. Evaluate the referral distribution and give suggestions for improvement.

Referral Source	*Code*	*Number*	*Percentage (%)*
1. Public welfare agency (state & local government)	40	155	30
2. Social Security Disability Determination Unit (State)	50	78	14
3. Physicians	72	51	13
4. Other interested person or individual	79	72	10
5. Self-referred person	70	43	9
6. State Employment Service	53	42	8
7. Public Health Dept.	38	29	6
8. General hospital	24	17	3
9. Area high school	14	8	1.50
10. Hospital or clinic, other	29	4	1
11. Vocational school	12	4	1
12. Chronic condition hospitals or sanatoriums	22	3	0.5
13. Rehabilitation facilities	30	2	.45
14. Schools for physically and mentally handicapped	16	2	.45
15. Other educational institutions	19	2	.45
16. Private welfare agencies	44	2	.45
17. Other public organizations or agencies	59	2	.45
18. State vocational rehabilitation facility	30	1	.25
19. Artificial appliance company	60	1	.25
20. Community mental health center	32	1	.25
Total		532	100.00

The above list represents the frequency distribution of referral sources of a general caseload. This caseload draws clients from the three-county area of Harlan, Leslie, and Bell in Kentucky. Bearing in mind the relative needs of the area and the vast sociological pattern within which this area of Appalachia falls, the distribution seems justifiable in regard to the service spectrum. The rationale behind this statement lies in the tone of operation of the service agencies and their dynamic effort to serve the handicapped, unemployed, and aged.

The largest source of rehabilitative material is the Public Assistance offices. Many persons are aware of this organization, whereas they may not be familiar with others. The work pattern in this region is maximally trended toward manual labor, particularly in the field of construction and mining. Illiteracy is rampant, and if a vocational handicap occurs to one of the people, it takes the maximum utilization of resources to return him to remunerative employment. The first thing that comes to mind of a person in their situation is to "sign up for welfare checks" and "draw food stamps." This in itself is the reason that Public Assistance is far ahead of any other referral source.

The next idea that occurs to the disabled worker is to apply for Social Security disability benefits. Although many apply, few are accepted, and thus the pattern becomes clearer. All rejectees for these benefits are referred to the Bureau of Rehabilitation Services and eventually to the counselor in which county these individuals reside. The rehabilitation process thus becomes a coordination of efforts and a team-minded approach to return these people to the labor market in order to relieve the welfare rolls. The Public Assistance Agency and Social Security Disability Determinations Unit comprise almost 50 percent of the referrals.

Family doctors are next in line as referral sources. They fall below the aforementioned agencies because of the fact that many people cannot afford to go to doctors unless they have a state medical card and they probably already have been referred by Public Assistance. If a person needs medical attention but cannot pay, then he is referred by the doctor to the Bureau of Rehabilitation Services. This is regrettable because many prospective clients are never referred because they can pay their own bill. I would recommend that the counselor talk personally to all physicians used as vendors in his area, explaining that many services provided by the Bureau of Rehabilitation Services are not initiated on the basis of economic need. This approach might very well increase the number of referrals from this particular source.

The State Employment Service and public health organizations also contribute to the number of possible applicants. They are, of course, part of the task force of dedicated personnel providing an umbrella of services to the community. They are aware of the rehabilitation process and function with emphasis toward it.

The small number that comes from high schools, hospitals, rehabilitation facilities, and schools for the physically and mentally handicapped is attributed to the hierarchy of the Division of Rehabilitation on the state level. In a planned and predetermined sequence, counselors are placed in these institutions for the primary purpose of working directly with the referrals from that institution. These would inevitably take the burden from the shoulders of the general caseload counselor.

In regard to chronic condition hospitals, sanatoriums, and private welfare organizations, there are few in this area, as the statistics indicate.

In retrospect one might say that the challenge lies in the counselor himself. It is his duty to seek out new vistas, adapt new and creative methods, and above all, have a good, well-rounded working relationship with the agencies and organizations in his area if he has any hopes of improving his referral sources.

Exercise 3

FREQUENCY DISTRIBUTION BY PRIMARY AND SECONDARY DISABILITY

RATIONALE

It is improbable that a vocational rehabilitation worker can provide adequate services until he has complete medical and psychological information on each client. Researchers in rehabilitation have found that the majority of clients eligible for vocational rehabilitation services have more than one disability. Since the counselor is responsible for determining the primary disability for statistical purposes, the secondary disability often is overlooked. To increase the probability of a successful rehabilitation, it is necessary to provide all services required to remove, decrease, or otherwise change the existing impairment(s).

The performance of this exercise also will allow you to gain a better perspective of adequate caseload balance; i.e. a vital equilibrium must exist so that caseload management is possible. Often the counselor does not know what percentage of his caseload is comprised of specific disability categories. Since there is no magic number stating how many quadriplegics, hysterectomies, hernias, or whatever should be represented on a counselor's caseload, it is difficult to reach such a balance. Realistically speaking, imagine how effective a general field counselor would be if the majority of his caseload was composed of spinal cord injuries. The time commitment to these clients would overwhelm him and, in turn, would not provide the counselor opportunity to serve other less severe disability categories. This assignment provides a method whereby the counselor can investigate the composition of his caseload and then make constructive suggestions to improve its management.

ASSIGNMENT

Prepare a frequency distribution of your active caseload by

39

primary and secondary disabilities. Arrange it in such a way that you know how many clients on your caseload fall within particular primary disability categories. As described in the format for Exercise 2, record both the number as well as the percentage found in each disability category. Then list the secondary disabilities appearing within your caseload in the same format as you did for primary disabilities. After this has been completed, examine and correlate the occurrence of disability patterns; for example, you have eight individuals on your caseload with a primary disability listed as alcoholism (let us say this represents 15 percent of your total caseload). Of those eight alcoholics, six have a secondary disability listed as stomach ulcers. After you have made this investigation, furnish some possible solutions as to how you might serve your clients. Also, correlate community resource referrals and primary disabilities. The reason for doing this is to see whether or not certain referral sources are sending clients to you with only one type of disability; for example, does Public Welfare refer to you only clients with back disabilities? If this is occurring, make recommendations to accommodate a more flexible plan for referring clients.

STUDENT WORK: SAMPLE 1

As seen in the following graph, the largest number of disabilities occurring in this counselor's caseload (61.4%) are in Category 1, "degenerative changes, congentital and acquired." A further breakdown of Category 1 shows the largest single disability to be cataracts, comprising 15 percent of the total caseload. It will also be observed that the majority of the referrals from the sources listed fall under Category 1, the one exception being those referred by general medical practitioners. Fifty percent of those individuals referred by general medical practitioners are suffering from traumas to the eye. Inasmuch as a general medical practitioner would be the most likely individual to contact persons suffering from traumas to the eye, this percentage breakdown is both logical and predictable.

It is more difficult to explain the percentage breakdown of self-referrals. Of those eight persons on this counselor's caseload who are self-referrals, 87.5 percent have primary disabilities in

TABLE OF DISABILITIES BY REFERRAL SOURCE
(*expressed as percent*)

PRIMARY DISABILITIES (OCULAR):
1. Degenerative changes, congenital and acquired
2. Traumatic conditions
3. Diseased, inflamed and/or infected
4. Congenital defect or deficiency
5. Due to other physical defect or disease
6. Total blindness, O.S., O.D., or O.U.
7. Primary disability other than ocular

SECONDARY DISABILITIES (OCULAR):
A. Degenerative changes, congenital and acquired
B. Traumatic conditions
C. Diseased, inflamed and/or infected
D. Congenital defect or deficiency
E. Due to other physical deficiency or disease
F. Secondary disability other than ocular
G. No secondary disability

	1	2	3	4	5	6	7	A	B	C	D	E	F	G	Total number referred by each source
Social Security Determination Unit	50	8.3	8.3	8.3	8.3	8.3	8.5	50				8.3	8.3	33.3	12
Department of Vocational Rehabilitation	75			12.5	12.5			37.5			12.5		12.5	37.5	8
Self-referrals	87.5	12.5						25					3.5	61.5	8
Departments of Welfare	57.1	14.2	14.2				14.5	14.2					28.7	57.1	7
Home Teaching Department (VCVH)	.50	16.6				16.6	16.8	33.3				16.6	16.6	50	6
Aid to the Blind Department (VCVH)	60			40				40	20		20			20	5
Ophthalmologists	60			20			20	20					40	40	5
Community Action Agencies	33.3				33.3		33.3	33.3						66.6	3
General medical practitioners	25	50	25					50					25	25	4
Optometrists	66.6	33.3						33.3					33.3	33.3	3
Public institutions	33.3		33.3	33.3									66.6	33.3	3
Individuals (private)	50			50									50	50	2
Veteran's Ad.	50					50							100		2
Educational Services (VCVH)	50			31.2	6.3		18.5	31.2			18.7	12.5		37.5	16
Total % disabilities for each type	61.4	8.4	4.8	14.4	4.8	3.6	7.2	31.3	1.2	0.0	6.1	4.5	16.8	40.9	

Total number on caseload at the time of the survey = 83

Category 1, 12.5 percent have primary disabilities in Category 2, and none have primary disabilities in Categories 3 through 7. Also difficult to explain is the fact that only 3.6 percent of the total caseload suffered total blindness in either eye or in both eyes. It is also interesting to note, but perhaps of no significant consequence statistically speaking, that 40.9 percent of the total caseload have no secondary disability.

It is difficult to make any assumptions regarding the frequency with which different referral sources tend to refer certain types of disabled persons to this agency. This distribution is indicative of one point and is not indicative of a general pattern. To be more valid and useful to the counselor, such a distribution would have to be taken over a period of time, such as every six months for a period of two years.

STUDENT WORK: SAMPLE 2

A Comparison of Primary and Secondary Disabilities with Referral Sources

A general field counselor in this state deals with a wide variety of disabilities which are brought to his attention by many different persons and agencies. An analysis of the counselor's caseload can be a valuable aid in discerning gaps or deficiencies in providing rehabilitation services to a given area. By the same token, it can reveal that which the counselor is doing well. The overall purpose in such an exercise is the promotion of counselor effectiveness since one can hardly plan constructively unless he has a concept of what is presently occurring.

This analysis is based upon an active caseload of 150. The first factor to be studied will be that of primary and secondary disabilities to be followed by a survey of referral sources. The numerical composition and the resulting implications for the counselor will be the primary areas of scrutiny.

Disability as used here will be defined as (1) any physical, mental, or emotional problem which can be documented medically or psychologically; (2) a primary disability shall be that problem which is the more severe when two or more disabilities are present. They will be listed according to numerical frequency in descending order. General categories rather than specific diag-

DISABILITY

Type	Primary	%	Secondary*	%
Mental retardation, mild	35	23.3	19	23.8
Mental retardation, functional	29	20.0	46	57.5
Orthopedic	20	13.3		
Behavioral disorders	18	12.0	5	6.2
Mental disorders	11	7.3	2	2.5
Bronchial asthma	6	4.0	3	3.0
Hernia	5	3.3	1	1.3
Hearing disorders	4	2.7		
Uterine fibroids	4	2.7		
Spinal cord injuries	3	2.0	1	1.3
Cerebral palsy	2	1.3		
Circulatory	2	1.3	1	1.3
Diabetes	2	1.3		
Epilepsy	2	1.3		
Rheumatic fever	2	1.3	2	2.5
Tuberculosis	2	1.3		
CVA	1	.7		
Drug abuse	1	.7		
Eyesight	1	.7		
Totals	150	100.5	80	99.4

* Many secondary disabilities were not documented prior to analysis, particularly with those functionally retarded.

noses are used for brevity's sake and are felt to be equally meaningful for discussion.

Analysis of Frequency

The most obvious fact to be gleaned from the foregoing chart is the preponderance of cases (50%) which are either mental retardation or mental illness. This denotes a significant trend since their inclusion as a disability in 1943. The prevalence of such disabilities in the society at large and the concern of vocational rehabilitation for these persons are amply demonstrated. There are many who feel that this will be the major handicap with which DVR will become involved. Sizable numbers of the mentally retarded are products of cultural and educational deprivation as one might expect from the lower end of the socioeconomic spectrum which constitutes the bulk of the DVR clientele.

The relatively small number of hernias and fibroids supports the contention that medical assistance programs and the ever-increasing employer-sponsored medical insurance plans have reduced DVR's traditional three H's—hernias, hysterectomies, and hemorrhoids—as physical restoration plans.

There are still a goodly number of orthopedic defects (20%) both congenital and traumatic, which are being brought to the attention of the agency and which frequently require extensive service, particularly in the area of vocational or college training.

Behavioral disorders which often are symptomatic of a more severe mental disturbance are, nevertheless, categorized separately. More recent legislation has opened rehabilitation avenues for problems of this nature especially with teenagers who have immense difficulty in adjusting to a rapidly changing environment and are victims of the upsurge in broken homes. This is another disability which seems to be on the increase and, in all probability, will continue to be so.

Scatterings of many other types of disabilities are present and will be dealt with as they arise, but they are limited in number and should not increase measurably except for drug abuse. Very few of the drug cases have been referred for various reasons although the effects of the drug culture are being felt now and will become a more significant factor later on. Too much vagueness and uncertainty surrounds the drug situation to attempt an accurate projection at this point.

Analysis of Referral Source

Source	Number of Referrals	Percentage (%)
Public schools	63	42.0
Physicians	17	10.9
Public welfare	16	10.6
Self	10	6.7
Friends	9	6.0
Public health	8	5.4
Corrections	6	4.0
SSDI	5	3.3
Prosthetic suppliers	4	2.7
VEC	4	2.7
TB sanatorium	2	1.3
Cerebral palsy center	2	1.3
Crippled children's hospital	2	1.3
Industrial commission	2	1.3
Totals	150	99.5

REFERRAL SOURCE

The largest number of active cases on this caseload were referred by the public schools in the area. There are three high schools and three junior high schools which are contacted on a regular basis. The primary contact person at each high school is the guidance counselor, whereas the visiting teacher acts as the liaison between the junior high schools and vocational rehabilitation. A relatively small percentage of school referrals have problems of a physical nature, chiefly because of improved medical and health services. Mild mental retardation, functional retardation, and behavioral disorders constitute the bulk of referrals. This reflects in part the growing concern of the school systems for students who are not college bound and the increasing flexibility of vocational rehabilitation to be of service to such persons. There remain, however, many more students who are in need of service.

Physicians also make referrals but not to the extent one might expect. Although their number of referrals is second, it is a poor second. This is due primarily to the increased recipients of Medicaid and to expanding group insurance programs in the area. There also appears to be a great gap between the conception of what rehabilitation is and what it ought to be in the minds of many doctors. It behooves the counselor to involve himself in an educational process.

Public health and welfare agencies are also somewhat in the dark and require constant updating as to vocational rehabilitation and what it is all about. The counselor will need to implement the cooperative agreements more actively at the local level.

Social Security Disability Insurance and the Industrial Commission refer persons regularly but with few being accepted. SSDI applicants are far too often deemed to be infeasible, whereas the majority of Industrial Commission referrals have simply been injured on the job and plan to return to work with little or no residual effect.

The remainder of the referred or transferred cases come from a variety of specialized institutions which can only be kept informed that vocational rehabilitation will do its part and will keep the institution informed as to its actions.

To narrow in on a specific referral source, the physician is necessary in order to explain the underlying rationale for the small percentage of referrals made to vocational rehabilitation. This counselor will identify this situation as it pertains to physicians.

There are a goodly number of physicians in the area who rarely if ever make a referral. There are three primary reasons: (1) the rapid increase of Medicaid recipients; (2) the expansion of employer-funded group insurance plans, and (3) the lack of understanding physicians have for rehabilitation.

For the first two factors to be dealt with adequately, there must be a thorough educational program undertaken by the local counselor to broaden the concepts held by doctors about DVR and to foment a greater understanding of the capabilities and activities. It is this third factor which is so crucial. Certainly the first two factors have made inroads, but there remains a large number of persons in need of physical restoration services who are not aware of DVR and who could be made so by their physicians. For this to occur the doctor must know who can benefit from DVR services and how to bring the prospective client and the counselor together. This can be done through the following steps:

1. A face-to-face meeting between counselor and doctor to create a common ground of understanding.

2. Subsequent regular contact by the counselor.

3. Appraisal of the counselor's itinerary and office hours for the doctor.

4. The speeding up of the rehabilitation process whenever advisable and possible.

5. A constant updating of DVR policy changes for the doctor.

6. Accurate procedural action to avoid undue delay and complications.

Exercise 4

FREQUENCY DISTRIBUTION IN STATE HOSPITALS OR INSTITUTIONS

RATIONALE

Often the counselor involved in a cooperative program in a state hospital or institution does not receive his referrals in the same manner as does the general counselor in the field. Usually the counselor in the institution receives his referrals from within and may receive his referrals from one particular source. As the rehabilitation counselor for this unit, you have responsibility to develop effective professional relationships with the various departments in that institution.

ASSIGNMENT

Part A. Trainees working in state institutions where referrals are from within will prepare a frequency distribution using referral sources from departments in that facility, such as guidance, nursing, medical, administration, social work, occupational therapy, physical therapy, and psychology. You are to make recommendations for improving the working relationships with a hospital staff and field program. If you are in an institution where the referrals are coming from only one person such as the chief psychiatrist or director of medical services, discuss an approach you might employ in order to insure that the other members of the hospital staff understand the role of vocational rehabilitation. If you do not attend hospital staff conferences, plan how you might be allowed to arrange this. Include your view of the interdisciplinary team approach to vocational rehabilitation and the role and function of each discipline as it relates to the philosophy of client rehabilitation.

Part B. The second part to this exercise will be to make a frequency distribution of primary and secondary disabilities (only if Exercise 3 was not assigned to you).

STUDENT WORK: SAMPLE 1
Part A: Referral Sources from Within the Hospital

Each vocational rehabilitation counselor in our hospital rehabilitation unit is assigned a specific geographic unit. As each patient is admitted to the hospital our unit receives an admission card on the individual. Depending upon his home county, a counselor is assigned to interview the patient. As the relationship and rehabilitation process develops, the counselor decides whether or not to continue working with the patient. However, there are no individual referrals from within the various hospital departments; i.e. social work, occupational therapy, physical therapy, recreation therapy, industrial therapy, and psychology. Therefore, a frequency distribution chart would show 100 percent via ADMISSIONS.

The following is a sample of an admission card to which the vocational rehabilitation counselor has access.

Name		*Ward*	*Social Security* #
DOE, John		IT/10	267-70-3069
Admission	*Type*	*Doctor*	*Marital Status*
12–16–69 10:45AM	Vol.	Dr. Jones	Divorced
Address			
6th Street, Central City, Kentucky		Muhlenberg 089	

Sex	*Race*	*Religion*	*Birthdate*	*Age*	*# Children*	*Birthplace*
Male	White	Baptist	02–02–32	37	no children	Born in Muhlenberg County, Kentucky

Education	*Occupation*
4th grade	Truck Driver

Previous Psychiatric Treatment	*Annual Family Income*
State Hospital (2) admissions	None

Admission Diagnostic Impression:	*Referral Source*
Schizophrenic, Chronic Undifferentiated Type.	Self

Comments:

Recommendations and newly developed procedures for improving the working relationships with the hospital staff and field program are as follows:

1. Team meetings recently have been instituted in which the ward doctor, vocational rehabilitation counselor, ward nurse, social worker, industrial therapist, chaplain, and occupational therapist meet bimonthly to discuss all patients. There is updated exchange of information. Specifically, the vocational rehabilitation counselor makes his or her recommendations and informs the other team members of all vocational endeavors.

2. This counselor also holds conferences with various ward doctors when there is a question concerning the progress of the patient.

3. Also, our unit has begun to keep detailed progress reports. (Notations in the vocational rehabilitation folder have always been complete.) However, now this counselor sends a copy of all interviews and meetings to the following:

   a. Mental health center.
   b. Medical records for the main chart.
   c. Notes to the ward (discussion during team meetings).
   d. Vocational rehabilitation folder.

Each report states where the meeting or interview was held and what was discussed.

4. There is also a work training center meeting held twice a month. It is held in the Rehabilitation Unit. Present are members from social service, occupational therapy, recreation, industrial therapy, the chaplancy, the work training center, and vocational rehabilitation. The psychologist and doctors have standing invitations to all meetings. Again, each patient working in the center is discussed in terms of progress made and ability. At this time any member present may report on his progress with the patient. Also, new referrals to the work training center are made through the vocational rehabilitation counselor.

5. Lastly, each week the vocational rehabilitation supervisor meets with the hospital superintendent, nursing staff, and all doctors. Then after each meeting the unit supervisor meets with all staff members in the rehabilitation unit. In this way each

member is kept informed as to all new policies being developed in the hospital.

Part B: Frequency Distribution of Caseload by Primary Disability

Code	Disability	Number	%
500	Psychotic disorders	57	43.2
	1. Manic depressive (3)		
	2. Psychotic reaction (0)		
	3. Schizophrenia (45)		
	4. Paranoid (6)		
	5. Chronic brain syndrome (3)		
510	Psychoneurotic disorders	9	6.1
	1. Psychoneurotic reaction (4)		
	2. Anxiety reaction (2)		
	3. Dissociative reaction (2)		
	4. Conversive reaction (1)		
	5. Phobic reaction (0)		
	6. Obsessive compulsive reaction (0)		
520	Alcoholism	49	37.2
522	Personality disorder	8	6.3
521	Drug addiction	3	2.4
530	Mental retardation and deficiency	6	4.7
	1. Mild (5)		
	2. Moderate (0)		
	3. Severe (1)		
	Total	132	99.9%*

* Error due to numbers having been rounded off.

According to this particular caseload (numbering 132 active cases), 43.2 percent are classified psychotic disorder (code 500), and of this group 79.1 percent are schizophrenia, 10.59 percent are paranoid, 5.2 percent are manic depressive, and 5.29 percent are CBS. Next, 37.2 percent of the entire caseload carry a final psychiatric diagnosis of alcoholism. Remember these figures denote primary disability only.

Psychoneurotic disorders at present make up only 6.10 percent (code 510) of the total caseload. Naturally the percentage of mentally retarded is quite small, being 4.7 percent. Also code 521, Drug Addicition, 2.4 percent and code 522, Personality Disorders, 6.3 percent are relatively low in comparison to two years ago.

Why? Upon investigation the following was indicated:

1. Two years ago psychoneurotic disorders made up approximately 63 percent of the caseload at this hospital unit. Today this figure has dropped to 6.10 percent, the reason being the effectiveness of mental health centers. Rather than admitting these people to hospitals where there is a strong chance of institutionalization, they are remaining at home and on the job. Periodically they are seen at their local mental health center.*

2. Alcoholism (code 520) has risen sharply from 8 percent two years ago to 37.2 percent. Why? To begin with, there are not more alcoholics today; rather this hospital has instituted a very effective alcoholic rehabilitation program. Secondly, our hospital is admitting alcoholics on a voluntary basis whereas several years ago they were not. In fact, two-to-four years ago alcoholics were admitted carrying a primary disability of personality disorder (522). The alcoholism was considered a secondary disability.

3. Mental retardation figures have always been very low because of another local hospital (State School) which specializes with mental retardation and deficiency. Secondly, the middle-aged elderly retarded are being placed more and more into nursing homes. However, it should be noted that there are a few patients in our facility at State Hospital who do carry mental retardataion as a primary disability. Why are these people here? In each case there is a personality and/or psychotic disorder compounding their mental deficiency, and thus there is a possibility of physical danger. In these cases the most effective treatment is brought about at our facility. Thus, there is less of a danger to the other mentally retarded if they were here rather than stay at State School. They now have a patient population of 435 and a doctor's staff numbering one. The rationale behind the decision to move these patients is self-evident.

---

*1. The percentage regarding psychoneurotic disorders of two years ago (63%) was obtained by the following method: A counselor conference was held between this counselor and the principal counselor present in this unit. He helped me review the caseloads of past years as to primary disability. Hospital admission records were checked in the medical records room. A sampling was taken; and the approximate percentage resulted.

4. Psychotic disorders have vacillated very little during the last four years. The figures vary between 35 percent and 45 percent. This, I feel, is very stable. Today it is this group which is the most difficult to keep out of the hospital. Today's percentage actually denotes chronic, "revolving-door" patients. These are the people who leave for a while but always seem to return. It is my opinion that the average readmission rate on this group is 80 percent. Further, the readmission rate of alcoholics is 85 percent, but their employability rate is also 85 percent. Alcoholics always seem to have something to fall back on but those patients suffering with a psychotic disorder rarely do.

5. Lastly, drug addiction has always been quite small. Usually the diagnosis varies with that of personality disorder.

Frequency Distribution by Secondary Disability

To date in this counselor's active caseload of 132 cases there have been only five cases with a secondary disability: two carry a secondary disability of mental retardation (mild); one with a secondary disability of deaf/mute; another has been diagnosed as chronic alcoholism; the fifth client suffers from a chronic brain syndrome.

Even though this is a relatively small percentage in relation to the total caseload, this counselor feels that other secondary disabilities do exist. The hospital staff is so overtaxed with admissions and understaffed with qualified help that comprehensive medical examinations are few and far between. Also, upon admission, the patient usually is under such a psychotic state that the medical emphasis is in the immediate control of maladaptive behavior. Once the staff does this, little time is left over to perform complete physicals.

Exercise 5

COOPERATIVE AGREEMENT

RATIONALE

As a vocational rehabilitation worker functioning within a cooperative program, it is necessary to understand the written document linking your agency with the related organization. All too often counselors have been functioning in a position under the auspices of a cooperative agreement and have not understood how these two agencies began working with one another for the welfare of clients and have not understood the responsibilities of each party.

ASSIGNMENT

Plan a meeting with your training coordinator and/or your supervisor to discuss the cooperative agreement. It is essential you have a copy of this agreement and understand every facet of it; therefore, after reading it over, discuss *in your own words* the essence of this contract. Plan a meeting with your counterpart in the other organization and discuss the rationale for the cooperative agreement. Record in a narrative fashion the results of this meeting. Identify the strength (s) as well as the weakness (es) of this cooperative agreement and include your recommendations for improvements.

STUDENT WORK: SAMPLE 1

A cooperative relationship between the Division of Vocational Rehabilitation and the Goodwill Industries has existed for more than 30 years in this state. The Goodwill Industries Workshop had a small beginning, but apparently in the 1930's occasional training placements were made by vocational rehabilitation counselors. Unfortunately, no documentation is available in the files of either agency prior to the establishment in 1961 of the present Goodwill Industries Rehabilitation Center. Although the

53

interest that prompted the establishment of the center was primarily local, the Division of Vocational Rehabilitation gave strong support to the planning for such a center.

Prominent local citizens became interested to the extent of setting up a local fund, estimated variously between 100 and 150 thousand dollars, in order to attract other funds. Initially the largest outside fund attracted was provided by the State Medical Care Association, which agreed to contribute only after the Division of Vocational Rehabilitation gave assurance that they would support the center by placing clients there. The original center, which opened in 1961, did not have dormitory facilities, and this weakness was noted at once. Without dormitory facilities, the center could not, of course, play a significant part in the rehabilitation of handicapped persons on a state-wide basis. Consequently, the Division of Vocational Rehabilitation took the lead in attracting federal funds which made the construction of the dormitory addition possible by 1963.

The first formal interagency agreement took place in late 1963, and it provided for training course outlines, referral procedures, and progress reports. This was a general agreement and was followed shortly by an agreement providing for board and room rates. This agreement concerning rates has been renegotiated four times since 1963, and there will undoubtedly be other negotiations soon.

There has never been a formal agreement between the two agencies as to referral procedures, but letters to and from agency heads throughout the years have served in lieu of a formal agreement. Vocational rehabilitation counselors have been instructed to follow the Goodwill Industries manual of services in this regard, and the Goodwill Rehabilitation Center has been careful to supply the counselors with copies of this manual. The contact person at Goodwill Rehabilitation Center has always been the director of rehabilitation and training. From time to time the Division of Rehabilitation has urged its counselors to visit the center, and the center has dispatched public relations teams to the various district offices of the rehabilitation agencies in order to explain services and policies.

As the number of referrals increased, the needs for a liaison counselor at the center became apparent. In 1965 a counselor position was established at the center for this express purpose. This counselor has served as the contact person through whom the vocational rehabilitation counselors served their clients, and as the contact person between the center and the vocational rehabilitation counselors. This contact role has never extended to matters of the admission of clients to the center. This judgmental activity has remained exclusively with the center.

When the Training Services Grant Program was established in 1966 under the aegis of the Rehabilitation Services Administration, the Division of Vocational Rehabilitation played the major role in arranging the organization of the Goodwill Rehabilitation Center as a government-approved facility. The administration of this grant became the responsibility of the liaison counselor and added greatly to his work load. The Goodwill Center also felt the need of more efficient services with respect to the administration of the grant. In 1967, when the grant request was renewed for another year, a request was made for a placement counselor position, and this was granted. Therefore, two contact persons were available; one dealing primarily with training services allowances, and the other with general liaison activities. This is the situation prevailing at the time of writing.

STUDENT WORK: SAMPLE 2
County Mental Health Clinic
Staff

Clinical Director	Field Service Guide
Consultation in Child and Adult Psychiatry	Vocational Rehabilitation
Psychiatric Social Worker (half-time)	Two Secretaries
Consultant Psychologists	Coordinator

I talked with the director of the clinic about its beginning and purpose, and the following is a summary of that discussion.

The clinic began in October 1964 as a satellite clinic of the local mental hospital. It was started by a doctor while on an elective rotation from the Duke University residency program. This doctor is now the director of the clinic as well as unit director of the northeastern unit at the hospital. A social worker assisted the director, and the clinic was held once a week. This operation continued for about two and a half years. About half of the patient load was aftercare, and in addition they averaged about three new patients a week, accepting referrals directly from private practitioners and agencies. The clinic did some screening prior to admission. The operation was almost entirely clinical work with patients, although one of the nurses did some consultation for a few months with the public health nurses. The original plan was to operate the clinic free to the county for only one year, but because of the excellent use made of the clinic, it was continued until June 1966, when county commissioners were told that the operation could not be continued free of charge. The director also felt that he needed more time on the unit, and so the clinic was held on Saturday once every two weeks. This was quite a reduction in service, but the previous experience seemed to create a demand for a clinic and it was well supported by the medical association, agencies, etc. In the spring of 1967, the commissioners appropriated $10,000 for the coming year, making them eligible to apply for $20,000 in matching funds.

The functions of the clinic have been rather flexible. During the time it was held weekly, new referrals from the community were plentiful and encouraged. For the past year, the waiting period for a new referral has been four to six weeks and naturally the requests have subsided. Most of the patients seen are now aftercare, though community referral has still continued. The clinic is now held five times a week and on Tuesday evenings, and the program is daily expanding.

Summary of Clinical Staff Duties

DIRECTOR. The director is responsible for the selection of the staff and for planning their duties, and the administration of the overall clinical services program. He will do clinical work as well as consultations with other staff members, agencies, and so forth, to help others become involved in the clinic program.

SOCIAL WORKER. This position is a joint position with the

Northeastern Unit, and the person spends two and a half days in each place, the county reimbursing the hospital for one-half of the salary. In addition, the social worker will be present at the Tuesday evening clinic and is paid a consultant fee for this service. She assists in taking social histories and also becomes thoroughly familiar with another similar program so that she can coordinate the two programs. She will help develop teaching programs for nursing and boarding home operators and develop a group therapy program for alcoholics.

CONSULTANT PSYCHOLOGIST. These persons are often residents from the nearby state university. Their duties are to test clients and work in conjunction with the psychiatrist to do what is necessary to evaluate a patient for treatment.

COORDINATOR. It will be this person's duty to keep the clinic's various activities running smoothly when the unit director is not there. This person will also serve basically as a public relations manager in the community for the clinic. She shall set up clinics, workshops, programs, and other projects that will boost the interest of the community in mental health.

FIELD SERVICE GUIDE. It is this person's duty to keep in touch with all discharged persons from the mental hospital to see that they are taking their medication and keeping appointments at the clinic if necessary. He will also visit the hospital every Friday for the purpose of seeing patients in the hospital, bringing patients in the hospital, bringing patients home who do not have transportation, and consulting with doctors on the patient's progress.

VOCATIONAL REHABILITATION COUNSELOR. This person shall take referrals from the doctor who needs help in job assistance or training. He shall be at the clinic one full day a week, free to the county. This worker will be provided by the Northeastern Unit. This counselor will also do follow-up work on hospital referrals and cases.

Summary

As can be gleaned from all the information above, the clinic is a multi-purpose unit. It is one of the steps toward preventive mental health care and participates in everything from school programs and PTA meetings to free marriage counseling clinics. All services are free to the public in an effort to increase the interest of the community in mental health. Certainly this clinic and others like it are providing wonderful services to the communities around it, and very often are enabling persons to obtain psychiatric help but remain in the community.

With the recent addition of the vocational rehabilitation counselor and family service guide, the client is followed from beginning to end, and for the client leaving the hospital to return to the community, there is someone to help them make the transition. Certainly for vocational rehabilitation specifically, the clinic is a wonderful source for testing and evaluation as well as therapy.

This sort of program not only helps the mentally ill, but almost more important it helps the community to understand the problems of others who may have mental problems or family difficulties so that the road back is made easier for the mentally ill.

Exercise 6

INITIAL INTERVIEW

RATIONALE

Upon returning to the local office, you will immediately assume a caseload as well as initiate service for new clients. The initial interview often has a direct bearing on the final outcome of a case; if the counselor does not begin to establish rapport with his client, the counselor may find it difficult to be of service to the client in future contacts. On the other hand, an effective initial interview can promote client motivation and trust.

ASSIGNMENT

The trainee is to submit a discussion of an initial interview. As a minimum, the written report should include this information:

A. How was the appointment made?

B. What plans were used to put the client at ease?

C. What methods did you use to gain the client's confidence and get him to talk freely without controlling the interview?

D. How did you assess:

  1. "Can do" factors (abilities, skills, knowledges)?

  2. "Will do" factors (motivation, interest, personality)?

E. What were some of the factors you took into consideration to evaluate the client's "emotional maturity"?

F. How did you assess his readiness for work and his attitudes toward work?

STUDENT WORK: SAMPLE 1

Initial Interview with Mrs. J

Since as a counselor I am institution-based, there is not, as a consequence, a variety of referral sources. Rather our procedure is a structured one and consists of a referral by a doctor from either the receiving department or one of the regular wards. Before the initial interview, the counselors already have obtained medical reports, progress notes, and diagnoses from the files; and appointments are set up through notification of the nursing staff in the client's building.

Mrs. J, the client I have chosen for the "initial interview," was a new admittance to the hospital. She was referred from the receiving department, and prior to my talk with her the following information (which I have abbreviated somewhat) was made available:

> Mrs. J, a 50-year-old Negro female, with a diagnosis of Schizophrenia, Chronic Undifferentiated Type, was admitted to State Hospital in April, 1969, on voluntary papers. Mrs. J has a history of being a patient at another state hospital on several different occasions. More recently, she was at the local sanitorium because of suspected pulmonary tuberculosis. At the present time, this is arrested. The patient admits to a history of hearing voices, accusatory in nature, and having visual hallucinations. During the staff conference she was still worried about the voices, and stated that they bothered her a lot. However, she was well oriented and in contact although somewhat depressed.

While the overall purpose of the opening interview is to (1) find out whether the client is interested in rehabilitation services, and (2) allow the counselor to assess client motivation, capabilities, etc., these aims are achieved most successfully, I believe, by relying on a nonstructured approach during the first meeting with the client, allowing him to carry the main part of the "conversational ball." The counselor is in effect trying to "sound out" the client in a number of areas, and this is best achieved by nondirective, reflective techniques.

The exception to this rule would operate in the case of a hyperactive or very manipulative client where directiveness by the counselor might be necessary to keep the interview on a logical track or to avoid the counselor being drawn into a "game" situation as projected by the client. Indeed, "many studies have pointed out that . . . the counselor should be active in the initial interview. This activity does not imply that the counselor has to lead the client because of his own needs; but rather he should take the initiative to reinforce those client behaviors which are positive steps toward rehabilitation." *

With the majority of clients, however, who are apt to be somewhat hesitant, anxious, shy, and even hostile, the counselor is concerned with creating a warm, receptive atmosphere in which the client can relax and express what he wants to say.

Because the rehabilitation client is in a dependent position when he approaches a vocational rehabilitation agency, it is important that his first contact with the agency be positive and rapport should be established as soon as possible.

This can be accomplished in a variety of ways, but the procedure I usually follow is to greet the client in an informal manner, ask a few questions, general in nature (avoiding emotion-packed subject matter) but specific enough so that the client knows you are interested in his or her case and aware of the problems that may be involved, and from there, after having established some kind of meaningful though tenuous response from the client, go on to briefly explain just what rehabilitation at State Hospital is set up to do, the aims of the program, services provided, etc. This explanation, in addition to supplying information to the client, allows him to "take stock" of the situation; i.e. become accustomed to the counselor and adjust to the unfamiliar surroundings.

After drawing a picture of rehabilitation services, the interview is ready to proceed to a more "in-depth" level and get down to the "meat" of the client's vocational situation. This may be accomplished by such open-ended questions as: How do you feel vocational rehabilitation could help you? Have you thought about the kind of job you might wish to look for after you leave the hospital? Were you satisfied with the kind of jobs you have held in the past?

In general, I would say the counselor should keep in mind the following considerations in his attempts to set the client at ease:

1. Talk on the client's level, using vocabulary consistent with

---

* See "Rehabilitation Counseling in a Dyad," by William McPhee, Frederick Janse, Gary O. Jorgensen, and Cecil O. Samuelson. *Journal of Rehabilitation,* January-February 1969, Vol. 35, pp. 19-22.

the latter's socioeconomic background. Do not, however, attempt to "talk down" to a client, but try to strike a happy medium where you indicate a basic respect for the client as a person (speak, as necessary, in terms he will understand). Communication is of the utmost importance in the client-counselor relationship, and a corollary of communication is empathy or understanding the client from his own frame of reference. Rogers defined empathy as "sensing the client's private world as if it were your own without ever losing the 'as if' quality." * In effect, a counselor must be able to convey his understanding of a client's feelings and attitudes while avoiding a perhaps natural tendency to prejudge and evaluate. In line with this, a counselor should be aware of situational and background factors as they are relevant to a client. Failure to communicate is of course one of the greatest barriers to an interpersonal relationship and may result in defensiveness, hostility, apathy, or other undesirable responses.

2. Use open-ended questions to elicit the fullest possible expression on the part of the client.

3. Rely—except in the instance previously noted of hyperactivity or manipulativeness—on a reflective technique to establish sympathy and reduce anxiety. A client should never feel threatened by a counselor's directiveness, and often, especially with mental patients, the solution does indeed seem to rest with the individual. By receptive listening, a counselor may not only encourage a client to define his problem, but arrive at an awareness of possible solutions.

4. The counselor, if attuned to the client, will be aware that the nuances, the *feeling-tone* underlying the words are often more important than the words themselves and should proceed to act on that basis; i.e. in the case of Mrs. J even though she reiterated she could not work because of "the voices," the tone in which she spoke indicated to the counselor that she really wanted help and someone to reassure her that she could work and function again in society.

5. Adopt a positive attitude and be genuinely supportive of

---

* See "An Instrument for the Measurement of Counselor Orientation," by William S. Sather, George N. Wright, and Alfred J. Butler. In *Wisconsin Studies in Vocational Rehabilitation*. Madison, Wisconsin, 1968, p. 13.

the client's efforts towards rehabilitation. The client will be sensitive to false optimism, and the expectancy on your part that the client does have the potential for improved functioning seems to be a vital determinant of counselor evaluations and client progress.

6. Importance of interview dynamics: Counselors should avoid a rigid, "deskside" manner and be responsive to shifts in client attitudes, mood, etc. For example, the use of direct eye contact is helpful in maintaining a continuous flow during an interview but there may be times when pauses will be necessary to allow a client to get his bearings. Beware of such negative factors as tardiness for interviews, insincerity, and unwarranted interruptions.

Assuming now that the counselor has established an initial rapport by use of the aforementioned considerations, the best way to assess a client's abilities and skills as well as motivation and interest is by inquiries into social attitudes and past job performance—proceeding on the assumption that the most reliable projection of future functioning is derived from observation and knowledge of the client's past.

In the case of Mrs. J, such questions as "What kind of work have you done? Have you had any special kinds of training—in school, on the job? Which job did you like the most . . . the least? What is the longest period of time you have held any job?" resulted in the following information. Mrs. J had been employed as a cook in several nursing homes for a number of years; following contraction of tuberculosis her vocational skill was rendered untenable, and subsequently the client found work in a janitorial capacity at the nearby sanitorium in her home town.

One criterion I think a counselor is always on the lookout for with regard to motivation is the degree of initiative displayed by clients in securing positions. Were there lengthy periods between jobs, and if so, was the client a passive recipient of welfare allotments at these times or was there an active effort on his part to find a job?

As a corollary of the latter, were most of his positions secured through the auspices of a welfare worker, a rehabilitation agency, or social service caseworker? Has he in effect played an active or a passive role with regard to job placement?

To continue this train of thought and delve further into motivation, it is important to ascertain the extent of past vocational aspirations. Has the client ever attempted to raise his vocational level by applying for training, either by classroom instruction or an apprentice on-the-job type of situation? Whether he actually entered into and completed the training is of course also relevant, but particularly in the case of culturally deprived clients, the doors to further training may have been barred by economic, racial, or other considerations. Thus, of primary concern to the counselor is whether initial impetus of ambition existed.

Frankness and responsiveness on the part of the client are also key considerations in assessing "will do" factors. Is the client honest in his appraisal of past failures or difficulty, vocationally, or does he try to cover up a discharge from employment? Does the client react in a positive fashion to suggestions of vocational opportunities by the counselor? Is he stimulated to consider possible new areas of employment? Admittedly, in the latter instance, the amount of stimulation often depends on the counselor's skill at presentation; but especially in the case of younger clients where ignorance of vocational areas may have appeared as a lack of motivation, the response to new vocational outlooks is particularly important.

Emotional readiness is often a rather nebulous area, especially in the case of mental patients where their behavior during an interview may be subsequently contradicted by reports of the nursing staff. However, there are certain guideposts which help the counselor in his determination. The most obvious of these are appearance and general physical condition, eye contact, affect, orientation, and ability to express oneself. A client who is sloppy in dress, disoriented and vague as to time and place, exhibits an inappropriate effect, or has difficulty in talking to the counselor (either by reason of a speech defect or emotional problem), is evidently not ready for work despite protestations to the contrary. Work adjustment and social reorientation may thus become necessary before the client is in a position to compete in the labor market.

Less obvious aspects of emotional maturity involve the degree of insight achieved by the client; i.e. does he realize the extent to which emotional blocks may have hindered job performance? Does he face difficult situations, or does he seek escape? Are his vocational goals realistic, or does he indulge in flights of ambition which seem to bear little relation to apparent mental level or past academic performance?

Emotional stability also can be assessed by the degree of dependence exhibited. Is the client still tied to parental authority, or conversely does he seem eager to effect a transference to the counselor? Does he tell a tale of woe or does he appear to be somewhat self-reliant, abstaining from entreaties or "begging" of the counselor, such as asking for pocket money, etc.?

Another essential ingredient vis-à-vis maturity is the client's self-image. Does he flog himself mentally with guilt feelings, or does he consider himself basically a worthwhile, productive person, capable of playing an active role in society?

In dealing with mental patients, a counselor must also attempt to assess during the interview the extent to which the client may be debilitated vocationally by suspiciousness, undue anxiety, hostility, irrationality, and other more obvious symptoms of mental illness such as hallucinations, delusions, hyperactivity, and flight of ideas. Some of these drawbacks are also operative, of course, with physically handicapped or culturally deprived clients but to a much less aggravated extent.

In the case of Mrs. J—while the client's motivation and desire to return to work were admittedly strong, although clouded at first by her anxiety over hearing voices—the counselor was faced with the realization that if this client were to function at all, it would have to be on the basis of acceptance of the hallucinations as a continuing state, not markedly amenable to medication. The question now was: Could the client be successfully rehabilitated despite a severe mental handicap?

The tentative conclusion reached by the counselor as a result of this initial interview was that Mrs. J probably could be rehabilitated and a job placement secured because of (1) the client's past industriousness and excellent work record and (2) the degree of insight achieved by Mrs. J, i.e. a partial acceptance of her condition and the prospect of awareness that to allow the hallucinations to which she was subject to disrupt the lives of those around her would, in the end, work against her own best interests. Thus Mrs. J, while at present requiring hospitalization, can look forward in the near future to the prospect of job placement.

The matter of assessing an initial interview as well as subsequent ones actually rests on a counselor's ability to maintain a delicate equilibrium. On the one hand, he must not merely "skim the surface" conversationally, but should be able to explore at some depth vocational abilities and potential. On the other hand, he should not engage in therapy per se, or attempts to restructure the personality, and so must avoid, where possible, emotion-charged areas that will merely result in an impasse between client and counselor or a "squaring off" into defensive and offensive positions.

The techniques employed to maintain this equilibrium and yet establish rapport are many and varied, and while I personally incline toward the approaches detailed above, in particular a nondirective orientation, I do not, however, feel that research on counseling has conclusively demonstrated that any particular group of techniques or "school of counseling" achieves better results than another. Basically I subscribe to the belief that the outcome of counseling is not so much a matter of theoretical orientation but is rather related to the counselor being warm, accepting, and empathetic. Above all, he should display a genuine respect for the client and the client-counselor relationship.

STUDENT WORK: SAMPLE 2
Initial Interview with Mr. A

The following is a documentation of an "initial interview" concerning one Mr. A.

Part A: How the Appointment Was Made

This appointment was brought about by an entirely different

method than I ordinarily use. Usually after the individual has been admitted I routinely receive a copy of the admission card; then an appointment is made. In the case of Mr. A, however, I tried something new.

While visiting the mental health center in Henderson I held a conference with the social workers. Upon conclusion of the meeting I held a private conference with one of the social workers. I asked if there was anyone coming to the clinic whom he felt would soon be going to the hospital for intensive treatment. The reply was positive; Mr. A, a young man of twenty, had recently been medically discharged from the Army. He was not improving while attending the center. In fact, he was deteriorating rapidly. The center psychiatrist had already recommended admission.

Thus this counselor felt that this particular young man would be hospitalized quite soon. Further discussion with the doctor revealed that admission would occur the following Monday.

I called my unit and had my secretary schedule an appointment on the Friday of the same week of admission. This was done due to the following reasons: The first three days following admission are reserved for complete physical, psychological, and psychiatric examinations and testing. A complete social history is taken. Therapy assignments are made. And lastly, time is needed for the new patient to orient himself to the hospital structure and routine.

Part B: Steps Used to Determine the Approach During the Initial Interview

Before the client was seen the counselor did the following:

1. The counselor held a conference with both the doctor and social worker. Both of these gentlemen had been following Mr. A for four years.

2. The medical/social material was read and evaluated by the vocational rehabilitation counselor.

3. The counselor met with his civilian employers, his family, and high school guidance counselor.

4. The information obtained revealed that this young man had been hospitalized several times for psychiatric purposes. His conversations had always been loose; he continually had auditory

hallucinations; and he had demonstrated confused thinking processes as early as the ninth grade of school. His affect frequently was inappropriate. While in high school Mr. A experienced a psychotic episode. It was also noted that his mother had been a patient in the hospital for several years and has had no contact with her son since he was a child. Lastly, Mr. A served eight months in the Army and was stationed in Germany. While there he suffered another psychotic break.

5. The psychological testing supported the above findings. Tests administered were the Minnesota Multiphasic Personality Inventory, the Rotter Sentence Completion, and Draw-A-Person. In addition, Mr. A expressed ideas of reference and paranoid ideations. In summary, the tests are highly supportive of Schizophrenia, Chronic Undifferentiated Type. All sources indicated a severe impairment.

Part C: *The Plan Used in the Initial Interview*

This counselor determined that the approach used had to be one which was direct yet warm. The questions had to be very simple and had to be asked several times. It was also felt that Mr. A needed a tremendous amount of encouragement and, above all, patience. During his life Mr. A had met with very little success. All reinforcement had been quite negative and had also been of a severe degree. Mr. A had had no "father figure" and lacked any male friends. When Mr. A asked questions, the counselor replied in concrete, real terms. Responses on the part of the counselor were never vague nor were they colored to make him "feel better." The counselor also pushed him to think. By this is meant that Mr. A suffered psychomotor retardation and therefore his thinking process was confused. But by pushing him to respond to each question, Mr. A finally replied in a coherent manner. When he did correctly reply, the reinforcement was a smile, nod, or touch. After a period of time Mr. A relaxed slightly. (Naturally, it would take prolonged counseling sessions to even begin to gain Mr. A's trust and confidence. This comes with day-by-day contact.) After Mr. A relaxed, the counselor then took Mr. A on a tour of the educational department and work training center. The tour went slowly so that as each visible area, machine, and tool was described, Mr. A could ask questions as he touched them. The walking and seeing while the talking continued relaxed the young man even more.

The interview ended in the work training center with Mr. A, the counselor, and work training center manager having a cup of coffee.

Part D: Factors Assessed

1. "Can Do" factors (abilities, skills, and knowledges). Mr. A had worked periodically in an aluminum siding company. His main function dealt with aluminum molds. Thus, when he was shown the plastic mold injectors in the work training center, he became more interested and asked comparatively more questions than he had in the beginning. However, the scope of his questions was far below normal. His employer had stated that when he did work he was slow, but after being shown how to do a particular task several times he could perform on a slightly below-average level. The knowledge, according to his foreman, was there but he was greatly limited in putting it into practice.

2. "Will Do" factors (motivation, interest, and personality). Due to the severity of Mr. A's illness, his motivation, interest, and personality were at the time of the initial interview very poor. His affect during the bulk of the interview must still be regarded as flat. However, this counselor felt that even though his illness had not yet begun to regress, Mr. A should be placed into extended evaluation.

Part E: Factors for Evaluation

The factors which were considered in evaluating Mr. A's emotional maturity and work attitudes were as follows:

1. The results from the psychological testing were reviewed. Results: Poor.

2. Mr. A's high school aptitude test scores and academic progress reports were reviewed. Results: Poor.

3. Lastly, his work attitudes and habits and personal interaction were considered by this counselor. This information was obtained from his former employer and social worker. Results: Poor to below average.

Decision: Continued counseling sessions while placed in extended evaluation.

Exercise 7

EVALUATION AND ACTIVITY ON A CLOSED CASE

RATIONALE

A counselor has numerous responsibilities when he is working with a client. In fact, when casually talking with another counselor about a particular case, one often loses sight of the total rehabilitation process as it has taken place. There is more to working with a client than manipulating paper work and making numerous telephone calls. It is the professional responsibility of each counselor to decide upon the array of services to provide and when a particular service is necessary for his client. Evaluation of a closed case (from status 26) should enable the counselor to gain insight into a proper perspective of this total rehabilitation process.

ASSIGNMENT

Write a narrative in-depth summary of one case which has been closed rehabilitated. Study the case carefully and write the report using the following as guides for evaluation:
- A. Eligibility.
- B. Needs identified.
- C. Services provided.
- D. Counselor's role.
- E. Case recording.
- F. Use of community resources.
- G. Placement.
- H. Job suitability at closure.
- I. Follow-up.

Also discuss which forms were executed, the sequence in which they were used, and their purpose. Relate in the report the points in the process at which prior approval was required and the rationale for its being required. If in your position you have as-

71

sumed a new caseload and there are no cases in this status, borrow one from a fellow counselor. The standards for evaluation of this case should be identical to agency policies and regulations. In your analysis particularly be aware of case recording and case management. Describe the strengths and weaknesses of this counselor's approach to this case. (It must be kept in mind you are not concerned solely with the criticism of the other counselor's work, but you are using a case as a learning device in an attempt to increase the effectiveness of your own professional attitudes.)

STUDENT WORK: SAMPLE 1

Evaluation and Activity on Closed Cases

Below is a narrative evaluation concerning Mr. P who was successfully closed in status 26.

Part A: Eligibility

Mr. P entered Western State Hospital with a final psychiatric diagnosis of Alcoholism, Chronic Addiction. He advised that this illness caused him to have blackouts and to act violently toward his wife, children, and employer. In addition, his memory had become defective; that is, during long periods of drinking there would be a complete loss of memory. This, of course, prevented him from working in any capacity and completely limited all of his activities. All social interaction with friends, associates, and family members ceased. Thus, it is quite apparent that Mr. P did suffer from a disability which was a substantial handicap to employment. For instance, Mr. P held three grocery jobs in two months. Continual drinking caused him to be terminated from all three. Physically, this man has extirpation of the left kidney, the reason being polycystic degeneration. He also suffered a bilateral inguinal rupture and was in need of extensive dental care.

Psychological testing indicated no signs of psychosis; however, Mr. P suffered deep depression and was in a general state of confusion. Evaluation from our alcoholic rehabilitation program showed much vocational potential even though during the initial weeks a defeatist attitude was evident.

Part B: Needs Identified

Mr. P's excessive drinking problem seems to be an external symptom with a life-long habit. It is my opinion that his drinking serves as an escape by which he "forgets" failures. It is apparent that he feels inferior as a husband and has not been able to provide adequately for his family.

1. Mr. P is in need of a program whereby he will have time to readjust socially. He has become a loner and is suspicious of anyone who approaches him; e.g. his employer, wife, or life-long friends.

2. Physically, Mr. P needs extensive dental care and a vast reconstruction in and of his diet, as his general state of health has deteriorated grossly over the past year.

3. Vocationally, this client needs placement into a job that would be supportive with his attempts toward sobriety. He has above-average intelligence and is quite aware of his vocational reputation.

4. Lastly, extensive guidance and counseling sessions are indicated, as Mr. P's rehabilitation process will be quite prolonged. Counseling will center around constructing a new self-image, the main focus being self-respect and how to regain it.

Part C: Services Provided

Through the facilities offered by this hospital and our rehabilitation department, Mr. P successfully participated in and completed the rehabilitation alcoholism program. Other services—guidance, counseling, and placement; group therapy; occupational, industrial, and recreational therapies—were initiated and resulted in Mr. P's full participation in all the above-listed areas. This active gentleman became the chairman of his ward and was so helpful to the other men that he was recommended and considered for the alcoholism coordinator's position in the hospital. He was hired for this position upon our recommendation after scoring 97.3 on the merit examination. Lastly, our rehabilitation services provided maintenance and transportation for this client during his first month of work and also supplied dental care (complete examination, fillings, extractions, and partial plates) in order to make the client more comfortable in his new position. Thus, he now functions confidently with the public.

Part D: Counselor's Role

Since Mr. P is a very active and sensitive man, the counselor chose to take a very nondirective approach. The counselor was very supportive of all gains made by this client and also gave a great deal of encouragement to Mr. P when he began participating in all ward activities. Over a period of time, this client decided that he would very much like to work with the alcoholics in the hospital. Therefore, the counselor arranged the following:

1. An interview with the personnel director in the hospital was established.

2. Recommendations were made to the hospital as to Mr. P's ability and vocational potential. These were substantiated by test scores such as the GATB and Mr. P's performance for the GED. Also his participation in the alcoholic program and progressive suggestions made by Mr. P served as a basis by which he was hired.

3. The rehabilitation counselor also arranged for Mr. P to take the merit examination on which he scored 97.3.

Lastly, as the counselor developed a sincere relationship with Mr. P, it was noted by the counselor that Mr. P refused to smile and often covered his mouth. Thus, the counselor suggested dental care and Mr. P beamed with satisfaction. He had made no mention of his teeth as he was "too embarrassed." This was the only time the counselor made a direct suggestion. As to maintenance and transportation, again it was Mr. P who made the decision to accept our funds. This approach was taken as Mr. P greatly needed to develop his self-image as a "doer" and "decision-maker."

Part E: Case Recording

All recordings are quite explicit and detailed. Progress notes as well as follow-up entries began in January 1969, and concluded in December 1969. Full notations are made first on a weekly basis and then on a bimonthly basis. Included within the notations is a progression which shows the attitude and behavioral changes developed within Mr. P. Also indicated are his vocational and social decisions with the "why" fully developed. For instance, his decision to reconcile with his wife and family are fully discussed. Also his views as to why he wishes to work with alcoholics are expressed; i.e. "They [other alcoholics] can't tell me I don't know that I'm talking about, 'cause I've been lower than any of 'em . . . ."

Part F: Use of Community Resources

Since our rehabilitation unit works cooperatively with the hospital, combined efforts have produced a program for our alcoholic ward.

1. Rather than evaluating these men in a workshop setting, evaluation is derived from an extensive alcoholic rehabilitation program. Here the participating members are afforded counseling, group therapy, pastoral sessions, and lectures from personnel directors.

2. Local employment offices schedule interviews and offer MDTA and OJT programs.

3. AA chapters receive letters concerning our discharged residents.

4. Our educational evaluator tests various clients with the GATB. He also tutors patients and prepares them for the GED which can be given in our rehabilitation office setting. Upon testing, various training programs are initiated (in this case the hospital hired and trained Mr. P). Our services then provided maintenance in a local home and transportation from the local cab company.

5. Lastly, cooperatively diagnostic services and physical restoration services were brought about through the hospital and rehabilitation unit.

Part G: Placement

The placement objective was determined to be that of a completely new profession. Mr. P has intelligence, willpower, and ambition. He wanted to advance; thus, placing him back as an unskilled laborer was felt to be a rather negative reinforcement to his potential. He is keenly aware of what he can do, and he has a great desire to help other people. He sold himself to the ward, the counselor, and personnel director. In addition, he ranked number one on the register. Since he has accepted his new position, the entire alcoholism program has progressed. To date their success range is 85 percent.

Part H: Job Suitability at Closure

Mr. P showed great insight when he decided to work with other persons who explicitly were handicapped because of alcoholism. As he put it, "I've been there and I know how low you can go. I've lost everything and everyone I've ever loved because I refused to face the facts about me." He is in a position to really "tell it like it is" and he does. The other members listen to him before they consider even talking to another person. Since he has experienced even greater obstacles than some of them, they cannot say, "You don't know about it." In addition to serving as coordinator, Mr. P also has established several local AA chapters.

Part I: Follow-up

Follow-up in the case of Mr. P has been extensive. Counseling sessions continued on a weekly basis after discharge. These sessions occurred at various times in different locations. For instance, the counselor met with Mr. P at one of his AA meetings; Mr. P was also seen several times while on the job; and the counselor has met with both Mr. P and his wife on several occasions. Even though this case is now closed, this counselor continues to see Mr. P frequently in regard to his new vocation.

STUDENT WORK: SAMPLE 2

Case Closure: Narrative on Mrs. K
(Review of closed case, status 26)

REFERRAL. By ward physician at Eastern State Hospital.

DISABILITY. Diagnosis of Affective Reaction, Manic Depressive Reaction, Manic Type. Client exhibited depression, hyperactivity, and flight of ideas. No physical defects noted.

SOCIAL HISTORY. This 38-year-old white female was hospitalized in March of 1966 and remained at Eastern State until furloughed in January 1969. There were three previous admissions.

Client is the mother of five children, four of whom have been placed in a foster home in Richmond under the auspices of the welfare department. The fifth child, her oldest son, is in another home located in Norfolk. The client's husband is deceased, and the client's mother, now in her 70's, is unable to cope with her daughter's illness and care of the grandchildren in a home situation. There has been a repetitive pattern in the case history where the client will live at home for a time, become dissatisfied and wander off, sometimes taking the children with her. She strongly resists hospitalization, and usually a court order has been required to secure readmittance.

From case reports, it would appear that the client exerts a serious detrimental effect on her children, evoking temper tantrums and other symptoms of misbehavior. Mrs. K's mother visits the children frequently, and in her opinion the State Home is the best solution in the present situation. She expresses herself as afraid of the consequences for the children if they are returned to their mother. The client, however, is anxious to regain custody.

Mrs. K has several older brothers and sisters but none of them wish to take her, so it will be necessary for client to seek independent living arrangements following vocational rehabilitation.

EDUCATIONAL BACKGROUND. Client graduated from a high school in South Carolina.

WORK HISTORY. Periods of employment included two years of office work at Medical College of Virginia, from 1947 to 1948; an office position with the Raleigh Company in 1949; office work with the Gill Directory in 1959, and various jobs as a waitress on a temporary basis. There was no continuous employment since 1959.

TESTS. A WAIS showed client with a full scale IQ of 99, verbal of 96 and with a performance of 103. In the opinion of the psychological tester, Mrs. K is suited intellectually for many areas of employment; however, a job involving independent decision-making would undoubtedly be too much of a challenge. According to the psychologist, Mrs. K would probably function best in a routine situation, although the task need not necessarily be simple or easy.

REHABILITATION OUTLOOK: 12-8-67. Following an expression of interest by Mrs. K in rehabilitation services, the client was determined to be eligible on the basis of disability connected with mental illness, and was accepted into the rehabilitation program. The client's emotional disturbances, (see diagnosis section) were felt to constitute an employment handicap at onset and to impede competition with the general labor force.

Brieflly, Mrs. K was in need of extensive social readjustment as well as vocational evaluation and trial training in order to accustom her, after the lapse of some years, to a work regimen. However, motivation on the client's part was strong, and this, combined with a reasonably high level of intellectual functioning, led the counselor to project that the vocational outlook was good, with a reasonable expectancy that the client would be able to obtain suitable employment following provision of rehabilitation services.

12-20-67. Believing that the client would benefit from group therapy and milieu therapy in conjunction with continued medication, Mrs. K was moved to the Rehabilitation House and scheduled for general evaluation.

1-3-68. Initial reports indicated that one of the most serious drawbacks for this client vocationally was an untidy appearance and work habits. To effect some change in this area, Mrs. K was scheduled for job readiness classes, which she attended regularly.

Final summary from the evaluators showed that Mrs. K got along well with others, but lacked industriousness, resourcefulness, and confidence. Retention, observation, and perception were judged poor. According to the evaluation, factory work (one of Mrs. K's vocational objectives) seemed unrealistic because of her lack of speed; however, her other interest in a cafeteria position was deemed feasible.

Overall, Mrs. K presented a classic picture of the discrepancy occasioned by emotional handicaps between a normal IQ as exhibited on the WAIS and a relatively low level of work functioning as demonstrated to the evaluators.

Since the client had expressed no further interest in office work where she had been employed in the past, and since a factory situation was thought to be unrealistic as a result of the evaluation process, Mrs. K accepted an assignment in the hospital cafeteria where, in the course of a few months, she performed well in a serving line capacity and indicated her liking for the job.

During this time also her appearance, manner of dress, and so forth improved considerably, and the case recording shows that she had frequent discussions with the counselor regarding family finances, personal problems, and vocational prospects. At the onset of counseling, Mrs. K had appeared as a rather timid but co-operative person, with a need to please which she met by acting like an obedient child. However, as in the counselor's opinion she was now reaching her maximum level of adjustment, attempts were made to upgrade the client's self-image, to increase assurance, and to encourage her to try to work out her own problems.

In response to the task group, Mrs. K was reported to be in good contact, amiable in disposition, and giving no evidence of irrationality. As might be expected from the foregoing, she declined leadership roles or participating to any great extent in decision making by the task group.

Considering the essentially passive nature of this client, except for the periods of manic swings when hyperactivity and irritability were employed to ward off depression, the counselor felt it would be necessary to assist with job placement to the extent of setting up initial interviews. From there, it was felt that Mrs. K had achieved a sufficient degree of assurance to make a good impression on the prospective employer.

Letters were accordingly sent to four cafeterias in the Richmond area, and when these failed to produce any response, the counselor utilized a vital community resource, i.e. the Virginia Employment Commission in Richmond, and arranged an interview for Mrs. K with a VEC counselor specializing in placement of the handicapped. At the same time, the counselor obtained productive results from a series of telephone calls on Mrs. K's behalf following a perusal of want-ad sections in the Richmond papers.

A conversation with the manager of the women's dining hall at the University of Richmond seemed especially promising. The manager was receptive to the idea of finding a position for Mrs. K and in general appeared to be a warm, sympathetic person, understanding of the problems involved with mental illness. A position was open in the cafeteria serving line in salad preparation and the manager also told the counselor that she hoped to find someone capable of acting as an assistant manager when it was necessary for her to be absent during the day.

Subsequently, through vocational rehabilitation financing, Mrs. K traveled to Richmond, was interviewed by several employers, and offered two positions, one with Shoney's Restaurants and the other with food services at the University of Richmond. It was indeed a foregone conclusion as to which Mrs. K would accept since they (the client and manager at the University of Richmond) had established an almost instant rapport at their first meeting. The extent of the cafeteria manager's favorable response to Mrs. K was shown by her offer to train the client as an assistant manager if she functioned well during her first few months on the job.

Maintenance until the client would be able to draw her first paycheck was arranged at a boarding house in Richmond, and Mrs. K appeared quite satisfied with her living accommodations, especially as several other rehabilitation clients were also rooming at the same address.

January 24 was the client's first day of employment, and during that week, the manager expressed to the counselor her satisfaction with Mrs. K's performance. Further telephone calls several weeks later informed the rehabilitation office that Mrs. K would be placed in training as an assistant manager.

The client's salary at $1.50 per hour was sufficient, enabling her to live independently, and the only major problem that arose from the time of her initial employment until closure was a repeated insistence on initiating legal proceedings to regain custody of her children. Fortunantely, the manager instinctively adopted the best possible approach in dealing with Mrs. K, using a firm manner and telling the client that she should not even consider the question of custody until after at least a year's employment and a stable financial position. Confirmation of this approach was given by the counselor in discussing the client over the telephone, and what appeared to be a possible forerunner of another manic swing was halted.

Follow-up was conducted chiefly by telephone, and after continued favorable reports from the boarding house and the client's employer, the case was closed in status 26. At this time, the client had been employed for a period of two months.

In summarizing this case, the following points may be mentioned: (1) The client was provided with a wide range and extensive scope of services which included counseling and guidance, personal adjustment training, room and board, clothing, transportation, laundry and incidentals, selective placement and follow-up; (2) without the benefits to be derived from milieu and group therapy in the Rehabilitation House, counseling, and on-the-job training in the hospital, the client would have been prepared inadequately for a return to the community and the prognosis for even a marginal adjustment would have been poor; and (3) a deciding factor in the client's successful retention of a job was undoubtedly due to the supportive help and insight of an employer who was familiar with this type of problem.

Exercise 8

CLOSE A CASE FROM STATUS 16, 18, or 22

RATIONALE

Upon acceptance of this position as a vocational rehabilitation worker, you are considered a full-time professional member of the agency; with this, certain responsibilities accrue immediately. You are responsible for taking over the existing caseload or assuming a new caseload with all of the professional qualifications of a seasoned counselor. As such, you will be responsible for working with cases which have gone through the initial stages of plan development and plan completion. You will be required to close cases from various statuses.

ASSIGNMENT

Select one case which is presently in status 16, 18, or 22. Use the same guides and standards for evaluation as outlined in Exercise 7. Close cooperation is needed with the local office in the selection and assignment of this case to be closed, especially if the counselor has not had the occasion to do such. Examine critically the justification for placing the client in one of the three statuses outlined in this exercise. Also, provide a descriptive analysis of the process used in determining the client's feasibility to enter the world of work.

STUDENT WORK: SAMPLE 1

Closing a Case from Status 22

Below is a narrative summary concerning Mr. W who has been in status 22, in employment, since December 11, 1969. This case is now being closed 26. The guidelines established are as follows: (A) eligibility; (B) needs identified; (C) services provided; (D) counselor's role; (E) case recording; (F) use of community resources; (G) placement; (H) job suitability at closure; (I) follow-up.

Part A: Eligibility

Mr. W being admitted to our hospital carried a final psychiatric diagnosis of alcohol addiction. He was tested by our psychology department for psychosis. Both the report from the psychologist and ward doctor indicated that Mr. W was a highly nervous man who, having experienced tremors and severe black-out spells, was generally confused. He has been extremely dependent upon alcohol for approximately twelve years and uses it in order to avoid making any decisions or facing any crises. He has been admitted to our hospital three times during the past four years. As a result of this disability, he has become vocationally and socially handicapped; that is, his work record has become irregular, his friends have drifted away, and his family is very depressed over his actions. He has not functioned on a satisfactory level (either in his home or on the job) for several months. Upon evaluation reports from our educational evaluation (Mr. W scored well in *all* areas of the GATB), progress notes from all therapy units (occupational, industrial, and recreational), and extensive counseling sessions, this counselor decided that there was an above-average chance that Mr. W could become effectively employable. The medical examination revealed no physical disorders; thus, it was determined that he could function quite well in his former position.

Part B: Needs Identified

1. Mr. W needed time to readjust socially both to his community and his co-workers.

2. He also needed to develop a constructive self-image by which he could come to terms with daily problems, major crises, and the "threat" of success.

3. Next, his religious concepts had manifested themselves in a very negative attitude toward "money," the world's problems, and marital relationships.

4. This client definitely needed to be encouraged. Reinforcement had to come quickly and immediately. In addition, gradual

responsibility had to be given—just enough for him to handle at a specific time.

5. Having such a contradicting work record, Mr. W needed a program whereby he could readjust vocationally.

6. It is true that his dependence needed to be transferred from "the bottle" to himself. In order to do this the counselor served as the medium. The rehabilitation plan was long-ranged. As he progressed in decision making and problem solving, the counselor withdrew into a more passive role.

Part C: Services Provided

1. Mr. W was afforded extensive counseling sessions by his rehabilitation counselor and local and hospital ministers.

2. He participated in the alcoholic rehabilitation program in which he was afforded group therapy. Extensive evaluation was obtained from this program.

3. Occupational, industrial, and recreational assignments were made. AA meetings were established for his benefit in which extensive lectures and audio-visual aids were employed.

4. Psychological, psychiatric, and physical examinations were ordered. Medication was prescribed.

5. Our educational evaluation helped Mr. W to recognize his vocational potential by means of the GATB.

6. Our social service department arranged for family visits and transportation.

7. The rehabilitation counselor established communication with the personnel director and supervisor. Meetings were held in which the employer agreed to work with Mr. W. The counselor also obtained a recovery slip from the doctor which was presented to the personnel director. At that time Mr. W was provided transportation.

8. Written referral was made to Mr. W's local mental health center as well as to his local AA chapter.

9. Follow-up services were extensive on the part of the counselor. They continued for four months on a bimonthly basis. Even though the case is being closed, correspondence is still continuing.

Part D: Counselor's Role

The counselor's main role in this case was more behind-the-scene. By that I mean that during interviews with the employment officer and work supervisor (while Mr. W was present) the counselor made no comments. However, at meetings with the above while Mr. W was not present, the counselor presented reports of evaluation from various departments and programs. The counselor also made recommendations. During initial counseling sessions, the counselor used the direct approach; then after approximately two months of encouragement and positive reinforcement, the eclectic approach was established. Nondirective tactics were utilized during the last two months of follow-up. To date there has been established a mutual relationship between Mr. W and his counselor.

Again the counselor held private meetings and interviews with the employer, social worker, family, and doctor. Programs were devised around the concepts of reality therapy for Mr. W. The communications between all agents were smooth and constantly updated.

Part E: Case Recording

All case recording reflects a detailed account of all meetings and interviews held with all interested parties. Goals are clearly stated in the follow-up notes. Attitude changes as well as personal self-care of Mr. W are notated in full. As his goals changed, his attitude improved. There is a concise updated summary of all counseling sessions held. Reports and copies of all materials concerning follow-up services are fully notated. In addition, the hospital medical records room received a full account of all services (i.e. counseling, follow-up, interviews) rendered to Mr. W since discharge. Each contact that the counselor made with Mr. W or with any interested party was explained in terms of (1) attitudes, (2) subject matter covered, and (3) goals.

Part F: Use of Community Resources

The following community resources were utilized in the case of Mr. W:

1. Mr. W was afforded guidance and counseling services

through our rehabilitation counselor and hospital chaplain. His own pastor was called upon to counsel him during hospitalization and after discharge.

2. Mental and physical restoration services were carried out by our hospital, Mr. W's local mental health center, and his local AA chapter.

3. Placement was secured by means of interviews with his former supervisor and personnel director.

4. Transportation was supplied by both our social service department and our rehabilitation counselor.

5. Lastly, diagnostic services and evaluation reports were obtained through our alcoholic rehabilitation program and psychology department.

Part G: Placement

Final placement of Mr. W into his original position was brought about through the combined efforts of Mr. W, the rehabilitation counselor, the former supervisor, and the doctor. To begin, Mr. W made known to his counselor that he wished to return to his old job. He sought assistance in securing an interview and recommendations. Mr. W then wrote to his former supervisor. Meanwhile the counselor evaluated the reports from the alcoholic rehabilitation program, the group therapist, and the doctor. In addition, the progress notes were reviewed during a rehabilitation counselor's conference. The counselor then made the decision that he could confidently recommend Mr. W to his former employer. Thus, a letter was written on behalf of Mr. W and an interview was scheduled the Monday following discharge. In addition, a recovery slip completed by his doctor verifying medically his ability to return to work was obtained and presented during the interview. The session proved successful; Mr. W returned to work December 1, 1969. Four months later it is noted that Mr. W is functioning on a very effective level and has gained the full approval of all concerned.

Part H: Job Suitability at Closure

Mr. W had been employed with the Whirlpool Corporation for approximately five years. He had established himself as a person of great initiative. Thus, he was well respected and had been offered a promotion prior to his admission to our hospital. However, Mr. W was frightened by advancement and success. He could only go so far vocationally before he would hide his fear by drinking. Therefore, he lost his job.

Mr. W has successfully been placed back into his old job. Responsibility was given to him slowly. Counseling sessions were held with his employer in which more encouragement was given initially.

Several weeks ago he was offered a promotion and accepted it. At that time he contacted his counselor and stated that he finally felt he could make it. To date he has succeeded. By placing Mr. W back into his old position it was felt that gradually he could face promotion and success. If he had been placed into a different position the basic problem would still face him. On his old job he realized that his friends and superiors were actually pulling for him. He faced the crisis and won.

Part I: Follow-up

Follow-up services were initiated on a bimonthly basis. Personal contact was alternated with telephone calls to the home and place of employment. Counseling sessions continued during these follow-up sessions; these sessions were held either in the home with Mrs. W also present or at the place of employment. It should be pointed out that permission to visit the client during working hours was granted prior to actual contact. The majority of our brief sessions were during his lunch hour so as not to disrupt his normal work routine.

The counselor continually pointed out the benefits of Mr. W's local AA chapter. Eventually he agreed to attend. To date, he is still attending regularly. Even though the case is now being closed Mr. W corresponds regularly with his counselor by mail. All follow-up was aimed toward encouraging Mr. W's sobriety and his decisions to go on with his work. Gradually, confidence was gained by this client. When he realized he could succeed, then his alcoholism was defeated. Follow-up services also brought the counselor into contact with Mr. W's supervisor, at which time a plan was devised in which he (Mr. W) was allowed to expand

and develop at his own rate. His supervisor encouraged him as he took on more responsibility. When he showed signs of wavering in his attempts to remain sober, his counselor was contacted. At that time a call or visit was made.

Exercise 9

THE COMPARISON OF TWO PHYSICAL RESTORATION CASES

RATIONALE

There is often the tendency for individuals working with the less complicated physical restoration cases to consider certain ones as "easy" and others as "difficult" not only in terms of disability, but in counselor's time and monetary expenditures. The purpose of this exercise is to create an awareness for the counselor that he is serving someone in need of services no matter what the degree of severity of the case and that there is far more similarity between disability groups than there is difference.

ASSIGNMENT

Describe the rehabilitation process of two different clients on your caseload. One of these should be what is considered a "routine" physical restoration case (e.g. hernia repair or hysterectomy) requiring little of the counselor's time; the other should be what is considered a difficult and time-consuming case (e.g. working with a severe arthritic or quadriplegic). After this has been done, compare the two cases for likenesses and differences and note how the counselor approached each of them. Explain the rationale the counselor used in accepting both of these cases. Briefly discuss how these clients seemed to accept or feel toward vocational rehabilitation as a result of the provision of these services.

STUDENT WORK: SAMPLE 1

Introduction

Vocational rehabilitation counselors are frequently faced with decisions regarding cases to be accepted, rejected, or, indeed,

89

sought. Agency expectations are such that the counselor must function in a manner consistent with policy guidelines in the provision of comprehensive and meaningful services to an ever-expanding clientele. The response to a given situation is conditioned by the counselor's interpretation of rehabilitation as a concept and the rehabilitation agency as a practical reality.

Within the context, the inevitable question arises as to whom shall be served so that maximum benefits are derived from the input of time and money. A legitimate judgment coordinating organizational goals and resources must be made and as such it should not be made in haste.

Far too often the tendency has been to accept the "easier" cases, particularly in the area of physical restoration, with some relish. The traditional three H's—hernias, hysterectomies, and hemorrhoids—have been welcomed primarily because they yield relatively quick closures and lend themselves well to a time-cost analysis.

Superficially, at least, the above statement is reasonable; however, inherent in this rationale is the assumption that disability may be categorically subdivided when, in principle, it cannot be. Disability by definition will not yield to arbitrary fragmentation. Indeed, there is a thread of commonality which binds the many degrees of disability together. It is the task of the counselor to grasp the full impact of basic similarities.

In essence, this exercise is designed to encourage a greater understanding and an awareness of persons in need of services and to urge safeguards against minimizing the effects of any disability on the individual.

Procedure

To further clarify the point, the summary of a hernia or so-called "routine" case will be compared with that of a quadriplegic to identify similarities and differences as each progresses through the rehabilitation process. Confidentiality will be preserved by referring to the clients in question as Mr. H and Mr. Q. The counselor's attitude in accepting the cases and the client's response to the provision of services will be points of discussion from which it is hoped some relevant observations and conclusions may be drawn.

Case Summary I

Mr. H came to the attention of vocational rehabilitation as a referral from the local welfare department. Having recently returned to his home community after residing for several years in Ohio, the client, his wife, and their four small children sought temporary refuge with the wife's family until employment could be secured. Upon applying for a position with an area industry, Mr. H was found to have a right inguinal hernia which precluded his employment.

The client presented a slovenly appearance reflecting the deprivation of his environment. As a seventh grade dropout, his general academic and verbal skills were quite low. Since he lacked both formal and vocational training, physical labor had been and would continue to be his principle means of livelihood. The vocational objective based upon his work history, ability, and expressed interest was merely to find a job as an unskilled industrial worker.

The counselor arranged for a general medical and surgical examination which confirmed the need for a herniorrhaphy. No psychological data was collected. After tentative approval of the medical consultant's prognosis, the case was accepted and physical restoration services were authorized.

Following convalescence, sporadic counseling related to job opportunities and potential work sites was given until Mr. H landed a marginal assembly line position. Both he and his employer were contacted several weeks later to find out if an adjustment had been made. Since each was apparently satisfied, the client was closed as successfully rehabilitated with an expenditure of roughly $700 and four hours of counselor time.

Case Summary II

Mr. Q, 18 years old, was referred to vocational rehabilitation by the visiting teacher at his former school after suffering a spinal contusion at C-6 with almost total paralysis. Although there was some return of function to the upper extremities, he was, for all practical purposes, a quadriplegic. His injury occurred in a diving accident.

The client was the product of a solid middle-class home which had afforded him most of the creature comforts, thereby elevating his definition of success and concept of an adequate standard of living. Nevertheless, Mr. Q had dropped out of school in the tenth grade and had worked several months as an apprentice electrician prior to his accident.

In formulating a rehabilitation plan, the counselor focused not on the disability, but on determining the extent of sensory-motor return and existing mental capacity. Since any vocational objective would be developed around these factors, the client was admitted to a comprehensive rehabilitation center where medical, psychological, and vocational evaluations could be conducted over an indefinite period.

Mr. Q remained at the center for a year progressing in self-care activities with the aid of skilled physical and occupational therapists. Special education personnel helped him in his quest for the General Education Development Certificate (GED). He did not, however, adjust socially and was terminated.

Upon his return home, there seemed to be an improvement in attitude. He completed the requirements for the GED and manifested general maturation. A KUB infection and several pressure sores were medically treated by the family physician. During the interim, several counseling sessions were arranged and conducted in the client's home.

The physical and mental state of Mr. Q warranted a request for readmission to the center for business training which was granted. The client received intensive counseling in conjunction with his vocational education for seven months until he and several compatriots were caught drinking, an action which culminated in their dismissal for disciplinary reasons.

The home counselor met with the client in his home on several occasions thereafter and succeeded in encouraging him to refine his avocation (drawing) into a vocational skill. Mr. Q did so and was able to locate homebound employment as a cartoonist with a local newspaper. After three months of satisfactory work adjustment, he was closed as employed. The time expended on his behalf was in excess of thirty hours, and the cost to DVR and the family ran into thousands of dollars.

Analysis

To be of value, any analytical review must be as objective as human error will permit. Preconceptions and prior opinions can influence conclusions so that validity is lost. By recognizing and remembering this limitation, a more fruitful discussion can ensue.

In perusing the aforementioned cases, two types of physical disabilities have been described, each of which has impaired the individual's ability to engage in gainful employment. There are certainly differences and similarities which should be assessed if insight is to be gained.

The first and most obvious fact gleaned from the case summaries is the disparity of effort and funds put forth for Mr. Q as opposed to that for Mr. H. This is the fundamental element in the "easy" case rationale to which many harried counselors adhere. Secondly, the time lapse, both in initiating service and in completing the rehabilitation process, was much lengthier for Mr. Q.

Further dissimilarities can be found. Mr. H's disability was surgically remedial whereas Mr. Q's was not, and no extended evaluation was requested for the former. As a result no psychological information was collected to indicate the effect of the handicap on Mr. H or to determine if he had unknown aptitudes, abilities, and interests which might be developed through training.

Coordination of services from a variety of sources, both public and private, were mandatory for Mr. Q while no professional persons except the counselor and the medical personnel were involved in assisting Mr. H.

While there are other differences, they are essentially irrelevant to the discussion. It is quite apparent that Mr Q received a greater range of services and they were justified. The view held of a hernia and its effects was not nearly so broad as that focused on quadriplegia. The question which comes to mind is: Why did Mr. H not get more assistance? Indeed, this is the crux of the matter. Examination of the similarities may be more revealing and productive.

It has been noted that each man is physically handicapped and unable to work, thus necessitating a medical evaluation by the appropriate specialists. A time element, financial considerations, proximity to the required specialists, and availability of mandated institutions are other factors which come into play, not only during evaluation, but at other points throughout the process.

What of the family members who are or may be dependent upon a client? Certainly no concrete plan can be conceived without an appraisal of their requirements. Now is the time to understand and coordinate the efforts of vocational rehabilitation with those of other agencies. For example, the Veteran's Administration, Employment Security Commission, welfare departments, insurance companies, and the Social Security Administration are prepared to handle claims in many cases.

Since neither client had a particular vocational skill, the feasibility of training becomes significant. Mr. Q was channeled into vocational education, but no data in the case summary can be found to verify its suggestion to Mr. H. In accepting the cases, there was a reasonable expectation that each client would become employed. Thus job placement and follow-up have several aspects worthy of mention: a client's social adjustment capacity, existing labor market conditions, maintenance until a paycheck is drawn, and transportation.

Counseling has gotten little reference, but it is expected to be continuous throughout the rehabilitation process. In fact, it may well be the most crucial component.

By now a number of significant similarities become apparent. The differences are of a technical nature, whereas the like factors are far more basic and influential to the restoration of a human life to a productive state of being.

The primary distinction between any two cases is not in the types of service rendered, but in the counselor's approach to a given disability. It is the impression that a particular handicap creates in the counselor's mind that is important. Whether one's attitude is positive or negative toward a client and the prospect of his employment is crucial to the selection of available resources or the proffering of suitable services.

Attitudinal response is a double-edged sword; it can work to both the advantage and disadvantage of a client. It need not be if a total person concept is cultivated. A narrow range of vision can lead to a limited extension of services. The dangers of such thinking are clarified in the December 1970 issue of *Research and Demonstrations Brief:*

> Our attitudes toward the disabled are more complex and less enlightened than we imagine. We need more light on the formation of such attitudes, for this can suggest points at which we can intervene to shape or alter them. Without such insight, negative rather than favorable attitudes are apt to be formed, and once formed are not only very hard to change but also quite damaging to the rehabilitation process.

Stereotyped ideas that a certain kind of disability will follow a predestined process must be avoided. Counselors through local orientation, experience, and/or carelessness may react to a given handicap in an automatic way. Mr. H is a case in point since there is no evidence to the contrary in the narrative. Frequently no more is required, but this in no way diminishes the responsibility to entertain and record all germane factors. To criticize counselors for not looking for extra work and expense is most unfair and is not intended; nontheless, the failure to grasp potential implications or to present a full array of realistic alternatives for the client's acceptance or rejection is not in keeping with professional standards.

Case acceptance in all instances is predicated on the belief that provision of services will render a person ready for gainful employment. There must be a thorough understanding of what the agency can and cannot do, and it must be subsequently transmitted to the client. Mr. Q's disability was permanent and compelled the counselor to ascertain his potential in other respects. It is precisely this attitude that this paper is designed to foment.

An interesting sidelight was the client's reaction to rehabilitation service. Mr. H was delighted that his physical problem was alleviated although he became disillusioned when employment was not immediately secured. On the other hand, the vast expenditures on Mr. Q's behalf did not bring an appreciable gesture of gratitude. Instead, he regarded them as his just due and was extremely bitter because his expectations were not met. Somato-psychological and socioeconomic influences were, no doubt, vital in shaping his response.

Conclusions

The interpretations and inferences are summarized and listed below with accompanying suggestions.

1. There are striking similarities in the elements surrounding any disability. It is the proper function of the counselor to ascertain and cope with those elements which have a bearing on the client's situation.

2. Avoid the stereotyping of disabilities by presenting all possible courses of action and available services.

3. Allow an adequate and thorough evaluation to proceed from an approach which embodies the total person concept. Focus on abilities as well as disabilities, both physical and mental.

4. The counselor through case reviews and other study techniques must reassess constantly his thinking to eliminate any trace of the dehumanization of clients.

Exercise 10

FUNCTIONAL CAPACITIES

RATIONALE

For those counselors with special assignments it is imperative to have a knowledge of the client's functional capacity to work within the labor market. Usually there is no formalized technique utilized by these counselors in arriving at a conclusion. This exercise should help you reach some tentative conclusions about your client's readiness for work.

ASSIGNMENT

Interview three random cases (arbitrarily select three cases from your active files) and write a narrative report describing present functional capabilities and limitations, such as work potential, relationship with other clients, relationship with hospital and rehabilitation staff, and relationship with therapy groups. During the interview have the client express his vocational preference, giving reasons why he made this choice. Evaluate the choice in light of information you received during the interview. Incorporate your views on how work conditioning and work adjustment programs can enhance the functional capacity of the client.

STUDENT WORK: SAMPLE 1

The following is a random sample of vocational rehabilitation cases. Each narrative report describes the present functional capabilities and limitations of each client. Areas to be covered in each report are work potential, relationship with other clients, relationship with hospital and rehabilitation staff, and relationship with therapy groups. Lastly, the vocational preference made by the client shall be stated with his or her reasons. The voca-

97

tional choice shall then be evaluated in light of the information obtained from the client during the interview.

Case A

This is the case of a 25-year-old, well-built white male in no apparent distress. Mr. A is divorced, has been jobless since March 1969, and has been unable to control his consumption of alcohol for the last two months. He finished his sophomore year in high school. His school record reflects a low "C" average. His last place of employment was with X Roofing Company in Owensboro, Kentucky. Length of employment was three years. Contact with his former employer revealed that Mr. A was hard-working, intelligent, and dependable. Reason for leaving: Mr. A quit. Recommendations from his former employer proved to be excellent. As to work potential, Mr. A was evaluated by our educational evaluator by means of the GATB. He qualified for patterns 22, 27, 33, 34, and 35. You will notice that patterns 27 and 34 include all types of welding (his projected interest). Mr. A reads on the seventh grade level and his arithmetical ability is weak. Thus, in order to prepare Mr. A for the GED, reading and math classes were scheduled into his alcoholic rehabilitation program. Three hours were set aside (8:00 A.M to 11:00 A.M.) five days a week for academic study. Progress notes from his hospital work assignments (OT, IT) also indicated that he was dependable, "a good worker." Application was made to a vocational-technical school in his local area, and Mr. A was accepted for welding instruction. The evaluations received concerning his physical and psychological status indicated that there were no physical limitations to his vocational choice. Finally, his IQ ranked within the normal range.

Mr. A is a very pleasant, jovial young man who interacted well with all members on his ward. He was an active participant in the alcoholic rehabilitation program and was selected by the other ward members to be ward chairman. The other men enjoyed Mr. A's company because he was always "down to earth" and really easy to talk to. In regard to hospital and rehabilitation staff members, Mr. A became a favorite. Why? He always tried to improve himself as to appearance and personal habits. He developed good manners, and made a sincere effort to be constructive in the program. Evaluations and reports from the occupational, industrial, and recreational departments indicated the above; i.e. "Mr. A was a real pleasure to work with; he is helpful and very active." In regard to therapy groups, Mr. A again participated. He even went so far as to encourage other group members to become involved.

Mr. A, as this counselor stated earlier, expressed the desire to go into welding. His reasons were as follows:

1. He wanted to increase his income and thus raise his standard of living.

2. He was twenty-five, had no trade or skilled experience.

3. He was a high school dropout who had learned that without an education and trade he could never really advance himself the way he wanted.

4. He hoped that by becoming a welder he could move into industry and eventually obtain a "high school equivalency diploma."

5. His last reason was that he had always thought he would like to try.

In evaluating his vocational choice, this counselor feels quite positive toward Mr. A's decision. Why? To begin with, this counselor feels that Mr. A's decisions are very concrete. In general, the reasons listed reflect desire and motivation on Mr. A's part. He is ambitious in wanting to get ahead, yet he isn't "pushy" or what could be considered "hard-headed." On the contrary, Mr. A shows a great deal of insight into his problem and in fact was admitted on a voluntary basis. He has offered a good deal of constructive criticism in regard to himself. Lastly, he has the intelligence and aptitude to perform as a welder. His sobriety should be maintained if he continues with present drive and attitude.

Case B

Miss B is a 44-year-old woman who was admitted to Western State Hospital due to mental deficiency, moderate with a neurotic reaction. At the time of admission Miss B was very agitated, overactive, and uncooperative in her domestic placement.

Physically, Miss B suffers from cataracts in both eyes. There is esotropia of her left eye. Vision is limited to objects. The patient states she cannot see to read, write, or to watch television. Examination of the retina and nerve head cannot be completed because of the mature cataract. Examination of the left eye shows some immaturity around the edges of the lens, but the retina again cannot be seen. Lenses cannot improve the vision. It was decided that the lens in the right eye should be removed. Removing the left lens may give a better field of vision, but since this has always been an amblyopic eye, the vision will certainly be questionable. Also, the physical examination revealed that this client suffers from an ear infection resulting from the growth of fungus on the eardrum.

Miss B stated that she had always enjoyed her work as a maid but was so ill now she simply could not function. Upon checking with Miss B's former employers it was found that her services as a general maid always had been quite satisfactory. She had been efficient and cheerful until her sight failed. At that time she became depressed, anxious, and uncooperative. Recommendations are good.

Work evaluation from our home management program indicates that Miss B shows great enthusiasm in class, and at times her humor annoys a few of the other patients. Her activities are limited due to sight failure; however, after surgery it is felt she can be returned as a domestic placement. Miss B is trying very hard to improve her work ability and has shown a great desire for employment. Even with her sight problem, she manages very efficiently in the household routine. Evaluation from the occupational therapy department indicates that Miss B's work habits and quality of work are fair. She needs supervision but relates well with the staff and other patients. Lastly, she appears cooperative and neat.

Miss B's relationship with other clients and the hospital and rehabilitation staff members has been satisfactory. Of course, failing eyesight and a severe ear infection has greatly hampered Miss B's ability to interact. However, it should be noted that she does attempt to get along with humor and enthusiasm. At times Miss

B "overdoes it," but this, I think, is normal since she is trying to compensate for her present poor eyesight and hearing. Miss B has not participated in group therapy at all.

Miss B has expressed a desire to return to work as a general maid. Why? Miss B stated that she liked the work because it gave her a feeling of belonging to a home. She enjoys children and cooking. Lastly, this is what she has "always done."

In evaluating the client's decision this counselor feels that Miss B with corrective surgery could return to her community as a domestic placement. Naturally, she will need a sheltered environment with a very understanding family. Since Miss B's IQ falls within the range for the moderately retarded, this counselor does not expect her to deal successfully with very complex abstractions. She realizes what a home is as compared to a hospital; and she knows the meaning of work. This counselor also feels that as her physical condition improves, Miss B will return to her old behavior patterns, i.e. being cooperative and helpful.

Case C

REFERRAL. By a physician at Eastern State Hospital.

DISABILITY. Schizophrenic Reaction; Chronic Undifferentiated Type. Exhibits inappropriate affect, i.e. silly, giggling, laughing, and hyperactive. Physical health is excellent.

SOCIAL HISTORY. This is the second Eastern State Hospital admission for Mr. C, a 26-year-old Negro male, who was previously hospitalized in 1966. The client's childhood was described as being relatively normal, and no behavioral problems were noted; but there is a history of mental illness on both sides of the family.

Domestic conflict did occur, however, between the father, a postal clerk at the local Air Force base, and the mother, a frustrated vocalist who frequently left her family to go to New York and sing in jazz bands. The mother's frequent absence, relative to the home situation, caused the children to become very dependent on each other (Mr. C has two brothers and one sister), and the client's first breakdown came in 1965 when his brother Clarence, with whom the client had a very close relationship, went into the Air Force.

Mr. C was at this time jailed for reckless driving and while in prison, encountered homosexual advances from other males, which upset him a great deal. Upon his release, the client broke down completely, barricaded himself in his grandparents' house with several guns, and it took five policemen to remove him to Bayberry Hospital. Mr. C's condition since that time has been further aggravated by the mother's refusal to admit her son's illness. In general, her attitude has been overprotective and domineering towards the client.

EDUCATIONAL BACKGROUND. Mr. C has a high school education and attended State College for one semester, taking courses in mechanical drawing. Grade level was generally very low except in industrial arts and drawing where client maintained an "A" average.

WORK HISTORY. The client has worked as a short-order cook, a car attendant at a Volkswagon dealer, and as a bellboy at the Hotel Plaza for a nine-month period. The latter was his longest term of employment.

TESTS. Bender-Gestalt, MMPI, WAIS, Rorschach, Kuder, and GATB were administered. On the MMPI, Mr. C "succeeded in concealing grossly pathological thinking, but the shape of the profile was consistent with a schizophrenic diagnosis. The Bender-Gestalt and Rorschach were also indicative of a schizophrenic reaction with paranoid features. The patient received a full scale 1Q of 91, which placed him at the average level. The above score, however, is a low estimate of Mr. C's true intelligence due to the detrimental effects of poor test-taking attitudes and sociocultural deprivation" (psychological report).

REHABILITATION OUTLOOK. When he first entered the hospital in 1966, vocational rehabilitation attempted to work with Mr. C; but after several months the case was closed in status 08 due to the client's continued emotional instability and failure to make any kind of sustained effort during the evaluation process. However, in the interim, Mr. C's condition noticeably improved; and, on the recommendation of the staff psychologist in the vocational rehabilitation building, Mr. C was interviewed in January and the case was reopened.

1-22-69. During the initial interview, Mr. C seemed to be in good contact, but was still quite inappropriate, laughing frequently. The client showed little or no insight, failing to make any kind of realistic appraisal of his situation. Mr. C's demands as observed by the counselor varied from a request for an immediate return to State College to becoming an inventor and an aeronautical engineer. The only realistic point, vocationally, was his expressed interest in mechanical drawing.

The client's emotional condition at the time of this interview was far from satisfactory; but from all reports, Mr. C had entered on a period of remission and it was, in the counselor's opinion, possible that he would improve to the point where serious vocational plans could be discussed.

Subsequently, the client was placed in extended evaluation and transferred to the rehabilitation building where it was hoped that the structured discipline of task-group living would exert a "toning down" effect on his inappropriate behavior.

For the first two months, there was little change in Mr. C relative to his participation in the task group ("Mr. C is quite silly and sometimes hysterical about what he has to say—continues jumping and laughing, although he tries to control himself.") However, his conduct was somewhat better in the evaluation department, and reports began to come in that Mr. C can "take criticism and will redo anything if not just right."

A turning point seemed to come in the second month of our program when he established great rapport with one of our evaluators and for the first time carried out assigned tasks in a serious, interested manner. Subsequent progress notes from the evaluation department praised Mr. C in no uncertain terms: "This young man has attended general and extended evaluation for three weeks. Well-groomed and liked by others, he has an easygoing manner and draws on his many talented resources when required to do so. During evaluation, Mr. C has settled down to serious work on a small wooden table and it is evident he takes pride in it. Vocationally, Mr. C scored high on artistic interests in the Kuder Preference Test and showed marked drawing ability. He has good comprehension, organization, and retention, and appears to be a very personable, talented individual" (taken from evaluator's report).

His relationship with the task group was much slower to change, but by mid-April, the counselor had received word that Mr. C "does pay attention and volunteers helpful suggestions" although continuing to "act silly" at times. Part of Mr. C's problem in the past had been a great lack of confidence in being around other people, but now, according to the nurses' report, he "enjoys group participation."

Feeling that client had reached a stage where some vocational plans could be drawn, counselor arranged for an appointment.

4-17-69. The course of the interview, which the counselor was gratified to note, was conducted in a serious manner throughout. Mr. C admitted that he didn't think there was much basis for becoming an aeronautical engineer, considering his past grades in school, although he was still very interested in airplanes. From there, the talk shifted to the feasibility of a return to State College, concerning which Mr. C, surprisingly, appeared doubtful. An awakening of insight on the client's part was expressed by his statement that he had had trouble with socializing and getting along at the college.

The interview had now reached the point where both counselor and client were in agreement that Mr. C was not yet ready to live independently, but that he needed to decide upon and pursue a vocational goal while he was getting better. In an effort to have the client use his own resources to pose a solution, the counselor asked Mr. C if he had any ideas where he could receive training and still have a "live-in" situation. Mr. C's reply, after a few moments debate was "How about that school in Fishersville where they have courses? I could take drawing there." After some further discussion about Woodrow Wilson Rehabilitation Center, what kind of school it was, the programs offered, and so forth, Mr. C said that he liked mechanical drawing in high school and at college. He felt he was good in art and wondered if he could be enrolled in the drafting course at WWRC.

The client continued by saying the only reason he might have trouble making it was that he knew he was way behind in math.

However, when the counselor explained about the special education classes which might be able to remedy this situation, client was very enthusiastic and desired to have his application processed without delay.

In retrospect, the counselor knew that she was dealing with a talented individual whose major hurdle, an improvement of emotional condition, was dependent on time and the beneficial effects of structured living conditions. But the second obstacle towards progress, i.e. the acceptance of a realistic vocational goal and method to achieve it, could and had been resolved through the counseling process.

There was no question of Mr. C's artistic ability, but problems did arise in getting him to channel his natural aptitude into a field which would be consistent with his educational background.

Fortunately, the client had arrived at a more realistic appraisal of his situation by the time of the vocational interview so that his original intention of becoming an aeronautical engineer was laid aside in favor of draftsman. The only real hindrance with this goal was client's poor grade levels in school and his score of 66 percent on the special education test during evaluation. However, the counselor felt that the detrimental effects of poor test-taking attitudes and sociocultural deprivation had contributed to an invalid estimate of Mr. C's true intelligence and that the special education classes offered by WWRC could remedy the areas of academic deficiency.

The other problem to be resolved was recognition by the client that he was still not well enough to function independently and would continue for a time to need a structured situation. Mr. C showed enough insight on this matter to state the problem; i.e. his trouble with socializing and arriving at a solution might be remedied after enrollment at Woodrow Wilson Rehabilitation Center where the staff was skilled in handling emotional problems.

Motivation on the part of this client had increased considerably since his enrollment in the rehabilitation program (as compared with his earlier detached attitudes) and now was felt to be strong enough to give a reasonable expectation of success in the drafting program. This, combined with the client's achievement of some insight, led him to decide on a vocational goal which the counselor found to be realistic and compatible with ability and inclination.

Plans are underway at the present time to enroll Mr. C in trial training at Woodrow Wilson Rehabilitation Center.

Case J

REFERRAL. By physician at Eastern State Hospital.

DISABILITY. Nonpsychotic Organic Brain Syndrome with Epilepsy. Medical record indicates sporadic epileptic seizures which, although not appearing to result in loss of employment, have caused her to be depressed and nervous and have occasioned several voluntary admittances to other state hospitals since 1962. Client is obese.

SOCIAL HISTORY. A heavy-set 28-year-old woman from the Tidewater area of Virginia, Mrs. J has been separated from her husband for more than seven years. Client was living with her mother at the time her recent illness occurred. Mrs. Snaw is presently caring for the client's three children.

EDUCATIONAL BACKGROUND. Mrs. J completed the ninth grade.

WORK HISTORY. Employment included a variety of unskilled jobs such as picking crabmeat, field work for different farmers in crop harvest, and employment as a domestic.

TESTS. The WAIS and GATB tests were administered. Mrs. J's full scale IQ on the former test was 72 with a verbal of 64 and performance of 87. The full scale score is within the borderline range, but the higher performance IQ indicates basically average intellectual endowment.

REHABILITATION OUTLOOK, *2-14-69*. During initial interviews, the client's appearance was poor, (sloppily dressed, etc.) but she did talk at length about the difficulty of finding work in the area and seemed definitely motivated towards upgrading her vocational prospects and securing permanent employment. As Mrs. J had never been contacted by a rehabilitation agency before, I explained the evaluation procedures and, after consulting with the client, decided to schedule her for trial work assignments in the areas of cafeteria, domestic training, and nurses' aide. The client's personality at this time appeared to be agreeable and rather extrovertive.

Prior to the counselor's interview on April 16 to discuss vocational preference, Mrs. J attended the general evalution program and received trial assignments in the laundry room, janitorial program, and as a ward attendant.

Reports from the evaluation department, supervisors, and co-workers indicated that with regard to interpersonal relationships, Mrs. J was quite sociable and friendly toward others. Personal hygiene evidently improved rapidly, as she was reported to be neat and clean. On job performance, Mrs. J was shown to have good dexterity, strength, and coordination and was described as a neat, patient worker.

The major drawback on her skills testing was slowness in comprehending directions. However, the staff felt that once she understood what was required, the client would become quite industrious and resourceful. The client indicated preference for nurses' aide work at the end of evaluation, but told evaluator she realized her lack of education might prove a hindrance. Client also stated she liked dishwashing and housekeeping. She sews well but prefers not to.

Since Mrs. J was not a live-in client at the rehabilitation building, she was not exposed to the task group and step level incentives; but information received from the nursing staff in Building 10 where she resides indicates that she is cooperative and a likeable person.

Psychological tests showed that Mrs. J had scored on the GATB an average of 10 points below the required level for the nurse's aide program, occasioning some doubt in the counselor's mind as to the feasibility of this goal.

During the ensuing interview, however, when questioned by the counselor, the client expressed a great deal of interest in training as a nurses' aide. In her own words, she "likes people and wants to help them." Mrs. J said that she enjoys working on a hospital ward and that sick people do not bother her.

She also stated that she wanted to choose a job that would pay her a higher salary than she had been able to earn before and that would be permanent employment, not just seasonal work. She appeared concerned about the financial situation of her mother and three children, currently living on welfare allotments; and said she wanted a job "good enough so I can send money home."

In response to a query by the counselor she said that despite her excess weight, she did not feel the job would be too physically demanding and that she would be able to be on her feet most of the day as the job requires. The client also felt that she needed to make the most of her chance to be trained under the rehabilitation program, specifically as a nurse's aide.

In evaluation of this client both prior and subsequent to the vocational interview on April 16, and keeping in mind her expressed preference for nurse's aide training, the following considerations were uppermost.

PHYSICAL CONDITION. Of primary importance was (1) whether her epileptic condition was under sufficient control to ensure the safe handling of sick people and (2) whether the client's obesity was such as to interfere with job performance.

In answer to the first query, a change of medication during the client's first week of admittance to the hospital seems to have been effective with no recurrence of seizures during the last three months. The counselor does not foresee any rejection of medication problem, and the client appears grateful for the help the drugs have rendered. Further observation of the client during the training period will prove valuable, taking into account her past history of epilepsy.

With regard to the client's problem of overweight, the counselor did not feel this should be a determining factor, as the client has worked all her life at physically demanding jobs and appears quite capable of sustained work.

MENTAL ATTITUDES. Especially significant in a nurses' aide capacity was the client's ability to relate well with others. In this area, the counselor felt that the client had proved herself to be outgoing and responsive in her contacts with other rehabilitation clients and hospital personnel.

JOB PERFORMANCE AND MOTIVATION. Important here was the balancing of what was evidently strong motivation and diligence on the job against a somewhat limited mental capacity and slowness in absorbing new information.

Overall, in assessing Mrs. J's work potential and the feasibility of her vocational preference, the counselor concluded that the positive factors; i.e. control of the epileptic condition, likeable personality, good performance on work assignments, and motivation, outweighed any negative aspects and that her goal as a nurse's aide was realistic. Admittedly, this vocation will probably extend to the limit of her capabilities, but in terms of job satisfaction and the securing of a permanent vocational skill, it should prove worth the effort.

RESULT OF FINAL INTERVIEW PRIOR TO TRAINING. Mrs. J was enrolled in the nurse's aide program on a trial basis and subsequently as a regular student after satisfactory completion of initial assignments.

Exercise 11

RESEARCH DESIGN

RATIONALE

Many counselors enter the field of vocational rehabilitation thinking that they have no responsibility in developing the profession other than the provision of client services. As a professional, it is your responsibility to upgrade continually the methods of carrying out the basic charge of rehabilitating people. Many newly employed rehabilitation workers have had appropriate academic and practical experience in the design and execution of research projects. It is important that various state agencies profit from this educational and practical experience of their staff members.

ASSIGNMENT

Identify a problem area in rehabilitation of interest to you and develop a research design which could be utilized by you and/or other staff members to study this area of concern. Your objectives for this exercise are as follows:

1. Think about a definition of research.

2. Explore how you can utilize research methods in your case work.

3. Discuss the behavioral implications arising out of the use of this research method.

4. Develop some ideas regarding the use of this project data.

This assignment is intended to create an awareness which will enable you to begin formulating a plan for career development. If you develop a sincere interest in this exercise and would like to pursue it further, you may substitute this exercise for two others. This can be done only after confirming with your training coordinator or by written approval of the faculty supervisor prior to commencing on such a research project.

STUDENT WORK: SAMPLE 1

Research Project: Intake at the Armed Forces Examining Station

INTRODUCTION. Even though vocational rehabilitation has been involved to some degree with the Armed Forces examining centers, such a program has not been established in my area. There are several definitions of research, all of which aptly would apply to an investigation of the merits of establishing such a facility in our state.

The definition of research utilized in this paper is "a studious inquiry or examination; a critical or exhaustive investigation or experimentation having for its aim the discovery of new facts and their correct interpretation, the revision of accepted conclusions, theories, or laws in the light of newly discovered facts, or the practical application of such new revised conclusions, theories, or laws." Briefly paraphrasing the above, my intention is to investigate, in a systematic way, the feasibility of initiating a vocational rehabilitation sub-office at the Armed Forces examining station. I might add that vocational rehabilitation has given me 100 percent support for this project. Of course, the ultimate result of this paper will be the establishment of such an office and, in turn, the rehabilitation of selective service rejectees which normally would not be located by our agency.

PURPOSE OF REPORT: to examine the effectiveness of a procedure by which rehabilitation services are offered to disqualified selective service registrants (SSR's) at the time and place of their pre-induction medical examination; to present problems encountered in the procedure; and to suggest methods of enhancing its effectiveness.

BACKGROUND INFORMATION. No written document to state rehabilitation facilities that directed or encouraged proffering services to medically disqualified SSR's has been located. According to the district supervisor of the vocational rehabilitation agency, oral agreements were made between the state selective service system and VR whereby disqualified SSR's would be referred to this agency for services. Major J, processing officer at the Armed Forces examining station, also was unable to find any documentary basis for cooperation between the agencies or for his facility even to make space available. At both DVR and the Armed Forces Examining and Entrance Station (AFEES), the authorities involved apparently were aware only of spoken agreements.

A State Employment Service counselor—who daily takes applications from SSR's who fail the Armed Forces mental qualification test—produced a barely legible duplicate copy of a U.S. Department of Labor letter that throws some light on the background for the cooperation of the agencies, although it is in no sense a directive to vocational rehabilitation services. The pertinent substance of the letter follows:

> The Department of Labor letter number 733, subject: "Services to Young Men Who Do Not Meet Requirements for Induction into the Armed Forces," dated November 15, 1964, with reference to "GAL's No. 753 and 761."
>
> Purpose: To provide guidelines to state agencies in assisting young men rejected by the Armed Forces by conducting initial interviews at examining stations and making referrals to cooperating agencies. Experiments with different procedures indicate that selective service referrals through written notices produced insignificant responses; initial interviews at examining stations yielded consistently higher numbers in a nationwide program. Therefore, all selective service rejectees will be interviewed at examining stations. The Department of Defense will cooperate fully; commanders of examining stations are being notified to arrange for access, necessary records, and use of office space. The Department of Health, Education, and Welfare is responsible for rehabilitation of those rejected for medical reasons. Recent legislation has appropriated five million dollars to HEW for a new program to provide service to medical rejectees, to be administered by a state agency designated in each state by the Governor. The state director of selective service and the state agencies responsible for services to the mental and medical rejectees should negotiate with commanders of examining stations to determine facilities available for the program. The procedure that follows will be adhered to. A representative of the Armed Forces will assemble the rejectees, record their names and addresses (only) in interview referral forms, explain that state representatives may assist them with their health and employment problems, and divide them into two groups, one of mental (or mental and medical) rejections, and one of solely medical rejections. Each group will be "stimulated" by the appropriate agency representative to participate in the programs. Interested rejectees will be referred to

appropriate screening points where they will sign a release and be interviewed on an individual basis. If the load is consistently small, the employment service representative may do the intake processing for both agencies.

From about 1965 to 1968, a representative of this state's Department of Health daily briefed medical rejectees at the examining station and cooperated closely with the employment service representative. Rejectees were briefed by him in groups, and the group was informed that those who were interested should remain, after the group was dismissed, for individual interviews. There is no available information on the disposition of applications taken by the Department of Health representative. His services abruptly ended in 1968. Apparently, after withdrawal of the Department of Health representative, the state selective service agency approached vocational rehabilitation with a request that this agency provide a counselor at the examining stations.

It must be noted that the Armed Forces Examining and Entrance Station is in the military chain of command. The AFEES commander is responsible to an Army district recruiting commander, who is responsible to the Army recruiting command at Washington. Although AFEES is staffed by personnel from all three major Armed Forces components, it is commanded and operated by the U.S. Army with the mission of providing examining and entrance service for all three components. It is also charged with medical and mental examination of selective service registrants, but it is not under selective service command or authority.

In regard to responsibility for providing facilities to other agencies, including rehabilitation services, the Major reports that in early September, the district commander informed him that facilities will be provided at the convenience of the examining station commander, provided space is available and the cooperation with the state agency will not hamper the operation of the station.

ARRANGEMENTS. In mid-May 1969, the vocational rehabilitation district supervisor and this counselor conferred with the AFEES processing officer. Major B agreed to have medically rejected registrants brought to the counselor in small groups as they became available for briefing. Initial intake was begun in June, but only for rejectees from one county. Briefings were discontinued at the end of June until mid-August to permit the counselor to attend training in Virginia. The examining station was moved to new facilities downtown in early September. Originally, a cubicle was to be allocated to the counselor for interviews, but the district commander, on or about September 10, during an inspection of the station, directed that cubicles be used only by military personnel or relatives of inductees and enlistees who were being sworn into service. He directed that the rehabilitation counselor be given space at the medical examining room.

Since September 11, 1969, the counselor has been stationed at a desk near the entrance to the large examining room where examinees disrobe, are assembled for examination, weighed and measured, processed into other examining rooms, and returned for outprocessing in the same dressing room. Processing personnel tandem to the counselor's position complete the medical papers and refer all registrants permanently disqualified for medical reasons to the counselor. Rejectees are briefed on an individual basis whenever possible, their applications taken, and a signed release obtained. The release is given to a records clerk in another room at the end of the day, and copies of the medical records are produced in one, or occasionally, two days.

There is no reliable time table for outprocessing of rejectees. Generally, however, the peaks of outprocessing occur between 10:30 AM and 12:15 PM, and again, a lower peak at 2:00 or 3:00 PM. Noise levels in the morning are extremely high. The counselor's location is open and interviews can be monitored easily by nearby examinees. Most of the processing personnel are helpful and cooperative, and several go out of their way considerably to assist in the service or to alert a likely candidate for services to the program.

No telephone is available for regular use. Reference books on the counselor's desk were often removed by examinees. Completed interview forms cannot be secured; there has been evidence that one or two may have been perused.

The counselor, on days spent at the station, usually was present from 10:00 A.M. to 3:30 or 4:00 P.M. Occasionally a rejectee would be missed because he had been outprocessed prior to 10:00 or because the counselor was at lunch. The processing officer states that it is not practicable to delay the outprocessing of rejectees more than a few minutes because of bus schedules and other problems.

RESULTS. Statistical results are here reported only for the period from September 11 to November 26. During this period, registrants from this state were given pre-induction medical exams on 50 individual days, but the counselor was present on only 23 days, for reasons indicated later in this report.

It should be noted that applications taken from registrants who resided elsewhere than in this county were forwarded to other counselors or districts without being recorded on case log or caseload numbers.

Available days for state registrants	50
Days counselor on station at AFEES	23
Number of rejectees briefed	331
Total number of applications taken	41
Number of applicants from other districts	16
Number of applications assigned to my caseload	18
Number of applications assigned to other vocational rehabilitation counselors	7
Number of rejectees who stated that they would apply for services later	35
Number of rejectees already receiving services	7

Distribution of Disabilities
of 41 Rejectee Applicants

Hearing	5
Vision	12
Orthopedic, including spine	15
Heart and circulatory	4
Allergies and asthma	2
Other respiratory	1
Chronic hepatitis	1
Epilepsy	1

A statistical look at the number of applicants who are found ineligible because their disability does not meet our agency's re-

requirement is not reliable at this time because there has been insufficient time for medical eligibility determinations to be completed on many applicants. However, the counselor has noted many cases that are certainly doubtful and has already closed three on the basis of medical ineligibility. Military standards for acceptance, at this time, are more stringent than rehabilitation standards.

Work Status. A count of the number of applicants who were working will be made for a later report. The counselor has noted, however, that more than half are working full time at above minimum federal wage, and about 5 percent are attending school.

Applicants' Desires for Service. Most applicants wanted additional training or education. About 10 percent wanted assistance in determining vocational goals. About one-third were clear in asking for medical diagnosis and restoration.

Problems Encountered. Because no telephone, privacy, or clerical assistance is available at the examining station, the counselor is unable to perform normal case management there. Most of the days he was not on duty at the station were spent in managing his regular case-load, which is predominantly not of selective service origin.

Because of lack of privacy, interviews are difficult to pursue effectively. This is especially true during periods of high noise level. Many rejectees appeared to be reluctant to divulge personal information in the hearing range of others.

Rejectees usually are eager to leave the station. Many from other areas fear that they will miss their bus transportation. During periods of high outprocessing, individual briefings of rejectees cannot be executed without causing them to wait up to 45 minutes while applications are being taken. The counselor noted that when interested rejectees were asked to wait for more than a few minutes to have their application formalized, about half departed rather than sit in the station.

Property and records of vocational rehabilitation at the station are not secure. There is danger of theft of office equipment such as typewriters, and compromise of client records.

As indicated above, the eligibility of many applicants is questionable. The counselor should guard against overselling.

Follow-up with medical and vocational appraisals has been difficult because more than half the applicants are working. Apparently many, on finding that they will lose work time, have lost interest in rehabilitation services. A few rejectees have appeared to suspect that services are designed to make them eligible for induction.

INDICATIONS. Projecting the actual statistics obtained, the daily presence of a counselor at the station during the average 18 days per month that registrants are examined, would yield about 35 applications per month throughout all counties served by the station. This yield probably could easily be raised to 40 or more per month if the present rate of pre-induction examinations continue.

The probable ultimate rate of closure in rehabilitated status is expected to be significantly lower than for other referral sources because more clients are working at acceptable wages, and, probably, more will be found medically unqualified for service.

In the present situation, a counselor cannot provide briefing and interview service at the station and simultaneously maintain a reasonable caseload. Although he should spend at least seven hours at the station to be reasonably certain that all rejectees are exposed to the rehabilitation offer, about 70 percent of that time is not consumed in briefing or interviewing; but this amount cannot be directed to case management because of problems already discussed.

A more complete statistical study of this procedure is advisable to arrive at conclusions regarding yield, successful closure, eligibility, and effective use of manpower.

Recommendations

1. Provide semiprivate office space, a typewriter, and telephone for the counselor at the station. In this connection the processing officer has indicated that probably in late January, a cubicle can be provided. Telephone and typewriter will not be provided by the station, however. The cost risk of installing a telephone at rehabilitation's expense with the possibility of later

withdrawal of the space is, in the opinion of this counselor, out-weighed by the additional number of persons who can be served by vocational rehabilitation thereby.

2. As an alternative to counselor office space, the rehabilitation representative at the station might be freed from caseload responsibilities. A counselor's aide could conduct the briefings and take the applications. Manpower utilization considerations in this regard are not good, however, since so much of the representative's time at the station would be inactive.

3. A third solution, suggested by the employment service representative, is to allocate the tasks of orienting medical rejects to him, per suggestion in the USDL letter already discussed. Training for the employment service representative would be advisable if such procedure were adopted.

STUDENT WORK: SAMPLE 2

Operation Discovery: A United Effort To Identify Hearing Disabilities

According to Goodenough[*] and Baker [†] approximately 5 percent of the students attending regular school classes have impaired hearing. Baker further states that many of the students are unaware of defects and suffer great educational loss. Some are mistakenly misinterpreted for behavior problems or mental retardation.

A basic assumption for this research was that there were children in regular classrooms who had unidentified hearing defects. The number of hearing impairments discovered was to be compared to the 5 percent national average to determine if this sampling varied significantly from that number.

Through the close cooperation of Rockingham County School personnel, the Health Department, Madison College, and Vocational Rehabilitation, an effort was undertaken to identify and rehabilitate those students having hearing disabilities.

---

[*] Florence L. Goodenough: *Exceptional Children*. New York, Appleton-Century-Crofts, 1956, pp. 345-351.

[†] Harry J. Baker: *Introduction to Exceptional Children*. New York, The Macmillan Company, 1960, pp. 346-357.

The sample for testing consisted of all 518 students attending Elkton High School, Virginia, which included eighth through twelfth grades. Mr. Robert C. Morris, audiologist at Madison College, supervised the screening tests conducted by senior speech and hearing majors. Three testing sites were set up within the school, and each student underwent a screening test using the audiometer. A second complete evaluation with the audiometer was given to 63 students whose initial screening test indicated a hearing impairment. This second evaluation was scheduled a month later to help eliminate those having a temporary hearing loss due to a cold or congested condition.

A total number of 25 students were found to have a hearing impairment and were referred to Vocational Rehabilitation which arranged for otological evaluations for 23 of the 25 referrals. Two students refused to have an otological examination.

The findings of this research supported the basic assumption that there existed unidentified hearing impairments in the classroom. Of the 25 students found to have a deficiency only 2 had any indication of a hearing problem in the school records. The number of hearing impairments discovered equaled 4.85 percent of the total sample. When compared to the 5 percent national average there appears to be no significant variation.* The procedure used in this project appears to be effective in identifying hearing problems, and plans are being developed for further testing in other schools.

---

* These percentage numbers were not subjected to statistical analysis.

Exercise 12

UTILIZATION OF THE *DICTIONARY OF OCCUPATIONAL TITLES (D.O.T.)*

RATIONALE

Within the world of work, occupations, positions, and jobs have become increasingly complex. No longer can we rely on our knowledge of how jobs formerly were carried out; it is necessary that we formulate a new attitude toward work.

The three volumes of the *Dictionary of Occupational Titles* Volume I, *Definitions of Titles;* Volume II, *Occupational Classification; and A Supplement to the Dictionary of Occupational Titles, Selected Characteristics of Occupations* have become vital tools for professional people working toward the ultimate goal of placing individuals in positions suited to their particular needs and abilities.

ASSIGNMENT

Select three cases from your caseload and analyze the client's chosen vocation. Describe the information located in the various volumes of the *D.O.T.* in relation to each client's chosen vocation. List the other available resources which you might use in order to supplement this material. Schedule an interview with your clients individually and relate this pertinent information to them and include a narrative of their reaction.

Examining each client's vocation separately, prepare an occupational analysis using the sample following this exercise as a guide. Discuss the relevancy of this material in relation to your responsibility of serving handicapped clients. How can the *Supplement to the D.O.T.* help you?

This exercise should be duplicated for local office use.

120

STUDENT WORK: SAMPLE 1

Client Information

Bill is an 18-year-old white married male high school graduate with a newborn son as of the time his rehabilitation plan was developed. Physically average in height and weight, he has suffered from extensive allergies throughout his life, but at the time of his referral by a high school counselor to rehabilitation services, his allergies were under control with medication and environmental and diet restrictions. His high school record is erratic, with grades ranging from D to A in such subjects as mathematics and physical sciences. He had personality conflicts with some of his teachers and disliked his counselor, a capable man who went to some pains to help Bill make adjustments. Psychometric instruments reveal that Bill is well in the top decile of high school graduates in most mental abilities as well as in academic achievement tests. Exceptions in school achievement show in mathematics, in which he performed poorly, despite intelligence tests which reflected good quantitative abilities. He did not take Trigonometry or Algebra III. In art he was a straight-A student. He held a part-time job in his last four months of high school to help support his new pregnant wife and worked full time after his graduation until he set out for college prior to implementation of the rehabilitation plan.

Exploratory Interviews

Bill sought assistance in choosing his vocational goal and in paying for its training or educational costs. He definitely wanted to go to college, despite the impediment of a family, and he felt that with part-time employment in college, some parental assistance, and tuition paid by the Bureau of Rehabilitation Services, he could see his way through four years of study. He expressed only two areas of interest, art and chemistry. In both fields he was unsure of himself. He knew that he was unusually talented in art, but feared that the talents required for real success in that field were beyond his reach, especially since he eschewed commercial art and favored completely independent creative activity. He liked chemistry as an intellectual challenge, enjoyed his limited chemistry lab experience, and believed that it was a well-paid profession. Again, he was unsure of his ability to master chemistry. He spoke of having difficulty developing hypotheses and experimental procedures to verify them when confronted with such exercises in his accelerated chemistry class in high school. He was aware that preparation for the chemical professions involved the study of mathematics but he had not been aware of the extent of these studies which, for an effective background and graduate work, required calculus, differential equations, and the special applications in statistical mechanics and quantum mechanics. He had not considered possible allergenic hazards in chemistry until his interviews with this counselor.

Vocational Interests and Aptitudes

The counselor collected information on Bill's high school grades and achievement and intelligence tests administered while client was in school. Together with personality information gleaned from Bill's school counselor, this information was provided by a commercial psychological counseling firm recognized as one of the best in Kentucky by the Bureau of Rehabilitation Services. Subsequent evaluation by psychologists of the firm, using Wechsler, Bender-Gestalt, DAT, projective and other instruments, and personal interview, led to recommendations for development in engineering, drafting, the physical sciences, or art. The Kuder Preference Record confirmed interest in both artistic and scientific fields, and discouraged development in service or persuasive fields. Bill's Wechsler IQ was 132, his verbal, 127, with a full scale of 130.

The chemistry profession, for competent persons, is a well-paid field, but a baccalaureate is not sufficient to achieve true professional status. Both research and analytical chemists are apt to be exposed to toxic and noxious substances that could threaten the health of the client, a possibility that the client's allergist confirmed. The client's poor performance in high school math subjects, his completion of only three years of math, with low grades, and his dislike of the subject, combined with the allergenic hazards, weighed heavily against his pursuing this area.

According to his counselor, the client's high school art teachers considered him an excellent candidate for commercial art, but were dubious of his opportunities for success as a purely independent creative artist. Although no conclusions were made by any advisors, an exploratory approach to the subject of art was recommended by teachers, the school counselor, and concurred in by the commercial psychological consulting firm. Pay for commercial artists varied widely in business and industry; for real talent and application, an income of $8,000 a year following graduation was not out of reach as depicted in the *Occupational Outlook Handbook, 1970-71 Edition.*

An alternative goal, one which could allow modification into either concentration in chemistry or in art, and which could capitalize on the client's interests and abilities in both fields, was scientific artist or medical illustrator. This field requires both two- and three-dimensional presentations of physical phenomena for educational and technical reporting purposes, in line drawings, halftones, color, and spatial simulations. The artist must have a well-developed understanding of the scientific or medical fields for which he illustrates, and he must exercise creativity as well as draftmanship and structural ability. In addition to illustrating for scientific and technical journals and making physical mock-ups for such educational fields as medicine and the physical sciences, the competent artist so trained could find employment in developing training aids for all types of training facilities, including the Armed Forces. Local inquiry revealed that there is no supply of scientific artists in the large metropolitan area in which the client resides. Scientific and medical schools purchased their requirements from out of the area, copied many, or improvised their own models and illustrations using the time of staff and faculty charged primarily with other duties. Wayne State University was identified as an institution utilizing a scientific illustrator, and identification and contact with this individual is still being attempted.

In addition to education in art, sculpturing, drafting, and the appropriate natural sciences, the scientific artist should be familiar with educational methods, particularly visual aids. He must have a high spatial visualization aptitude, ability to readily grasp the desires of a writer or educator stated in hasty terms, a sense of the dramatic and emphatic, and ingenuity. A university degree would not be essential to effectiveness, perhaps, but certainly would enhance his acceptability to the scientific and educational community. During his last years of college preparation, the aspiring scientific illustrator, if he has demonstrated his ability, should be able to develop contacts for employment through his university faculty as well as through submission of examples of his work, and displays at exhibits and conferences.

The most significant aspect of this vocational goal for Bill, however, is the flexibility it allows him. He may transfer to commercial art, teaching, or technological professions with little or no modification of his first several years of college work.

Subsequent Interviews

The collection of information about my client, including the psychological-vocational assessment, had been completed prior to this counselor's departure for the summer session at Virginia Commonwealth University's counselor orientation program. On his return in mid-August, time was extremely limited for development and implementation of Bill's vocational educational plan. Fortunately, the idea of medical illustrator had been suggested to the counselor by the use of mock-ups and charts in the Orientation to Rehabilitation training course. A single interview with the client in late August was sufficient to arrive at an agreed goal. The information and speculation described above was developed with the client gradually, beginning with his health and math hazards in pursuing chemistry. He was enthused about the concept of combining art and chemistry studies in college. During the summer he had obtained a tentative commitment for employment at Morehead State University and had already been accepted there.

Recognizing the fact that the *Dictionary of Occupational Titles (D.O.T.)* is to be used as a guide describing categories of positions rather than as a description of a specific job as it exists in a specific work setting should enable the user of this resource material to assist his client in the selection of an appropriate vocation.

As a starting point, Volume I of the *D.O.T.* was utilized to gain a general understanding of the responsibilities of a medical illustrator. The definition in Volume I states:

MEDICAL ILLUSTRATOR (medical ser.) 141.081. artist, scientific. Makes sketches and constructs tri-dimensional models to illustrate surgical and medical research procedures, anatomical and pathological specimens, unusual clinical disorders, micro-organisms, and plant and animal tissues. Develops drawings, paintings, diagrams, and models illustrating medical findings for use in publications, exhibits, consultations, and research and teaching activities. Completes illustrations in pen and ink, monochromatic wash, water-color, carbon dust, and mixed media. Constructs, or advises in construction of teaching models in plaster, wax, plastics, and other materials. Devises visual aids to assist in interpreting research programs. May specialize in illustrations in a particular medical field. May specialize in drawings of plant and animal tissues and be designated as HISTOLOGICAL ILLUSTRA-TOR.

This definition allows the counselor and client an opportunity to examine the occupation in its broadest aspects. Specific analysis of the job must be gathered through additional resource material such as the *Occupational Outlook Handbook, 1970-71 Edition,* as well as Volume II of the *D.O.T.* and *A Supplement to the D.O.T.,* and actual work assignments as they exist in the labor market. As stated previously the client has procured a job at Morehead State University as a medical illustrator.

Since the client and the counselor tentatively had reached a point where Medical Illustrator seemed appropriate to the client's interests and previously determined aptitudes, Volume II (1965) was used to assess transferability of skills.

On page 232 of Volume II, the worker trait groups within areas of work are found. The following is an adapted form of the listing as found in Volume II:

ART WORK
.081

Work Performed

Work activities in this group primarily involve the creative expression of ideas, feelings, and moods in artistic designs, objects, and arrangements. Commercial arts are characteristically concerned with the creation and reproduction of commercial and industrial designs involving adherence to technical requirements or functional limitations specified by the client or employer.

Work Requirements

An occupationally significant combination of: aesthetic appreciation; creative imagination; artistic judgment concerning harmony of color and line; eye-hand coordination and finger and manual dexterity to paint or draw and to use handtools when working with materials; perception of form and design, color discrimination to perceive differences in hue, shade, and value; and spatial aptitude to visualize and depict three-dimensional objects and arrangements on two-dimensional surfaces.

Clues for Relating Applicants and Requirements

Demonstrated artistic ability, including hobbies, particularly if artwork has won prizes or been sold.

Training and Methods of Entry

Vocational high schools and art schools or institutes awarding diplomas upon completion of 2 to 3 years of theory and practice provide preparation generally acceptable for entry positions in commercial art. Commercial artists may find employment in printing and publishing houses, advertising agencies, commercial art studios, department stores, and Government agencies. Specialized skills, such as lettering, illustrating, or typography enhance employment prospects. Advancement to responsible positions involving planning and layout work depends largely on development of artistic and technical skills through experience and on-the-job training.

Art schools offering 4 years of study, particularly those connected with colleges or universities, commonly award the bachelor of fine arts degree which is generally considered evidence of preparation for entry into fine artwork. Preparation includes studying such subjects as history, and English, which are not ordinarily included in preparation for commercial artwork.

RELATED CLASSIFICATIONS

Decorating and Art Work
  (.031; .051; .061) p. 228

Drafting and Related Work
  (.181; .281) p. 377

QUALIFICATIONS PROFILE

GED: 5 4
SVP: 7 8 5

Apt:	GVN	SPQ	KFM	EC
	223	224	222	52
	13	1 3	333	41
				3

Int: 8 6
Temp: X 9
Phys. Dem: S L 4 6

The integration of client's professed interests in both chemistry and art seem compatible when compared to the Qualifications Profile.

Through additional academic training and on-the-job training, the counselor is confident Bill can become a superb medical illustrator. Restricting his future, vocationally, is not intended by focusing solely on this position as a medical illustrator; the client realizes his interests as well as labor market trends may alter, to some degree, his ultimate choice.

As noted in the above worker trait description of art work, the physical demands of the job are not strenuous, especially in relation to Bill's allergy disability.

A Supplement to the D.O.T. is a useful device for the vocational rehabilitation counselor since it is an abbreviated version of Volume II. Within the *Supplement* one can locate via the *D.O.T.* code number the job title as recorded in Volume I or Volume II. Also found are the physical demands, working conditions, and training time required for specific jobs. Once the counselor has mastered Volume II, he may then elect to scan the *Supplement* in order to define various worker traits required for specific vocations.

Summary

Because of the time limits in developing information about the occupation chosen, this counselor may have been imprudent in selecting this particular case for this exercise. Nevertheless, the case demonstrated how seemingly unrelated abilities and interests can be combined in vocational goals, and permit flexibility in ultimate career development. The client was especially intelligent and discerning, despite some personality problems, and did not tax the counselor's communicative and persuasive skills as some other active cases in his caseload have done. Again, the utilization of the *D.O.T.* has enabled the counselor as well as the client to assess the transferability of skills, the physical and mental demands of the job, and a general orientation of worker requirements necessary for average job performance.

Exercise 13

COMMUNITY RESOURCES

RATIONALE

Each vocational rehabilitation worker is responsible for developing a working relationship with a number of community resources within his territory. There are many which are available and it is the counselor's responsibility to select the appropriate one for his particular client's needs. Not only should the counselor have an in-depth knowledge of several of the larger community resources, but also he should have at his fingertips a list of resources that he might have occasion to use on a regular basis. This exercise is intended to acquaint the trainee with agencies and facilities which can supplement the services provided by vocational rehabilitation.

ASSIGNMENT

Part A. The trainee is to make an in-depth study of one major community resource and develop an agency understanding in areas such as relationships, responsibilities, agreements, referrals, and services. Lines of authority, identification of contact persons at each unit, ways the facility can help your agency, and ways your agency can help the facility should be treated as well. Pay particular attention to the role various community resources can play in assisting the client in the transition from hospital or unemployment to community living and greater participation in society. Examples of community resources that may be used are the Department of Social Services, State Employment Service, Goodwill Industries, a rehabilitation center, a workshop, special clinics, and teaching hospitals. Of course, this is not an exhaustive list. It is recommended that you discuss this exercise with your training coordinator and/or supervisor to see if there are any community resources in the area which have not been studied lately or have never been approached by vocational rehabilitation. The supervisor may elect to have the trainee study a community resource which has failed to refer clients to the agency. The training coordinator may approve another community resource for this exercise if he feels a study of that resource might better fill the training needs of the counselor trainee.

Part B. The counselor trainee is to list community resources and services in his territory. The following is a list of basic services (in italics) provided and the types of facilities rendering such services:

Diagnostic
    Medical Centers
    Rehabilitation Centers
    Workshops
    Clinics
    Evaluation and Guidance Services

Counseling and Guidance
    Guidance Clinics
    Family Service
    Churches
    Legal Aid
    Mental Health Association Office (NAMH)

Vocational Training
    Vocational Schools
    Business Schools
    Goodwill Industries

Placement
    U.S. Employment Services
    Private Employment Agencies

Maintenance
    YMCA
    YWCA
    Family Service
    Red Cross

Physical Restoration
    Hospitals
    Cancer Society
    Shriners Hospital
    TB Association

Transportation
   Family Service
   Church Groups
   Civic Clubs
Artificial Appliances and Braces
   Private Firms (i.e. hearing aid dealers, prosthetic and orthotic
      companys, etc.)
   Clinics
   Foundations
Education
   Colleges
   Universities
   Junior Colleges
   Private Schools
This exercise is not to be a "yellow pages listing" in which
the counselor merely utilizes the local community services direc-
tory and copies material; this is a learning experience which
enhances the effectiveness of the counselor. Choose those re-
sources which you may have occasion to use in the provision of
services for your clients. Within each listing should be the name
of the organization, a contact person you might rely upon, the
address and telephone number, and a thumbnail sketch of the
services provided.

Note: This exercise should be duplicated and placed in a
central file accessible to all professional staff in your territory.

STUDENT WORK: SAMPLE 1

Part A

The treatment mental health center of our county is located
on the grounds of Memorial Hospital and is governed through a
board composed of the county commissioners. The controlling
body, however, is the State Department of Mental Health for
quality control and for overall funding purposes.

Funding is through state funds with 25 percent for the first
year and 75 percent coming from the federal government; and
60 percent funding from the federal government after the second
year, with 40 percent from the state; and thereafter 40 percent
to the third year, and at the end of the fourth year, 30 percent

from federal funds. The remaining amount will be made up of funds from the state and/or county and local resources.

The community mental health center of this county is responsible for assembling a variety of services within a geographic area for the treatment of the mentally ill and the prevention of mental illness. The reason for the establishment of mental health centers, and this one in particular, is so that a variety range of coordinated mental health services will be available close to the home of the patient; and through the center's programs it provides the resources for and strengthening of existing resources in the community to prevent mental illness.

The treatment mental health center of Wake County provides five essential services to the citizens of this county:

1. In-patient Care. The unit offers treatment to patients needing 24-hour care. This is currently provided through contractual arrangements with two local hospitals.

2. Out-patient Care. This unit offers treatment programs for adults, children, and families.

3. Partial Hospitalization. This unit offers at least day care and treatment for patients able to return home evenings and weekends. In some cases, night care is also provided for patients able to work but in need of further care or without suitable home arrangements.

4. Emergency Care. 24-hour or emergency service is available in one of the three units named above. If a physician or psychiatrist is not on duty at the treatment mental health center, an answering service will provide him the name of a private psychiatrist under contractual service to the center or to the psychiatric section of the hospitals.

5. Consultation and Education. The center staff offers consultation and education to community agencies and professional personnel.

In addition to these five basic services, the treatment mental health center also provides the following additional comprehensive service areas:

1. Diagnostic Service. This service provides diagnostic evaluation and includes recommendations for appropriate care. The

concept here is that a patient no longer is admitted directly to the state mental hospital. The citizen is evaluated at the mental health center and then proper referral is made. This may be to the mental hospital, or recommendation may be made for in-patient care in a general hospital or out-patient care or partial hospitalization. This is the concept of one portal of entry into the psychiatric hospitals.

2. Rehabilitation Service. This service includes both social and vocational rehabilitation. It offers for those who need them services such as pre-vocational testing, guidance counseling, and sometimes job placement. This is the area in which the treatment mental health center wishes to establish a more direct relationship with the school systems' special education instructors and vocational rehabilitation counselors. For a while, it has had this as a basic concept and implementation is underway. The center wishes to broaden this area of contact so that referrals can be made both from the mental health center to vocational rehabilitation for job placement and from vocational rehabilitation to the mental health center for diagnostic evaluation follow-up and in some cases, medical and/or psychiatric treatment.

3. Pre-care and After-care. This service provides screening of patients prior to hospital admission and home visiting before and after hospitalization. Follow-up services for patients are available in out-patient clinics or in foster homes or half-way houses. This is the second area in which the vocational rehabilitation services are needed by the mental health center, for these patients in years past have been returned from a state hospital to their communities without any preparation, or at best, inadequate preparation being made for their reception in their home areas. This created a tremendously high readmission rate of patients to the state psychiatric hospitals. Through the utilization of the resources of vocational rehabilitation, the comprehensive mental health center will be able to provide the psychiatric follow-up for these patients and provide through family therapy an environment conducive to maintenance of average citizenship status. However, according to the center staff, the major area of need will be the provision for job opportunities and job place-

ments which the vocational rehabilitation services most assuredly can provide to these ex-patients. The center staff through expressed statements felt that the after-care program will be successful only through a broad-based cooperative venture of vocational rehabilitation services, the State Department of Mental Health, and the mental health center in this county.

4. Training. The mental health center carries on extensive programs of training for all types of mental health personnel. Former classifications such as aide/attendants at the hospital are rotated through the mental health center to train them on the concepts of community mental health. Mental health technology students from outlying community colleges are rotated through the center as part of their two-year associate of arts training. Students in the registered nurse programs of Memorial Hospital and two other state hospitals are rotated through the center to provide these students with the necessary introduction to community mental health services. Additionally, the psychiatric staff members of the state hospitals are rotated through the center to provide psychiatrists training and institutional types of psychiatry background in community psychiatry.

5. Research and Evaluation. The center has developed an extensive research program to evaluate its own effectiveness in its program activities. It has launched a research program into the problems of mental illness. Additionally, the center is joined in an interagency venture with the Department of Social Services, Department of Corrections, and Department of Public Health to research the effects of environmental activities and conditions upon creation of mental illness and also the prevention of mental illness.

By way of summary as to the purpose of the mental health center, its goals and philosophy, the staff of the treatment mental health center stated that in this program a patient can move easily from one type of treatment to another as his needs change. Treatment at any time will be appropriate to the course of his illness. This is called "continuity of care." It represents the most advanced psychiatric thinking in research concerning care of the mentally ill. It is a key concept of this mental health center program.

STAFFING PATTERNS. The treatment mental health center is administered by a psychiatric M.D. director. He is assisted by two full-time psychiatrists who provide the basic psychiatric care for patients at the center, and he represents the contact person for any type of demonstrated and approved psychiatric needs or services. He stated that if he was not able to be reached, then one of the other psychiatrists could be contacted and could provide the necessary treatment services or referrals.

PSYCHOLOGICAL SERVICES. Currently, there are two full-time psychologists on duty at the mental health center. They provide such services as psychological testing and behavior modification activities for adults. One is a specialist in children's services and has special expertise in problems of emotional adjustment of school children. This section represents an excellent resource for contact for vocational rehabilitation counselors in the school system and would either provide services for the students referred by the DVR counselor or refer the student and counselor to another section in the center for appropriate care.

SOCIAL SERVICES. The center employs four social workers full time. Two of these are specialists in children's maladjustment and provide a broad range of children's services including two active therapy groups in the morning and one active therapy group in the evening. Techniques of behavior modification through a token economy are utilized extensively in this unit. Also some modified attitudinal therapy activities based on the concepts developed at the Veterans Administration Hospital in Tuscaloosa, Alabama, are utilized as a part of the retraining activities for these children. The center staff stated that this unit would probably provide the greatest services to the school counselors of any unit at the center and encouraged the DVR counselor to contact this unit directly whenever a problem of apparent emotional adjustment was observed.

NURSING. The center employs two full-time mental health nurses. The RN's are responsible for assisting in medical care of patients who report to the clinic and providing for a degree of supervision over the children who require some type of medication and medical treatment. The RN staff is also an integral part of the after-care activities along with the social services section and follows up the patients once they have been discharged from the state psychiatric hospital and sees that they do report for medication and weekly or biweekly therapy sessions.

RESEARCH AND EVALUATION. The center employs under contract a part-time psychologist, a part-time educator, and a part-time sociologist to provide such services as community surveys, development of instruments to evaluate staff effectiveness and program effectiveness, and assessment of the need for various types of vocational rehabilitation job placement services. This section relies heavily upon a close cooperative agreement with the vocational rehabilitation services as to the availability of funds and partial underwriting of psychiatric and psychological services to enable the patient (ex-patient) to return as a fully productive citizen in the economy. The staff expressed a high degree of willingness to participate in such an activity.

ADMINISTRATIVE STAFF. Currently the center employs four full-time administrative secretaries, two receptionists, and two mental health workers with a two-year Associate of Applied Science degree. The administrative secretarial staff provides the necessary administrative support for follow-up contacts, initiation of certain completed forms, i.c. expense vouchers, Medicaid and Medicare vouchers, records completion for the Department of Mental Health, and in general seems to provide the basic structure for the administrative operation of the mental health center. The two receptionists are responsible for contacting those individuals who have not met appointments and for scheduling appointments. If an individual is contacted by the receptionists and presents a vague reason for not making the appointment, then the administrative secretary will contact the individual and discuss the matter further. If this is not fruitful, then either the social services section or the nursing section will be contacted. Usually, a mental health worker assigned to the section will accompany the nurse or social worker on a home visit to determine the basis of the problem preventing the attendance of this person at the appointed time.

The treatment mental health center appears to be a most useful resource for vocational rehabilitation to utilize. It has the broad range of services assigned to it which have been listed above and is attempting to fulfill those ten basic areas of services. Referrals can be made by this department, especially from our school programs to the children's therapy and diagnostic units, at very little if any difficulty and will enable vocational rehabilitation services to avail itself of a broad range of services which we, at this point, are not tapping. Conversely, vocational rehabilitation services can provide a great service to the mental health center by providing the job placement needed for patients or ex-patients being released from the state hospital and channeled back through the mental health center. Secondly, it can provide services by assisting in job placement for those people who do not require full hospitalization but for whom a position would be one of the basic avenues of treatment which would enable them to achieve a degree of emotional stability, economic security, and self-respect.

During the month of August, the mental health clinic served a county population of 216,000. During this period of time, the center began the month with 2,059 patients on the books. They admitted 176 patients during the month, terminated 114 patients, with an overall number of patients on the books of 2,121. There are currently 36 adult patients on the waiting list. It is noteworthy that there are no children on the waiting list. These services are being provided. There were 2,467 staff interviews held during this period of time, and 333 hours of community service were devoted by the staff during this period.

Part B

Diagnostic Facilities

1. Montgomery County Society for Crippled Children and Adults; Easter Seal Treatment Center. 1000 Twinbrook Parkway, Rockville, Maryland. Phone: 424-5000. Contact Person: Mr. K. M. McManes. Offers diagnostic services in

speech and language disorders, occupational and physical therapy evaluations.

2. Hope Day Care Center for Retarded Children. 6100 South Gate Drive, Temple Hills, Maryland. Phone: 894-4411. Director: Mrs. Lee Anna Mielzarek. Personal adjustment training and academic program for retarded (severely). There is no maximum age limit.

3. The Potomac Foundation for Mental Health. 5413 West Cedar Lane, Bethesda, Maryland. Phone: 530-6333. Director: Brian Crowley, M.D. Provides diagnostic evaluation of children and adolescents by psychologist, psychiatrist and psychological testing.

4. Occupational Training Center and Workshop. 4501 Hamilton Street, Hyattesville, Maryland. Phone: 864-1603. Director: Joseph C. Walter. Programs offered include an evaluation program to determine employability, a personal adjustment training program and work adjustment training, as well as vocational training.

5. Montgomery County Mental Health Center for Adults. 8500 Colesville Road, Silver Spring, Maryland. Phone: 587-2200. Director: Paul G. Yessler, M.D. Services offered include diagnosis, evaluation consultation, and psychological testing.

6. Heart Association. 7847 Old Georgetown Road, Bethesda, Maryland. Phone: 657-8878. Director: James R. Thomas. Offers a work evaluation program consisting of a cardiologist, vocational counselor, and medical social worker to evaluate work potential of cardiac patients.

7. Jeanne Bussard Workshop. W. South Street, Frederick, Maryland. Phone: 301-663-9588. Contact Person: Mrs. Helen Nessear, director. Diagnostic and PAT training facility for retarded, usually for more severely retarded.

8. Montgomery Workshop. Connecticut Avenue and Plyers Mill Road, Kensington, Maryland. Phone: 933-2200. Contact Person: Mr. Bill Scott, director. Diagnostic and PAT training for retarded and some emotional.

9. Psychological Evaluation. Staff Psychologist, Mr. Joel Billy.

Located in our facility, 390 Martins Lane, Rockville, Maryland. Does psychological testing and is a resource person on cases requiring a psychological diagnosis.

10. Psychological Evaluation. Kreger Associates. Suite 917, 5530 Wisconsin Avenue, Chevy Chase, Maryland. Phone: 656-7650. Contact Person: Mrs. Jewels Kreger. Provides psychologicals; will test at schools.

11. Psychiatric Evaluation. Adrian Cohen, M.D. 8224 Woodmont Avenue, Bethesda, Maryland. Phone: 652-2377. Does psychiatric evaluation and works as an advisor regarding the handling of emotional cases.

12. Medical Consultant. C. James Duke. Holy Cross Hospital, Silver Spring, Maryland. Phone: 495-1351. Provides consulting on medical questions.

13. University of Maryland Speech and Hearing Clinic. University of Maryland, College Park, Maryland. Phone: 301-454-2546. Contact Person: Dr. Doudna, director. Provides speech and hearing examinations and therapeutical services for employable adults referred by us.

14. The George Washington University Medical Center. Rehabilitation Research and Training Center. 901 23rd St., N.W., Washington, D. C. 20037. Phone: 331-6666. Provides diagnostic and total vocational evaluation for physical handicapped, especially cerebral palsy.

Counseling and Guidance Facilities

1. Over "60" Counseling and Employment Service. 4700 Norwood Dr., Chevy Chase, Maryland. Phone: 652-9339. Offers counseling employment service to persons over 60 on adjusting to problems brought on by aging and pre-retirement counseling.

2. Pastoral Counseling and Consultation Center of Greater Washington. 3000 Connecticut Avenue, N.W., Washington, D.C. Phone: 234-8081. Provides evaluation and diagnostic services for individuals, marriages, and family groups. Group therapy, individual and family counseling offered.

3. Psychiatric Service. Veterans Administration Hospital, 50 Irving Street, N.W., Washington, D.C. Phone: 483-6666.

Provides psychiatric diagnosis and group therapy; primarily for veterans.

4. **Red Cross, Montgomery County Chapter.** 2020 East-West Highway, Silver Spring, Maryland. Phone: 588-2515. Provides counseling, guidance, and financial assistance for Armed Forces personnel and their families.

5. Washington Opportunities for Women, Inc. 1000 16th Street, N.W., Washington, D.C. Phone: 393-6151. Acts as an advisory service and clearing house for current local information about college and university programs and part-time opportunities for paid employment, and provides individual interview and referral services to women seeking such opportunities.

6. U.S. Public Health Service, Out-Patient Clinic. H.E.W., South Building, 330 E Street, S.W., Washington, D.C. Phone: 962-7418. Services include out-patient consultation and treatment for individual, group, or family.

7. Community Mental Health Services. 8500 Colesville Road, Silver Spring, Maryland. Phone: 279-1605. Contact Person: James Read, M.D., psychiatrist. Provides counseling and therapeutic services to adult residents of Montgomery County; fee based on income, run by Montgomery County Health Department.

8. Catholic Charities of the Archdiocese of Washington. 1710 N Street, N.W., Washington, D.C. 20036. Phone: 783-0581. Director: Very Reverend Leo J. Coady. Provides casework services and financial help to Catholic families and unwed mothers.

9. Child Mental Health. 12701 Twinbrook Parkway, Rockville, Maryland. Phone: 279-1671. Contact Person: Florence Weiner, psychiatric social worker and acting director. Provides counseling and therapeutic services for youth population of Montgomery County, part of Montgomery County Health Department.

10. Consultation and Guidance Center, Inc. 1105 D Spring Street, Silver Spring, Maryland 20910. Phone: 585-7777. Contact Person: Co-directors, Dr. Harvey Sweethaum and Dr.

Irving Raifman. Provides diagnostic and treatment facilities for emotionally disturbed. Treatment offered through combined approach of several disciplines, including individual, child marriage, and group psychotherapy.

11. Family Service of Montgomery County, Inc. 350 Hungerford Drive, Rockville, Maryland. Phone: 762-0300. Contact Person: Francis J. Ryan. Provides counseling services to children, adults, and families with problems.

12. Jewish Social Services Agency. Wheaton Plaza Office Building, Wheaton, Maryland 20902. Phone: 946-1202. Provides counseling for family and marital problems, and service to unwed mothers.

Vocational Training Facilities

1. Institute of Modern Procedures. 1701 North Fort Myer Drive, Arlington, Virginia. Phone: .525-4890. Registrar: Mr. Robert A. Stutsman. Provides a training program in the fields of key punch operator, computer operator, and programmer; printing and drafting.

2. Bethesda Beauty Academy. 7810 Old Georgetown Road, Bethesda, Maryland. Phone: 657-3333. Director: Joseph Perron. Provides a course in hair styling and cosmetology.

3. Washington Drafting School. 2045 University Blvd., Langley Park, Maryland. Phone: 439-7777. Director: Charles P. Janssen. Offers both certificate and degree programs in general, architectural, mechanical, electronic, structural, statistical, and technical drafting; as well as courses in heating and air conditioning.

4. Control Data Institute. 11428 Rockville Pike, Rockville, Maryland. Phone: 521-3700. Contact Person: Mr. Dwight Spear. Offers a program in computer technology and programming technology.

5. Temple School. 7940 Wisconsin Avenue, Bethesda, Maryland. Phone: OL2-1300. Contact Person: Myrna Bailey. Temple is a business school and offers courses in business, secretarial skills, and accounting.

6. Lewis Hotel-Motel Schools. 2301 Pennsylvania Avenue, N.W., Washington, D.C. Phone: 333-4692. Director: L. E. Fuhrmann. One of the few schools in area which offers courses in hotel

management, including maitre d'hotel, bartender, steward, chef, as well as sales and public relations.

7. Technical Institute of America. 7600 Georgia Avenue, Washington, D.C. Phone: 588-2425. Director: Mr. Spitzer. Offers training for technical writers, illustrators, color rendering technicians, opaquers, junior draftsmen, drawing letterers, and proofreaders.

8. Cashiers Training Institute. 711 14th Street, N.W., Washington, D.C. (Suite 600). Phone: 783-8488. Offers courses for cashiers and checkers, PBX, receptionist, IBM keypunch and typing.

9. Professional Barber School. 2401 Blue Ridge Avenue, Wheaton, Maryland. Phone: 942-2260. Director: Mr. Casey Cassidy. Offers course in barber techniques to qualify student to pass state board.

10. Columbia School of Broadcasting. 4641 Montgomery Avenue, Suite 401, Washington, D.C. Phone: 657-3190. Director: Mr. Frank Feller. Offers courses in all phases of broadcasting and announcing.

11. Davis Memorial Goodwill Industries. 1218 New Hampshire Avenue, N.W., Washington, D.C. 20036. Phone: 337-5900. Contact Person: Richard A. Nelson, executive director. Provides a comprehensive rehabilitation facility for medical, social, and prevocational services; work evaluation training; and sheltered employment for handicapped persons.

12. Maryland State Employment Agency. 1126 Georgia Avenue, Wheaton, Maryland. Phone: 949-5300. Contact Person: Miss Pat Wheeler, MDTA Coordinator. MDTA training courses.

13. Lear Siegler Institute. 640 University Boulevard, E., Silver Spring, Maryland. Phone: 439-8000. Contact Person: Mr. Mel Siegel. Provides computer training, fashion merchandising, secretarial and business training.

14. Information Systems School. 11141 Georgia Avenue, Wheaton, Maryland 20902. Phone: 942-4423. Contact Person: Mr. Al Himmelbau. Provides training in computer careers.

15. Rockville Beauty Academy. 808 Baltimore Road, Rockville, Maryland. Phone: 762-3332. Contact Person: Mr. Belle, owner.

Provides training in beauty culture.

16. Lincoln Technical Institute. 901 New Jersey Avenue, S.E., Washington, D.C. Phone: 547-8600. Contact Person: Mr. Shaw, director. Provides training in auto mechanics, auto air-conditioning, and all aspects of automobile maintenance.

Placement Facilities

1. General Services Administration (part of Civil Service Commission). 7th & D Streets, S.W., Washington, D.C. Phone: 963-5384. Contact Person: Mr. Arthur Palman. For jobs as guards and custodial service.

2. Mr. Mount. Placement officer with D.C. DVR. Coordinates placement services for the entire metropolitan area. Phone: 629-0252.

3. Handicapped Workers Group. 1310 Apple Ave., Takoma Park, Maryland. Phone: 270-4341. Contact: Mrs. Roberta Jack. Jobs involve selling light bulbs from a telephone sales office. There are no special work requirements for job.

4. Maryland State Employment Service. See above. Contact Person: Mrs. Seigle, Counselor.

5. Employers Advisory Council. Joint effort of DVR and personnel officers of various employers in area; meets once a month and counselor presents difficult cases for placement and advise on placement and receives advice concerning possible placement of the client.

6. Federal Government, Civil Service Commission, Selective Placement Programs for the Handicapped. 1900 E Street, N.W., Washington, D.C. Phone: 632-5687. Contact Person: Mr. Ed Rose, Director. Provides help in placing handicapped persons in federal government.

7. Schedule "A" employment with federal government. Contact individual federal agencies for openings and DVR must certify them (head of program on federal level). Mrs. Mary S. Douglas, Placement Specialist for Handicapped. 1900 E Street, N.W., Washington, D.C. Phone: 632-4488.

8. GEICO (a private industry). Wisconsin and Western Avenue, Chevy Chase, Maryland. Phone: OL 6-1000. Contact Per-

son: Mr. Ford, director of personnel. Government employees Insurance Company is very open to the hiring of handicapped persons. Serves on Employment Advisory Committee.

Maintenance Facilities

1. Help Unincorporated. 580 University Blvd., Silver Spring, Maryland. Phone: JU-8-1600. This is a cooperative mission service project of the council of churches, serving as a central point of contact for emergency assistance in time of need.

2. Housing Counseling Service. 400 First Street, N.W., Washington, D.C. Phone: 386-6145. Aids in finding dwellings for low and moderate income families.

3. Housing Authority of Montgomery County. 1010 Rockville Pike, Rockville, Maryland. Phone: 279-1318. Provides housing for low income residents of Montgomery County.

4. Mrs. Miriam Gloyd. 1 Lawrence Court, Rockville, Maryland 20850. Phone: 762-3419. Provides boarding house, half-way facilities for people with emotional problems. Cost $170 per month.

5. Montgomery County Boy's Home. Fall Road, Rockville, Maryland. Phone: 762-8417. Contact: John Travis, director. Provides half-way house facilities for youthful male offenders.

Physical Restoration Facilities

1. Health Department, Montgomery County, County Office Bldg., Rockville, Maryland. Phone: 279-1671. Through their home health services, both physical and occupational therapy services are provided to homebound patients at a nominal fee. They also conduct an alcoholic and drug dependency clinic for people with problems of alcoholism or drug abuse, consisting of individual and group therapy.

2. Chestnut Lodge. 500 W. Montgomery Ave., Rockville, Maryland. Phone: 424-8300. Director: Dr. Dexter M. Bullard. It is an intensive psychoanalytic therapy hospital.

3. Anchor House. 1212 Monroe St., N.E., Washington, D.C. Phone: 832-5555. It is a residential home for men and women between 21 and 55 years old with emotional or mental problems. Must be employable after one year of treatment.

4. Center for Handicapped; Cerebral Palsy Association of Montgomery County, Inc. 9421 Colesville Rd., Silver Spring, Maryland 20901. Phone: 588-4075. Contact: Elwood E. Swarmer. Out-patient clinic provides physical, occupational and speech therapy.

5. Montgomery County Society for Crippled Children and Adults, Inc. (Easter Seal Treatment Center). 1000 Twinbrook Parkway, Rockville, Maryland. Phone: 424-5200. Contact: Mrs. Steward. Out-patient center provides physical, occupational, and speech therapy and psychological and audiological evaluation.

6. Multiple Sclerosis Association of Greater Washington. Gorman Building, 3800 Reservoir Rd. Phone: 625-7765. Contact: Mrs. Pauline M. Walker. Serves persons with multiple sclerosis and related disorders with physical therapy and occupational therapy.

7. Holy Cross Hospital of Silver Spring. 1500 Forest Glen Road, Silver Spring, Maryland. Phone: JU-9-2600. Contact: Dr. Duke. Through their rehabilitation unit they provide physical therapy and other restoration services.

8. Washington Sanitarium and Hospital. 7600 Carroll Avenue, Takoma Park, Maryland. Phone: JU-9-8800. Contact: John Ruffcorn. Provides the services found in most prosthetic clinics.

Transportation Facilities

1. Community Action Committee, Montgomery County. 1010 Rockville Pike, Rockville, Maryland. Phone: 279-1245. Contact: Miss Joyce Walker. Will provide transportation or money for such in order to place a client on a job.

2. FISH. A volunteer community organization. Part of UGF in Rockville, Maryland. Phone: 924-4362. Contact: Mrs. Carolyn Roslund. They will provide free transportation in emergencies as well as to bring persons to and from interviews and appointments.

3. American Cancer Society, Maryland Division, Inc. 8510 Dixon Ave., Silver Spring, Maryland. Phone: 587-1555. Contact: E. Larue Lunt. Will provide transportation money.

4. Health Fund, Montgomery County. 27 W. Jefferson St.,

Rockville, Maryland. Phone: 762-2202. Contact: Dorothy Dimmilt. Will provide money in an emergency for transportation.

Artificial Appliances and Braces Facilities

1. Universal Artificial Limb Company. 938 Wayne Avenue, Silver Spring, Maryland. Phone 587-6892. Contact: Mr. Caron. Handles artificial limbs and braces.

2. Accredited Surgical Company. 8705 Colesville Road, Silver Spring, Maryland. Phone: 585-7711. Contact: Mrs. Mascourtz. Rents and sells all sorts of hospital supplies and orthopedic appliances including the "helping hand" for wheelchair clients.

3. Center For the Handicapped; Cerebral Palsy of Montgomery County, Inc. Maintains special funds for braces, orthopedic appliances, and dental care.

4. Capitol Orthopedic, Inc. 8818 Cameron Street, Silver Spring, Maryland. Phone: 588-5088. Contact Person: Ivan Sabel. Handles artificial limbs and orthopedic braces.

5. Silver Spring Surgical Supply, Orthopedic Brace Company. 12910 Grenoble Drive, Rockville, Maryland. Phone: 946-2929. Specializes in custom-made braces, prescription and manufactured, functional-type hand splints, Milwaukee Braces.

6. Hanger, J.E., Inc. 40 Patterson Street, N.E., Washington, D.C. Phone: 628-1037. Deals in artificial limbs and braces.

Education Facilities

1. Galluadet College, 7th St. & Florida Ave., N.E., Washington, D.C. Phone: 543-9515. Provides liberal arts and college courses for all qualified deaf students in U.S.

2. University of Maryland. College Park, Maryland. Four-year college leading to BA and BS degrees and higher.

3. Montgomery Community College. Two campuses. Rockville Maryland. Phone: 762-7400. Takoma Park, Maryland. Phone: 587-0415. Provides two-year courses. leading to associate degrees and two-year transfer programs.

4. The George Washington University. Washington, D.C. 20006. Phone: 676-6000. Undergraduate and graduate programs.

5. The American University. Massachusetts and Nebraska

Avenue, N.W., Washington, D.C. Phone: 244-6800. Undergraduate and graduate programs.

6. Towson State College. Baltimore, Maryland 21204. State school. Undergraduate and graduate programs.

Exercise 14

INNOVATIVE PROGRAMS RELATIVE TO REHABILITATION

RATIONALE

There are many new programs being developed throughout the county of which the professionally employed rehabilitation workers should be aware. Almost every week one learns through public media or through conversation of a new program being developed to serve a certain population; e.g. New Careers, Manpower Development Training Act (MDTA), and JOBS sponsored by the Department of Labor; the establishment of a Commission on Aging, the Office of Economic Opportunity's Public Defender Program as well as other legal programs; and the federal government's emphasis on hiring the mentally retarded. It is essential that one acquaint himself with these new programs and lend assistance when possible. In turn, they will be acting as new referral and service sources for vocational rehabilitation.

ASSIGNMENT

List several of these new programs in your community. Investigate one of them and write a narrative description of its responsibilities including services provided, types of clients served, eligibility criteria, priorities, and types of expenditures of funds. Discuss how this organization might utilize the services of vocational rehabilitation. Also, decide if this program can be of service in providing aid to *your* clients. List some possible innovative approaches which might be used by both organizations. Go out on a limb and make some suggestions which one might normally cast aside as being infeasible.

147

STUDENT WORK: SAMPLE 1

This agency uses the NOTE program, the WARE program, Goodwill Industries of Kentucky, Urban League On-the-Job Training, and several other types of training areas to provide services in addition to the work of this agency, but I have selected the NOTE program for a brief in-depth view of the work which this agency and NOTE provide.

NOTE Program

The initials of this organization stand for Neighborhood Opportunities to Train and Earn. It provides training in a suitable work area for those boys and girls between the ages of 16 and 21 who are out of work and are also out of school. The program lasts for twenty-six weeks if successfully completed. It can be terminated by the individual client at his own will, but will not give him credit and does not permit him to enter another similar type of program until three months have passed by. Upon the completion of this training, placement is also provided and the choice of either returning to school or to continuing to work is explained to each individual trainee. Many of these persons will continue to work in various settlement houses or have other places in which they can work. The family income is checked very thoroughly and it must meet the standard or else the client will be refused services of NOTE.

At the present time—and it should continue thus—this rehabilitation office and NOTE share a warm reception. We have been able almost to keep the quota full with candidates who meet all the requirements into this program. It should nevertheless be mentioned here that because this is an outside agency, anyone who qualifies may apply for admission into the NOTE program. They also are asked by the Department of Child Welfare, with whom we work in cooperation, to take the ones which they can send direct to this program.

In order to work under the NOTE program, a worker's permit is required. This form can be completed by taking it to either the county board of education or the city board of education and having an official record of school attendance filled in on the proper card. Then a tuberculin test must be given to the client either by a private physician or the health department.

The initial interview to be made at the NOTE office which is located at 809 E. Washington Street, telephone 585-5247, is to be set up with the secretary. The interviewer will most likely be the program director. After the interview, the client will be placed in either one of four locations. The Presbyterian Community Center has utilized these clients and it provides a very worthwhile follow-up group therapy session. Some of our clients have worked as child-care attendants, seamstresses, typists, and kitchen aides.

Work reports are provided by telephone or in-person on-the-job type check-ups. This program has continued to accept our young male clients, but they are not able to use the young female clients as often.

Our agency provides bus transportation by the city buses if this is needed. Another feature which is good about this particular program is that the clients are paid an average wage of about $1.40 an hour. The workers are permitted to work about 25 to 32 hours a week until they are 18 years old and then they can work longer.

There are no charges to either our agency or by the client to NOTE. We can continue to use this facility and they, in turn, are always reminding us that we can send them any good boys that want to work. By their use of group therapy and the encouragement of continuing education, I personally feel that some clients might reevaluate their decision to drop out of school.

This NOTE program has been the definite holding stay of some clients who would have otherwise returned to an institution for punishment as a juvenile delinquent. Because of the placement which is provided by this particular program, many clients have been able to find permanent work and become rehabilitated. Such work as is being done by rehabilitation services and the NOTE program is actually real work experience and has been the means of retaining certain young persons by the courts. There have been failures with some of the clients in this program, but on the whole there is a value to be achieved by successfully completing this program. Neither our agency nor the work of all such programs can reach every client successfully but we are working to improve the ones who are concerned and want to learn as well as earn. The financial rewards of this program are not very great during the training period, but they are worth setting our eyes upon and trying to reach out for higher goals.

The NOTE program has provided this agency with referral information, and in the field of social service I feel this has been a great opportunity for those who were very sincere in their efforts. We must continue to work together in an effort of cooperation to see just how we can produce trained and more educated individuals. This is the basic philosophy of such organizations.

STUDENT WORK: SAMPLE 2

One of the community resources which I have found very useful is the CAC, Community Action Committee. It is an anti-poverty agency for Montgomery County. It depends on the Office of Economic Opportunity for funding and staff. It basically provides services and programs of self-help.

My first contact with them was when they referred a rather indigent resident to the county to DVR for assistance in finding a job. They provided the transportation for the client to come to the interview. Since that time, a sort of cooperative-reciprocal agreement has been worked out between the Department of Vocational Rehabilitation and the agency. They have sent us referrals and we in turn call on them to provide either service or appropriate referrals for our clients. Some of their services and objectives include making social services more readily accessible to those who need them and to better inform communities of existing social programs. They encourage county housing developers to meet the needs of low-income families and assist in finding suitable housing for these people. They have neighborhood workers who work in the poor communities. They also sponsor a day care center which provides youngsters with day care so that the parents may complete their education, undergo job training, or return to work. They operate two clinics where legal advice is available to low-income persons in the county. They provide job development opportunities and have a job development specialist who negotiates with employers and encourages them to provide training programs and job opportunities for the underemployed. They also provide transportation as mentioned earlier. In cooperation with the extension service, classes are provided for instruction in sewing, child care, and nutrition at no cost.

Especially since the funds have been so tight this year with our organization, CAC has been a valuable resource to us in providing services free of charge. Most of the workers are volunteers, and some even work from their homes.

Exercise 15

THE CLOSING OF CASES FROM 08 STATUS*

RATIONALE

You will probably have the occasion, if you already have not done so, to close one or more of your cases in the 08 status—infeasible for rehabilitation services. Too often the counselor gives a scant justification for closing his client in this status. Federal and state regulations require an in-depth and extensive justification prior to closure. Unfortunately, many counselors take advantage of this closure category to remove what is called "deadwood" from their pending files rather than working on a constructive plan for the individual's rehabilitation. A few counselors use this status as a scapegoat for their own inadequacies. For example, if he starts working with someone and feels the client has no potential, usually this reflects the counselor's own biased attitudes and opinions, if he is unable to contact this client, the counselor will close the client as 08 with a justification of "uncooperative and unable to locate." The purpose of this exercise is to allow one to examine this status in depth rather than giving it only cursory attention.

ASSIGNMENT

Describe in depth the 08 status. Examine five 08 cases chosen at random and describe why they were closed in this status. Justify these 08 closures in relation to agency policy. Discuss how you or someone else might have used professional skills to successfully rehabilitate these clients. Clues to look for relative to 08 closures which should be included in this report would be the following:

---

* This exercise was adapted from a special study committee formulated by the North Carolina Division of Vocational Rehabilitation.

1. Applicant's age.

2. Applicant's refusal of services; if so, why?

3. Did applicant respond to counselor's communications and appear for appointments? What were the methods used to communicate (letter, telephone call, personal visit by counselor)?

4. Was applicant unable to be located, or had he moved? How many times did counselor attempt to contact person? Method used (letter, telephone, visit, other).

5. Did he have insufficient financial need? Explain briefly the circumstances and why counselor made this decision.

6. Was there no disabling condition present? How was this determined?

    A. Available medical diagnosis.

    B. Available psychological diagnosis.

    C. Available psychiatric information.

    D. Counselor's interview with applicant; briefly describe this situation.

7. Was there no vocational handicap? How was this determined?

    A. Available medical diagnosis.

    B. Available psychological diagnosis.

    C. Available psychiatric diagnosis.

    D. Counselor's interview with applicant; briefly describe this situation.

8. Was rehabilitation not feasible due to a too severe handicapping condition? Describe the condition and tell why counselor made this decision.

9. Was applicant denied services because the counselor felt the probable services would be too expensive? If so, describe the situation.

10. Did applicant have multiple disabilities or a terminal illness? Describe condition and relate why counselor made this decision.

11. Are there services or programs available for this client in your state or surrounding states? Describe briefly such programs and decide how they might benefit your client (s).

12. Describe the last contact with the client.

STUDENT WORK: SAMPLE 1

Status 08, "Closed After Evaluation," is the first of three stages in the rehabilitation process where citizens may be denied further agency services. As such, it is the primary screening device used by rehabilitation counselors and serves as a tool in shaping the character of the caseload.

Under the terms of Public Law 333 rehabilitation services are not to be provided if the referral or applicant does not exhibit a physical or emotional handicap which places significant limitations upon the individual's functional activities, a handicap to employment based upon the existence of the disability, and a reasonable expectation that agency services will render the disabled individual fit to engage in gainful employment as defined by rehabilitation agencies to include placement in the competitive labor market, professional practice, self-employment, farm labor, housekeeping, family work where payment is in kind, sheltered employment, and home industry.

While it is true that the person closed from status 08 never became a "client," it cannot be said that he did not receive substantial services. Medical diagnostic services include several of the following: medical and surgical examinations, psychiatric evaluation services, dental examinations, consultations with and examinations by specialists in all medical specialty fields, in-patient hospitalization for study or exploration, clinical laboratory tests, diagnostic x-ray procedures, trial treatment, and other medically recognized diagnostic services. Psychological services determine the extent and nature of intellectual functioning, interests, aptitudes, and personality.

It is obvious that the disabled person must be physically fit to undertake the necessary training required for employment and to function in the position in which he is placed for some time. Acute illnesses will render applicants ineligible, at least until their condition stabilizes. There are also people who, because of general debility, malnutrition, and constitutional inadequacies, do not possess the potential to make effective use of rehabilitation services.

In determining eligibility, the counselor must recognize that the disabled person will have to possess the mental capacities to learn or to perform those functions required on the job. In addition, the handicapped individual must be emotionally equipped to manage personal affairs and social relationships without excessive supervision.

If, following the completion of a standard diagnostic work-up, the counselor cannot determine eligibility and requires more information, the applicant may be placed in six or eighteen-month evaluation. To be placed in eighteen-month extended evaluation, status 06, the handicapped individual must have one of the following disabling conditions: mental retardation, deafness, blindness, a spinal cord injury or disease, heart disease, cancer, stroke, epilepsy, mental illness, cerebral palsy, brain damage, arthritis, muscular dystrophy, cystic fibrosis, or renal failure. An extended evaluation period, status, 04, not exceeding six months, may be provided for all disabling conditions not covered in status 06. Often the multiple handicapped will be placed in this status.

While in either of the extended evaluation statuses, a multitude of services may be provided, including physical restoration services which include medical and surgical treatment, psychiatric services, dental care, hospitalization and clinic treatment, nursing service, convalescent or rest home care, drugs and supplies, orthotic and prosthetic devices, physical therapy, occupational therapy, speech and hearing therapy, psychological services, and visual services. Trial training and trial placement also are used.

If at any time during the periods provided the counselor feels that the client does not possess the qualities which would fulfill the "reasonable expectation" criterion, the client may be closed in status 08. At that time, the counselor should prepare a summary of the medical, vocational, social, psychological, or other case data which served as the basis for his decision to deny further services. At the same time he should submit an analysis showing why the evaluation material led to the decision to close the case at that stage in the process.

Status 08 can be considered one of the important administrative tools used by the vocational rehabilitation counselor. Effective use of this screening device will assure not only quality service to the handicapped, but realistic services to the general taxpayer who supports this program.

Arnold F

Arnold F was referred to the division of vocational rehabilitation through the pupil guidance office of a large suburban comprehensive high school as a physically handicapped student who wanted to enter into the retail sales and management field. The applicant was rejected by the United States Army for induction because of a missing left pectoralis major muscle.

The general medical examination of the family physician confirmed the reported physical anomaly and recommended an orthopedic evaluation. The specialist's report found the anterior chest wall contour on the left side to be flat when compared to the right, and the anterior wall of the axilla to be markedly deficient when compared to the right anterior wall. The pectoralis minor muscle was well developed and active. The shoulder joint showed a full range of motion.

The radiological report found the shoulder to be essentially normal in structure. The orthopedist described the condition as not disabling for normal activity, including such activities as heavy lifting. Consequently, no treatment was indicated.

Under normal circumstances this physical anomaly would be hidden under the clothing of the applicant. Therefore, the counselor believed that there was no cosmetic handicap relative to his possible functioning in the retail sales field.

In view of the orthopedic evaluation, the radiologist's report, a normal general medical evaluation except for the reported anomaly, the applicant's apparent adequate adjustment to the condition, and the applicant's expressed vocational interest, the counselor did not believe that the missing muscle constituted a vocational handicap, and the case was consequently closed in status 08.

At our last meeting the counselor summarized his findings and explained the reason for the denial of services to the applicant, while reminding him of his right to appeal the counselor's decision. The counselor then administered the Strong Vocational

Interest Blank, giving the applicant a completed summary sheet to be used in his private vocational planning.

Finally, the counselor reviewed with the client what the counselor felt to be his advantages in the competition of the job market as a high school graduate rejected for induction into the armed services for a condition that in no way affected his functional activity. The counselor provided the client with the names of business schools where he could further his education, and the name, address, and telephone number of the state employment service counselor in a nearby branch office.

William P

William P was also referred to vocational rehabilitation through the school system. The guidance office of a comprehensive high school, while preparing a survey of handicapped seniors, noticed that he had received speech therapy in the elementary grades and that his teachers mentioned a stuttering problem which they felt made him reluctant to take part in class discussions.

A review of his school records revealed a senior student with honor grades for six consecutive years. He wanted to continue his education by enrolling in the state university to study chemistry, with the goal of becoming a research biochemist.

The general medical examination was normal with the exception of what the physician described as a "mild speech impediment." In order to obtain a professional evaluation of this obvious speech problem, the applicant was referred to the speech and hearing diagnostic clinic of the county health department.

The stuttering problem was noted by the consultant to be of a mild to moderate degree containing sound repetitions and some word repetitions. However, this did not seem to detract from the applicant's ability to express himself. The consultant found him to be "in general, quite articulate." The client reported significant improvement in the past three years without the aid of speech therapy.

The recommendation from the speech and hearing diagnostic clinic was to the effect that no further speech therapy was appropriate and that the stuttering problem would not interfere significantly with his academic objectives or vocational plan. The counselor agreed.

In the final meeting, the counselor again reported the conclusion of the speech and hearing consultant. The applicant agreed that it was a fair evaluation and a just decision but was concerned about funding for his college program. The guidance department at the high school had assured him that he would be eligible for vocational rehabilitation services because another stutterer had been accepted. The counselor explained that the guidance office was in error in promising the services of another agency, but this did nothing to relieve William's disappointment.

The counselor provided the applicant with the necessary information and forms to apply for the college entrance examinations, National Defense Education Association student loans, and various state scholarships. He also recommended that William see his guidance counselor to map out alternative strategies to obtain scholarships and other financial support for his continuing educational plans.

The counselor scheduled a special visit to the high school to remind the guidance counselor of the individualistic approach taken by the rehabilitation agency in dealing with handicaps and to ask him not to obligate this agency or foster false hopes by assuming the role of the rehabilitation counselor.

Larry K

This 18-year-old boy was referred to vocational rehabilitation through the special education department of the public school system. Larry recently received his special education high school diploma after two years of home teaching.

Three years ago he was hit by an automobile, suffering extensive brain damage. The general medical examination noted a paralysis of the left hand, a tremor in the right hand, and a paralysis of the left leg, causing him to walk with a limp. His speech is slurred and child-like in quality.

An ophthalmological examination found visual acuity with best correction to be 10/200 in the right eye and 20/200 in the left eye. The ophthalmologist expected the condition to remain stable and noted subnormal accommodation as another result of the accident.

It was obvious that the client could best be considered a candidate for sheltered employment. Upon visiting the home and seeing how completely dependent he was upon his mother, the counselor requested a teacher of the blind to meet Larry and his mother to determine if he was capable of learning more self-care activities. In order to provide this service, the applicant was placed in status 06, eighteen-month extended evaluation. The teacher made nine visits. As a result of her efforts, Larry was able to wash himself, brush his teeth, shave with an electric shaver, and dress with the exception of tying his shoelaces. She was unsuccessful in trying to teach him to walk along the roadside or to make use of public transportation in mobility training.

The counselor then obtained a full psychological evaluation through a corporation specializing in psychological services for the visually handicapped. The report concluded that if it were not for the physical handicaps, he could perform in a situation where the job was broken down into simple concrete tasks requiring no judgment. He was unable to perform any of the performance tasks which required coordination of both hands. Even when administered tests requiring the use of his better hand, he encountered great difficulty.

From the medical and psychological evaluations, the counselor concluded that Larry might be able to function in a limited way in a sheltered facility. However, at the time of evaluation Larry did not grasp the concepts of success and failure. The counselor feared that in the sheltered workshop he might come to realize how handicapped he was and as a result become unnecessarily depressed.

The only sheltered workshop available to Larry was more of a day care center operated by special interest groups for their own children rather than a legitimate workshop as defined by vocational rehabilitation. It was not productive or vocationally directed and, as such, unacceptable to our agency.

In view of all of the above, the counselor closed this case in status 08 with a notation that the disability was too severe. In our final meeting with Larry's mother, this counselor explained the findings and explained that she might in the future consider the sheltered workshop if changes were made in its operation. This is doubtful since she is an extremely overprotective person. The counselor also explained that Larry could be considered as a dependent child and become a permanent income tax deduction. The counselor additionally provided the mother with information concerning travel concessions, property tax exemptions, and other special considerations given by the state and federal government to the legally blind citizen.

Alice T

Alice T is a student in a joint vocational rehabilitation public school program for the educable mentally retarded. Alice was 20 years old and would soon be forced legally to leave the special school which she had attended for ten years. As a student in this cooperative program, Alice worked on a part-time basis in a beauty shop and a hardware store. She especially enjoyed the hardware store because she had little to do and could spend most of her time sitting on the front step watching the cars go by.

Alice's teacher removed her from the position at the hardware store thinking that she had the ability to do more. Indeed, a Wechsler Intelligence Scale for Children, administered by the rehabilitation counselor yielded a performance 1Q of 87. As a result of this testing, the teacher decided that Alice could function as a salesgirl in a local department store. Her trial placement was terminated after three days. She said she did not like the people at the store and refused to return. The counselor then arranged a tour for the family at a work evaluation center. During the tour Alice said nothing. When asked later what she thought of the facility she answered that it reminded her of a factory and that there were obscene pictures on the walls. This was a complete fabrication. The counselor asked Alice and her family to reconsider entrance into the evaluation unit in view of her impending graduation.

When the counselor telephoned three days later, the mother hung up. On four succeeding occasions she again hung up after the counselor identified himself. Because of these actions a conference of school administrators, parents, and the counselor was held. The parents felt that the counselor was "picking on our daughter." They did not see why Alice could not continue in the school or at the hardware store. It was explained that the placement in the hardware store was only for work adjustment and that no wages were involved and that she could not continue in school after her twenty-first birthday. The parents refused to believe this and demanded that Alice be permanently placed in the position she liked so well. The school, the store owner, and the counselor all agreed that this could not be done.

The counselor closed the case in status 08 due to "lack of cooperation." To accede to the desires of the family would be to deny to many other children in the special school the benefits of adjustment training derived from short term placement in the hardware store.

In that no compromise could be reached between the parents and the counselor, the rehabilitation process could not begin. The student was returned to the school to graduate with her class. The parents were reminded of their right to reapply at a future date for vocational rehabilitation services. The counselor fully believed that they would do so soon after Alice graduated. Intense family counseling might have been used to convince the family that the counselor and the school were not picking on Alice; however, due to the intensely emotional nature of the parents' response, this was impossible.

Calvin S

Calvin is a 52-year-old self-referral to the vocational rehabilitation agency. He was last employed ten years ago by the federal government as a chemist earning over $10,000 per year. He is now supported solely by a civil service disability grant of $4,000 per annum. Fortunately for Calvin S and his wife, their children are grown and self-supporting. The grant is adequate to maintain them in modest circumstances.

The medical history dates back seventeen years to the onset of tremor which was subsequently followed by rigidity and akinesia. He displays the classical stigma of Parkinson's disease including tremor, increased salivation, rigidity, and retropulsive gate. In addition, childhood polio left him with an atrophied left leg. The cumulative effect of these disabilities left him immobile. However, he is mentally alert and interested in improving his situation.

The applicant was placed in status 06, eighteen-month extended evaluation, to afford the counselor an opportunity through appropriate medical facilities, to provide trial medication using the experimental drug L-Dopa. The applicant was referred to the neurological department of a medical school which would follow him in the course of the chemotherapy. The medical school indicated to the counselor that dramatic improvement was possible. Because of the limited financial resources of the applicant, the rehabilitation agency sponsored the entire cost of the treatment. At the end of one year of trial treatment the medical school reported limited improvement, although Calvin S was quite pleased with the results. The counselor believed that the applicant's only possibility for employment would be in a sheltered situation which he would not accept. His only desire was to continue using L-Dopa. Treatment with this drug could continue indefinitely. In view of the prohibitive costs of this experiment, the counselor could not justify the expenditures involved for continued agency sponsorship.

Before closing the case in status 08—because the disease was too disabling and potentially progressive—the counselor brought a social service worker to Calvin's home to explain the special buy in provisions of the Medicaid program that would allow the department of social services to use Medicare funds to provide continuing chemotherapy. At first he was reluctant to apply for his medical assistance card feeling that it was charity. However, because there was no monthly check involved or exchange of money he was able to justify his own participation in the program.

The counselor also provided the applicant and his wife with information relating to special tax concessions allowed to disabled property owners. Before concluding our last meeting, the counselor assured both husband and wife that if the continued treatment proved successful, he would be reconsidered at a later date for other agency services.

Exercise 16

COUNSELING APPROACHES AND TECHNIQUES UTILIZED BY THE VOCATIONAL REHABILITATION PROFESSIONAL

RATIONALE

One of the inherent responsibilities of a rehabilitation counselor is to provide the people in the community with services not ordinarily provided by other professional people or agencies. A fundamental and basic service is the provision of counseling and guidance. Yet, this is sometimes overlooked and is one reason why the rehabilitation counselor often is viewed as only a "coordinator" by other disciplines. The purpose of this exercise is to provide one with an opportunity to investigate in depth a counseling approach utilized while working with clients.

ASSIGNMENT

Choose a representative case from your caseload, preferably one with which you recently have initiated services, and describe how the client was counseled. Describe the counseling approach(es) you used and your rationale in view of the client's disability, emotional status, and level of intellectual functioning. Why was this approach employed rather than one of the other methods usually discussed in an academic program, in one of your in-service training programs or in your professional reading? Discuss the client's reaction to such counseling in relation to his immediate plans and to his long-range goals. How will you utilize this evaluation of your approach in helping your client with future problems and planning?

STUDENT WORK: SAMPLE 1

Counseling Within the Vocational Rehabilitation Process

Roy is an 18-year-old with no apparent physical complications

163

but has a WAIS verbal IQ of 74 and performance IQ of 76. He received a high school completion certificate based on special classes and limited shop work. His widowed mother has provided little supervision and admittedly is not able to meet even his basic needs for food, clothing, and shelter. He lives in a foster home with interested and responsible foster parents. As a result of comprehensive vocational evaluation, he was enrolled in the hospital orderly course offered by the community hospital and the Biscoe Vocational-Technical School. An energetic and affable person, he is socially immature and often is socially and vocationally irresponsible. His physical and mental abilities seem adequate for his present training but definite progress in self-discipline and responsibility must be evident if he is to utilize his training upon completion of the course. Roy's pleasant personality and energetic approach to assignments for which he is positively motivated have to some extent offset his deficiencies in the training.

Roy's DPW caseworker, a recent college graduate, carries an extemely heavy caseload and has limited contact with the client.

The client's need for guidance and his positive response to supervision and direction have suggested to me the need for directive counseling from his instructor, caseworker, and me. A case conference attended by the three of us resulted in the establishment of certain levels of behavior and responsibility that all will expect from him, with the imposition of restrictions on the use of his leisure time when he behaves irresponsibly socially or in training. Reinforcement of responsible behavior is made very obvious to him. This client does not seem to be able to benefit from long-range planning, and only immediate, obvious forms of reward seem meaningful to him. Although Roy has far to go before he may be a responsible employee, we are pleased with his present rate of progress.

The caseworker and I have both encouraged the foster parents to be straightforward with Roy, letting him know specifically what they expect of him and vice versa. The foster parents have been encouraged in giving Roy responsibility for helping on their small farm and attending to regular outdoor chores. This seems to help him feel more a part of things, is an outlet for excess energy, and is an opportunity for him to earn a little spending money. It is imperative that Roy learn to stick with a schedule. The foster parents often have to remind him of what he is expected to do at certain times.

I anticipate giving him more responsibility as the advantages of responsible behavior become more obvious to him. I believe that he may realize that there is more to making a living than just being agreeable and being good company. We have talked about what effect his completion of assignments at the hospital has on the health and happiness of individual patients. This is a real thing to him and hopefully, with close supervision by his instructor and hospital staff, he can learn to get his assignments done and still be appropriately kind to patients. Often Roy has to be told very definitely that his inclination to talk and play with fellow students interferes with the quality and quantity of his work.

This young client has made some progress which I believe has been due partly to his knowing where he stands with all who are working with him. This seems to be helping him establish a framework of what is acceptable behavior and vocational performance as contrasted with his extreme immaturity of a few months ago. There is still an obvious need for structure and direction.

Without generalizing to an unrealistic extent, I feel that a person such as Roy with limited abstract abilities and an insecure, unsettled childhood often will benefit from the establishment of a definite understanding of what is expected of him. The satisfactions of more acceptable behavior will, hopefully, gradually replace the direction that to me seems necessary and beneficial for an individual of little self-direction and maturity.

STUDENT WORK: SAMPLE 2

The Role of Counseling in Vocational Rehabilitation

Since counseling is the backbone of rehabilitation services, would the geographical area in which the counselor works and the educational background of the individual client determine the method of counseling to be used?

The types and techniques of counseling are many and varied, but the outcome is always hopefully similar—to enable the client to see a situation that will help him better adjust to his environment.

Many counselors have a particular counseling method which they will argue is the best approach. I personally feel that the situation, location, and the counselor himself should determine the approach used by the counselor.

Of the four main types of counseling, nondirective, client-centered or Rogerian counseling is probably the most widely used. Named for its originator, Carl Rogers, this method is used when the counselor feels that he can take a passive role. He allows the client to do most of the talking and take sole responsibility for any decisions reached. Testing and other information giving procedures are kept at a minimum. This method is used widely on the college level and may be used by the rehabilitation counselor if he thinks his client has the intelligence and perception to make his own decisions.

The directive or counselor-centered technique is utilized when the counselor feels that he must take an active part in a counseling session. He will guide the counselee toward choices that he considers best for the future well-being of the client. He strongly suggests possible answers for pertinent questions and freely gives advice. Tests and other sociometric devices are commonly used to gain information about the client's attitudes, interests, and abilities. This technique may be used at the counselor's discretion if information reveals that the client is not capable of making the best decisions for his own well-being.

The eclectic type is a median point between the two above-mentioned methods. Followers of this form of counseling utilize the best approaches from both and adapt it to the particular situation. I believe that an effective rehabilitation counselor would find this approach more fitted to his needs since he draws his clientele from many backgrounds, even though he may only cover a small area. This fact is certainly true in my particular caseload area.

Another approach that is not as widely used but would certainly deserve attention before any conclusions are drawn is the behavioral technique. To use this method, the counselor would have to have a working knowledge of psychology and the learning theories. Punishment and reward are used discriminatingly to accomplish a desired result. In counseling a client, the counselor will make use of certain effective stimuli which will in turn initiate the desired response. This operant technique "conditions" the client to respond in the proper manner. Stimuli used may be as subtle as a smile, an attentive stare, an encouraging gesture or a simple spoken word such as good, excellent, or yes. The counselor can also extinguish undesired responses by some form of punishment. Punishment may also be subtle, such as turning away and ignoring the client, nodding in disagreement or complete indifference to a statement.

This could perhaps be the most effective method of counseling although it does have its disadvantages in reference to rehabilitation. First of all, it is time consuming. The counselor may have to meet with the client several times before he can gain complete effectiveness. Secondly, this form of directive counseling demands prolonged exposure to encouraging stimuli or "extinction" may occur. This simply means that unless continued encouragement is given, the desired response of the client may vanish and all preceding work was done in vain.

No matter what approach the rehabilitation counselor seeks to use, I feel that the personal intelligence and sociological background of the client play the most important role in success. Motivational factors must certainly be taken into consideration. Although some motivation may be instilled by the counselor, there must be some present to begin with or success is questionable.

I feel that in the geographic area of Harlan, Bell, and Leslie counties in Kentucky where motivation and education is almost always at a low level, for a counselor to achieve the desired results he must take the eclectic route, drawing the best techniques from all methods. In one interview he may be on one end of the eclectic continuum bordering on directiveness, while in another interview, he may lean toward nondirectiveness if the situation warrants this approach. Other methods will be brought in as needed, such as testing and other sociometric materials to develop an overall understanding of the client's need, but I believe the word that would sum up the rehabilitation counselor's approach should be *flexibility*.

Exercise 17

CORRECTIONAL REHABILITATION AND THE CLASSIFICATION PROCESS

RATIONALE

Vocational rehabilitation's involvement in corrections has increased substantially in recent years. To insure the continuation of this cooperative relationship it is imperative that the counselor understands the various ramifications of correctional policy. Classification procedures have been and will continue to be permanent fixtures in the correctional setting. With the advent of vocational rehabilitation there has been a necessity for various state departments of correction to modify and in some cases completely revise their classification procedures in an effort to involve the services of this traditionally community action program. Correctional personnel recognize the significance of accepting rehabilitation personnel as team members.

ASSIGNMENT

As a counselor assigned to a correctional unit, describe in detail the classification procedure used by this institution. Analyze it in such a way that you can make constructive suggestions especially in relation to the inclusion of vocational rehabilitation representation on the classification committee. It is important to discuss this exercise in terms of a realistic approach to inmate rehabilitation rather than a theoretical and/or clinical approach.

STUDENT WORK: SAMPLE 1

The classification process in penal institutions is *in theory* an attempt to diagnose, categorize, and on the basis of these efforts to formulate a program geared to the rehabilitative potential of the individual inmate. I emphasize the phrase *in theory* since the above broad description of the classification connotes a treatment-

169

centered approach. In actuality classification historically has **been** and still is custody centered; i.e. the focus is more on punishment than rehabilitation.

In my work setting the classification process has three basic functions: diagnosis-orientation, treatment, and custody. The diagnostic phase of classification begins when the inmate arrives at the reformatory and is sent to a reception and orientation unit, commonly referred to as "the fish tank." Here the individual undergoes a physical, psychological, and educational evaluation. He is examined by a physician and dentist, given a blood and urine test, chest x-ray, etc.

The inmate also is interviewed briefly by the reception unit psychologist in an effort to detect any obvious emotional disturbances. I personally question the validity of any information derived from this interview since most inmates experience a culture shock when they first enter the institution. The initial emotional impact of incarceration in many cases definitely precludes a realistic assessment of the inmate's usual (for him "normal") psychological state.

The new inmate is additionally given a battery of aptitude and achievement tests. The results of these tests are used later as a factor to determine what responsibilities the inmate will have within the institution. However, I also have qualms regarding the validity of these test results. During the three weeks spent in the "fish tank," the inmate is literally "not himself." Often an inmate, after he has grown accustomed to the institution, will score significantly higher on these tests than he did during the diagnosis-orientation period.

During this three-week period various professional personnel —from custody and treatment—talk to the new inmates. In a group setting some representative of each department describes the purposes of that department, be it custody, psychological services, or chaplaincy, and relates how the inmate may utilize the resources available.

It is in these introductory speeches that the inmate first learns of the vocational rehabilitation program. Both the supervisor of rehabilitation and the principal of our vocational school delineate the purposes, services available, and application procedures regarding vocational rehabilitation. I have observed these introductions to rehabilitation, and they seem very adequate; but later as I talk with inmates, they report no recollection or at best a vague idea of what vocational rehabilitation is all about. Apparently the inmate is bombarded with so much both emotionally and informationally that vocational rehabilitation often is lost in the concomitant confusion.

Also, during the diagnosis-orientation period the inmates are informed of various reformatory organizations such as the Jaycees and SPADE. Usually the inmate presidents of the various clubs give the presentation.

The last phase in the initial diagnostic process is an interview with the inmate's social worker. During this encounter—usually too brief because of the sheer pressure of numbers—information of a rather objective nature is gleaned (family data, social history, interests, and what role the inmate would like to fulfill within the institution).

Considering the pressure of increasing admission rates, the diagnosis-orientation phase of classification cannot be criticized too sharply. However, on the basis of my conversations with inmates, particularly my clients, this three-week period is a very unpleasant experience. As one of my clients (now out on parole and employed) recently put it, "It's a real bummer. You get up and they say, 'Today you're going to have a chest x-ray.' Big deal. So you sit around with a bunch of people you don't know and wait for the damn x-ray. You're always waiting for something. After a few days it gets next to you. It's the longest three weeks I ever spent in my life."

After the diagnosis-orientation phase, the inmate is ready to go before the classification board. Where I work, the associate warden of the treatment staff is the head of the classification board. Theoretically, the data gleaned during the diagnostic period comprises the basis of the inmate's crucial encounter with this committee.

I use the phrase "crucial encounter" because virtually every phase of the inmate's life within the institution will be determined by the classification board. The board is comprised of representatives from treatment, custody, and social services. The number on the board rarely exceeds five. With the exception of the associate warden of the treatment staff, the individuals comprising the board vary.

As was cited earlier, the classification process is, *in theory,* treatment centered. Treatment covers those areas of reformatory life not directly related to security or custody. The avowed goal of the treatment program is the rehabilitation of the inmate. The whole point of the diagnosis-orientation phase in the classification process is to guide the classification board in formulating a realistic treatment program for the inmate, which hopefully will best facilitate his rehabilitation.

As opposed to treatment, custody involves keeping the inmate under surveillance, i.e. physically confined. The stark fact is that although the major avowed purpose of the classification process is treatment, historically and in my work setting, custodial categories determine treatment. Each inmate is given a custody category, and this category determines whatever else the inmate might do. In my institution there are four custody or security designations:

1. Medium I—The inmate may work any place within the institution, i.e. the buildings and fences.

2. Medium II—The inmate may go outside the fence if escorted by a guard.

3. Minimum—The inmate may go outside the fence without an escort.

4. Minimum OKO—The equivalent of what used to be called the "trustee."

Most men go into Medium I and probably remain there for the duration of their incarceration. The lower security levels have to be earned through a good work record and a history of cooperation with the institution.

After a man's custody status is determined (usually Medium I), the classification board determines the treatment program. Basically, the factors considered here are the man's work and dormitory assignment. The inmate is consulted regarding what he wants to do. The man's request may vary from attending school all day to serving as a dormitory janitor. The board examines the man's request by four major criteria: custody assignment, the inmate's own request, the results of his diagnostic period, and the needs of the institution. Foremost is the man's custody assignment. For example, a man classified Medium I could not work on a farm detail.

Since the custody limitation is paramount, every man's job request obviously cannot be met. However, from my contacts with personnel and inmates, the classification board does make a genuine effort to accommodate a man's request. Although factors such as the needs of the institution override the inmate's job request, he is at least given the opportunity to make his request.

A vital part of an inmate's treatment program is his dormitory assignment. The classification committee does make an attempt to maintain some homogeneity within the dormitories. Factors such as age, work assignment, and physical and mental limitations determine the man's dormitory assignment. Many inmates I have spoken with feel that this is the most important factor in a man's social adjustment and rehabilitation. A man must feel as much "at home" as possible, which means his environment must be as compatible as possible to his temperament and serve as an asset, not a deterrent, to his rehabilitation.

It is rather ironic that a classification board whose avowed purpose is rehabilitation does not have a rehabilitation professional in its membership. This fact is ironic but not surprising. Notwithstanding noble paper guidelines, most penal settings (my own included) still act on the premise of retributive justice and not rehabilitation. Thus in a custody-oriented setting, it is not too surprising that rehabilitation is not represented on the classification board. Thus before the rehabilitation staff can be represented on the classification board, much less have a powerful voice, the reformatory must alter at least slightly from what I view as an inordinate preoccupation with custody (i.e. determining where a man's body can and cannot go) to a recognition that rehabilitation is the major task of the reformatory.

Regarding a more active entry into the activities of the classification board, the department of rehabilitation cannot be the bull at the tea party. Merely pushing for recognition, especially in my work setting, inevitably would result only in intensifying the distrust many correctional workers have toward rehabilitation workers. Vocational rehabilitation is a new arrival on the corrections scene. Since our focus on the inmate is that of one to be helped instead of one to be punished, the vocational rehabilitation worker represents a threat to the old order.

If vocational rehabilitation becomes a more powerful force in the classification process, its workers must be willing to endure the onus of any agent of change: active patience. The rehabilitation worker must go out of his way to work closer with the correctional staff and eventually break down the barriers which separate his agency from certain reformatory personnel. Only as the rehabilitation department gets more and more into the main stream of institutional life and policy can it hope to be more than a peripheral influence in the crucial classification process.

In my work setting the place to concentrate vocational rehabilitation effort in terms of classification is at the diagnostic phase. We need to utilize data gained there and perhaps even have a rehabilitation worker assigned part time to the diagnosis-orientation center. We would, by working closer with the department, be in a position to locate the prospective vocational rehabilitation client early in his institutional stay. We could then work with both the inmate and his caseworker and if the individual's situation warranted it, work toward classification to a vocational school. The extent to which vocational rehabilitation can establish a precedent for rehabilitating inmates will determine the extent to which the agency can become involved in the classification process.

In summary, vocational rehabilitation will have to earn a voice on the classification board through active patience, a closer working relationship with the correctional staff, especially diagnostic professionals, and ultimately a demonstrated record of actively assisting the inmates with whom we work in their rehabilitation.

Exercise 18

BUSINESS SURVEYS AND LABOR
MARKET ANALYSIS

RATIONALE

There are many responsibilities which are considered of prime importance when discussing the vocational rehabilitation counselor's role. One of the most important would be his ability to provide placement and follow-up for his client. Since 1920, this has been one of the services provided by vocational rehabilitation; yet it is one of the services which is "losing its strength." Many counselors seem to rely solely on the other individuals to provide the placement services his client so desperately needs even though the ultimate responsibility for placement is the counselor's.

Not only should the counselor be concerned with specific jobs existing in various businesses in his territory, but he should also be aware of general labor market trends within a large geographic area. Additionally, this exercise should initiate fundamental concepts of public relations.

ASSIGNMENT

Part A. The counselor trainee is to make a report on one business survey per week as a part of his training in placement and public relations (a placement survey form in Appendix B has been provided for your convenience). Each person contacted during the business survey becomes a potential employer and is to be treated as such. Each survey should be made for the purpose of gaining occupational information about the company or business visited. It is not the intention of this exercise to make a specific job placement of a client.

These surveys have several purposes:

1. They enable the counselor to become acquainted with the employment opportunities in his territory.

175

2. They enable various businesses to become acquainted with vocational rehabilitation.

3. They provide the counselor an opportunity to increase self-confidence in the area of selling himself, his agency, and eventually his client.

See example of completed survey on page 177.

Part B. As a person working in vocational rehabilitation, it is very important that you continually be aware of the labor market in your area. Since the manpower needs of industries and corporations are indicative of the labor market trends in a locality, list such companies in the following format: name of company, address of company, name of employment office, telephone number, number of employees, and a brief statement of their service to the community (this would be areas of work the particular company might specialize in, such as packaging, assembling, and sorting). One of the requirements of this exercise is that you personally contact your local state employment officer and discuss this assignment with him. You should utilize his services in obtaining this information.

As you survey the labor market in your area, it is important to keep in mind the size of the geographic area you serve. For example, a counselor working in downtown Dallas, Texas, would need to investigate only the major industries within a one- or two-mile radius of his office; on the other hand, a counselor working in a small rural community, such as Harlan, Kentucky, might need to increase the radius to fifty miles from his office. In addition, you should concern yourself primarily with those jobs considered as blue collar since they comprise the majority of the labor market and, in turn, the clients on your caseload. There is no set number of labor market surveys to be completed; you and your training coordinator will determine this. Do not include in Part B any surveys previously done in Part A of this exercise. The following is a sample only; you may wish to devise your own format.

STUDENT WORK: SAMPLE 1, PART A
COUNSELOR TRAINEE BUSINESS AND INDUSTRY SURVEY

Establishment ACME VARIETY STORE City JACKSONVILLE, FLORIDA

Industry and Major Product(s) DEPARTMENT STORE Street 432 COMMERCE STREET

Employing Officer MR. JAMES SMITH Phone 337-1549 Date of Contact MARCH 18, 1971

Union Requirements: Yes No X Insurance Requirements: Yes No X Medical Requirements: Yes No X

VR Explained? Yes X No Employed in Plant 36 Number Disabled Employed 3

Is there a systematic training program? Yes X No Will they train? Yes X No

Is employment seasonal? Yes No X If so, peak Slack

Distance to transportation line? Blocks/miles 1 Block ramps? Yes No X Elevators? Yes X No

Parking facilities? Yes X No How far from office? BEHIND STORE How far from work area? 50 FEET

Architectural barriers? Yes Describe RESTROOM FACILITIES WILL NOT ACCOMMODATE WHEELCHAIRS

Type of reception received from business establishments: High receptive X receptive indifferent antagonistic

Job Titles (D.O.T.)	Number in Position	Percent Standing (%)	Age Requirements Min. Age	Age Requirements Max. Age	Physical Demands (D.O.T.)	Primary Function of Job (D.O.T.)	D.O.T. G.E.D.	S.V.P.
PRICE MARKER 209.588	1	50	18	—	S-4	Attaches price tickets to articles of merchandise.	2	2
INVENTORY CLERK 223.388	1	90	18	—	L-4,6	Receives and sorts incoming stock; compiles inventory reports.	3	4
PORTER II 381.887	1	100	18	—	M-3,4	Cleaning floors by sweeping, mopping, and waxing.	2	2
SALES CLERK 290-478	9	100	18	—	L-4,5	Provides assistance for customers in selecting merchandise.	3	3
CASHIER-CHECKER 299.468	3	60	18	—	M-4,5,6	Sells and totals customers' merchandise and bags it.	3	2
SECRETARY 201.368	2	10	18	—	S-4,5,6	Types and performs normal office routines.	4	6
DEPARTMENT HEADS 299.138	8	85	18	—	L-5	Supervises and coordinates other employees as well as a salesman.	4	7

Additional Comments: This company will hire the parolee, the controlled epileptic. Even though they strive for employees with a high school diploma, they will hire people without it.

STUDENT WORK: SAMPLE 1

Part B

I. *Name of Company*:   Kor's
    Address of Company: Rockville, Maryland
    Employment Officer: Mr. S
    Telephone Number: 881-8500

Comments: Kor's is a large retail chain store serving the Montgomery County area. It sells everything from cosmetics to household appliances at discount prices. It has about 300 employees, 1 percent of which is disabled. Mr. S has worked very closely with DVR in the past in hiring the handicapped. They will train people on the job for various positions in the store. There are no specific educational requirements for employees, and he would consider hiring a mentally retarded client providing he was educable. A wheelchair client would be a problem because there is a good deal of mobility involved in the jobs.

Their main areas of work would include sales personnel, cashiers, stock girls and boys, general office clerks, and janitorial help, as well as doormen. They would consider the handicapped for any of these positions.

II. *Name of Company*:   Government Employees Insurance Company
     Address of Company: Bethesda, Maryland
     Employment Officer: Mr. F
     Telephone Number: OL-8-1000

Comments: GEICO is one of the largest insurance companies in the metropolitan Washington area. It serves not only government employees, but a large sector of the population as well. They do require at least eight years of education, but no technical training. They will hire some mentally slow clients in the clerical fields, as well as wheelchair clients. Their main areas of work are as follows: mail clerks, receptionists, appointment clerks, file clerks, general office clerks, and of course the usual number of administrative, supervisory, and sales personnel involved in a large insurance company.

III.   *Name of Company*:   Tixon Electronics
      Address of Company: Silver Spring, Maryland
      Employment Officer: Mr. K
      Telephone Number: 622-2122

Comments: Tixon is a large electronics company which is involved in the manufacture of communication equipment for data transmission between computers. It has about 385 employees and a large number of handicapped employees. Although they employ a large number of professional engineers and electronic technicians, my inquiry dealt mostly with what sort of jobs would be available for the disabled. They would include electronics assembler, switchboard operator, and clerk-typist. These jobs require no specific educational background, although for the assembler, it would be wise to have some training. They will train on the job, however.

IV.   *Name of Company*:   A. L., Inc.
      Address of Company: Washington, D.C.
      Employment Officer: Mr. A
      Telephone Number: 859-8318

Comments: A. L., Inc. is a small architectural design company, which has only 15 employees. Mr. L has a genuine interest in the handicapped and has 5 disabled employees in his firm. Two of them are architects and three are draftsmen. Their disabilities include one amputee, one alcoholic, one emotional case, and two deaf clients. He also employs civil engineers and sales personnel to do public relations work. He is highly receptive to hiring the handicapped, and this is one of the few companies I have found which employs professional personnel who are handicapped, providing they meet the necessary educational requirements.

V.   *Name of Company*:   Suburban Auto Body
      Address of Company: Washington, D.C.

Employment Officer: Mr. L
Telephone Number: 624-2810

Comments: Suburban Auto Body is a well-known shop with a good reputation in the area. Mr. L has worked closely with DVR in the past in hiring the handicapped. Of his 10 employees, 3 of them are handicapped. One is deaf, one has emotional problems, and one has a language problem. The main jobs available are for auto body and fender repair. They do contract work for Sheehey Ford and Jack Amatucci Chevrolet as well as work on foreign cars. There is no educational requirement and he will provide them with on-the-job training in body and fender work.

VI.   *Name of Company*:   Marriott Corporation
       Address of Company: Washington, D.C. (main office)

       Employment Officer: Mr. Z
       Telephone Number   756-2700

Comments: Marriott is a nationwide corporation of hotels and resturants whose main office is in Washington, but there are hundreds of shops throughout the area. The number of employees depends on the size of the restaurant or hotel. They have been very receptive in hiring the handicapped, and Mr. Z serves on the Employer's Advisory Committee in Montgomery County. Except for the managerial and office personnel, many of their jobs are open to the handicapped. Some of these include kitchen clerks, waiters and waitresses, kitchen helpers, maids, and busboys. A severely physically handicapped person might be used as a cashier, and both emotional cases and mentally retarded would be considered for the other jobs.

VII.   *Name of Company*:   Speed Systems and Research Corporation
        Address of Company: Bethesda, Maryland
        Employment Officer: Mrs. M
        Telephone Number: 856-9500

Comments: Speed Systems does work involving the development of methods to speed and organize the storage, retrieval, manipulation, and display of technical and management information for the use of government and industry. They do basic research, consulting work, systems design, computer programming, engineering, and the operation information centers. They have about 700 employees and up until now have been reluctant to hire the handicapped. They recently employed two newly trained computer operators, one programmer, and several keypunch operators, who had been trained with assistance from vocational rehabilitation. They were very satisfied with them and are much more receptive to hiring a disabled person now. They will consider training clerical personnel for general office work as well.

VIII. *Name of Company*:   Montgomery County Department of Liquor Control

       Address of Company: Rockville, Maryland

       Employment Officer: Personnel Office, County Building

       Telephone Number: 279-1271

Comments: One of the positions open in the county is titled Warehouseman-Truck Driver's Helper. It would involve routine manual work assisting in the performance of warehouse and delivery duties. It involves loading and unloading delivery vehicles. Applicants must have completed the ninth grade, be at least 21 years of age, and have some experience in warehouse or similar work. They would consider a client with a slight emotional problem who has good physical endurance. Other positions available at various times in the county are as follows:

1. Watchman—involves making rounds inside and outside of buildings; watching for fires or prowlers; making phone reports to Police Department; and other related duties such as taking messages. The only prerequisite for the job is the ability to read and write.

2. Laboratory Helper—routine, nontechnical work. The applicant must have completed the eighth grade and be able to understand and carry out oral and written instructions.

3. Parking Meter Mechanic Helper—semiskilled work in the repair and maintenance of parking meters and related equipment. Qualifications include ninth grade education and some mechanical ability.

4. General Maintenance Man—unskilled maintenance repair work in the electrical plumbing and carpentry trades, with an eighth grade educational requirement.

IX. *Name of Company*:   Ferro Tech Inc.
Address of Company: Gaithersburg, Md.
Employment Officer: Mr. F
Telephone Number: 848-8800

Comments: Ferro Tech is a manufacturer of ferromagnetic materials for solid-state devices. It has research and development facilities to make non-catalog items. Makes dielectric materials for microwave use. There are about 40 employees, and they just recently hired their first handicapped employee, who received training through vocational rehabilitation at solid-state electronics school and was hired as an electronic technician. The company was pleased with the client, who was a cardiac case. Mr. F would consider hiring other handicapped persons who have specialized training and necessary skills. He would not offer on-the-job training.

X. *Name of Company*:   U.S. Civil Service Commission, Bureau of Recruiting & Examining
Address of Company: 1900 E St., N.W., Washington, D.C.
Telephone Number: 632-5687
Employment Officer: Mrs. Mary S. Douglas, Specialist for the Handicapped

Comments: Probably the largest single employer in the D.C. area. It serves as the agency coordinator for selective placement of the handicapped. The type of jobs vary from single custodial work to supervisory and administration duties.

Exercise 19

CORRECTIONAL REHABILITATION AND THE UTILIZATION OF INMATE INFORMATION

RATIONALE

A counselor is responsible for gathering pertinent information on all his clients. This sometimes becomes difficult in the correctional setting because inmates often give conflicting information to different people. One must sift through many irrelevant or inappropriate responses in order to reach a decision prior to providing rehabilitation services.

ASSIGNMENT

Discuss the following: To the extent that inmates of correctional institutions tend to give conflicting information to different professionals working with them and in fact often seek to manipulate institutional and vocational rehabilitation personnel to the inmate's own purposes, the rehabilitation counselor can take special steps and precautions to avoid being "used" by his public offender clients.

STUDENT WORK: SAMPLE 1

The matter of inmate information is a perennial maze of confusion to all the correctional staff and vocational rehabilitation personnel. In many cases, especially if the inmate has no known relatives or if they are inaccessible, the institution must depend upon the inmate for much personal information. Since there is no way to verify this information, it is obviously of questionable value.

On the other hand, occasional information the institution has gathered from sources other than the inmate is not exact. Usually the lists of arrests and convictions, are accurate. But the personal information is sometimes of questionable value. A case in point:

One vital factor in planning an inmate's rehabilitation pro-

184

gram is his family status. A client of mine reported that he had three children by his ex-wife. On the other hand, his institutional folder listed these three children plus four illegitimate children. I informed the inmate of this discrepancy. He seemed stunned and denied the existence of four illegitimate children. The source of the above information about the extra four children is unknown. Yet this information is a vital factor in the inmate's personal history and is recorded on every major report written regarding him, including the summary sent to the parole board.

Briefly, what the above observations mean is that it is often difficult for the vocational rehabilitation counselor and the correctional staff to determine whether the inmate is lying or not. Thus, the first major problem about inmate information is the absence of valid referential criteria for testing the truth of what the individual says. And this difficulty of discriminating truth from fiction is especially difficult in the area of strictly personal information.

It is a universally known fact that inmates do give conflicting information to various professional people within the institution. For example, an inmate might report horrendous family problems to a social worker, the rationale being, "I really need to get out so I can keep my family together." On the other hand, if a vocational rehabilitation counselor asks the same man if he has any domestic problems that might detract from his rehabilitation plan, the latter would be very likely to reply unequivocally, "No."

Thus, the inmate often determines his responses to correctional workers on the basis of the function of the particular professional with whom he is talking. The inmate sizes up the staff member's role, determines what would sound best to that particular set of ears, and acts accordingly. And as was mentioned earlier, the institution often has no guaranteed means of checking the validity of the inmate's responses.

The best test—next to the institutional folder, kaleidoscopic hodgepodge that it may be—of an inmate's truthfulness is his consistency in dealing with various professionals. This **means** interdepartmental collaboration; i.e. did he give the social worker one line and the rehabilitation counselor another?

Most inmates have a relatively vague idea of what comprises their institutional folder. Consequently, the man out to blatantly "use" the rehabilitation counselor with false information will easily be detected. Additionally, the counselor can check with the inmate's social worker to check the account given to him. If there is an inconsistency between an inmate's response, the institutional record, and/or the report he has given another staff member, the counselor should proceed with caution. If there are irreconcilable contradictions, the inmate should be informed; and the counselor should check out the discrepancy with the best (often meager) means at his disposal.

No one bats 1000, and truth *per se* is often a metaphysical dream in ascertaining accurate inmate information. But the counselor can, if he uses the methods discussed, avoid striking out (being "used" consistently).

Exercise 20

THE SOCIAL READJUSTMENT OF THE PUBLIC OFFENDER

RATIONALE

As a counselor working within a correctional unit, you have been charged with the responsibility of trying to develop a rehabilitation plan commensurate with the inmate's abilities, motivations, interests, and aptitudes. At the same time you must be acutely aware of the circumstances existing in the community in relation to your client's needs.

ASSIGNMENT

Discuss this situation as it exists in your work setting: Problems of social readjustment are probably greater causes of vocational rehabilitation failure in the cases of public offender clients than are lack of job skills. What steps can the counselor take to get some action to help resolve this situation?

STUDENT WORK: SAMPLE 1

The social readjustment of the public offender is a two-pronged problem. The correctional rehabilitation counselor must attempt simultaneously to deal with the dual nature of the problem.

Having been ejected from "normal" society, the inmate is thrust into a society whose structures differ radically from those of the outside world. Briefly stated, the inmate was removed from a larger "normal" society in which he failed to adjust properly and sent to a smaller "abnormal" (by conventional standards) society in which he *must* make some sort of social adjustment. This is a major problem for many inmates. This is the first prong of the problem.

In this correctional facility all vocational rehabilitation ac-

187

tivity—vocational training, counseling and guidance, and work adjustment—occurs within the institutional setting. Obviously, unless a client has made an adequate social adjustment to the institutional community, the counselor will be hard pressed to proceed with a rehabilitation program. In fact, the trauma of trying to adapt socially to prison life is often the major deterrent to an inmate's rehabilitation.

Recently one of my clients, a 22-year-old male enrolled in a vocational school, was severely beaten by several inmates in his dormitory. Apparently he had broken some inmate code and divulged certain esoteric information. He obviously was not functioning well in his social environment.

Fearing for his life (and justifiably so), the client requested to be placed in segregation which was a small single cubicle comprising one section of the maximum security unit of the reformatory. He remained there until he could be assigned to another dormitory. While in segregation for a week, he missed his vocational classes. I advised him to write his instructor and explain the situation. Frequently clients come in and complain that problems on the "yard" are distracting their minds from their vocational training. The case just cited was extreme, though not too uncommon.

Unless the client trusts his counselor to maintain confidentiality, it is exceedingly difficult for the counselor to help the inmate with his problem. However, if the client can openly discuss his social conflicts, the counselor is in a position to aid the man in defining his problems and determining feasible options for coping with them.

Most inmates' social adjustment problems go untreated. However, the blame cannot automatically be laid at the doorstep of the correctional staff. Chances are the correctional staff would take appropriate steps to help a man if they knew his problem. But in an institution housing over 1800 inmates an anonymity and concomitant depersonalization inevitably occurs. The inmate is distrustful of the correctional staff. Even if an inmate is willing to unburden his adjustment problems to a social worker or chaplain, the mere burden of numbers would preclude the in-depth counseling and planning needed to alleviate the difficulties.

However, vocational rehabilitation counselors in correctional settings carry considerably smaller caseloads than social workers. Thus the counselor has more time to spend with his clients. Also, it has been my experience that rehabilitation clients, once they realize that the department of rehabilitation is under the department of education and not corrections, are prone to talk more candidly to their counselor than to anyone else in the institution. This places the counselor in a unique position. Often he can detect and define problems which would otherwise go unnoticed. Once the counselor diagnoses the difficulty, he can recommend steps the inmate can take to cope with the situation. This could involve an interview with the chaplain or even the warden. The point is that if the client trusts his counselor and knows he is behind him, he often will seek out the help available within the institution.

Thus the first prong of the incarcerated client's social readjustment is the manner in which he copes with the pressures of institutional life. The second prong is perhaps even more baffling, namely the task of preparing the client to leave the circumscribed "abnormal" world of the institution and return to what I formally referred to as "normal" society. In other words, the client, if his rehabilitation program is to succeed, *must* make an adequate adjustment to institutional life. But he must not lose his vision of a place in society outside the institution.

If rehabilitation is to be effective, both social worlds simultaneously must be kept in mind. The counselor obviously has his work painfully outlined for him.

The problem places the counselor in a rather contradictory predicament. He must simultaneously aid the client in adjusting to the regimented existence of the institution and develop qualities of self-reliance and self-worth necessary to successful functioning in "normal" society. The irony is that the counselor is in the unenviable position of guiding a client through a rehabilitation program in a setting which repudiates, indeed, often does not tolerate, the virtues such as autonomy and personal actualization which the rehabilitated person is supposed to possess.

Inevitably incarceration results in depersonalization. But the counselor must work within this depersonalizing setting and lead the client toward self-actualization, i.e. developing his unique potentials to their maximal level and becoming a fulfilled person, not remaining a five-digit number.

If the client is to keep both social worlds in realistic perspective, guidance and counseling are imperative. The counselor must be acutely aware of the two social worlds and the adjustment problems inherent in both. One of my most difficult tasks as a counselor has been keeping clients' contacts with the outside world alive, i.e. the avoidance of total client institutionalization. This is a greater problem with older men.

I have found cultivating employment incentives to be the most effective means of keeping a client out of the psychic morass of that depersonalization which the totally institutionalized man embodies. From the first interview, we talk about "outside contacts." I avidly encourage letter writing, both as a means of finding employment leads and also of keeping a finger in the pie of reality. A case in point:

I have a client enrolled in a vocational class. He was visibly despondent and becoming more depressed all the time. When I asked him what was bothering him, he replied. "This goddamn place is eating my guts out." I reminded him that he would come up for parole in less than four months.

I asked him if he really wanted to get out. He replied that he did, but he didn't see much he could do. His next statement— indicative of his loss of contact with the "real" world—was, "Even if I make parole, who the hell's going to hire an ex-con?" I replied I didn't know, but he'd never find out wallowing in self-pity. I told him he was falling into a classic pattern: Sit on your hands until you either make parole or get a flop; then decide what to do.

I encouraged him to write letters to various meat-cutting establishments in the area. I practically dared him to land a job before he even went for parole. I told him he was wasting precious time and that if he'd get off his hands, I'd back him up if an employment opportunity did materialize. Somehow he got "turned on" to the idea and overnight became a fanatical letter writer. Recently I received a call from a local firm. The owner wanted to interview the client so I set up an appointment. He got the job.

Briefly the client contacted the outside world, received recognition beyond his belief, and is already well on his way to effecting a social readjustment to this outside world, this other dimension of existence. Of course he has to make parole; but his efforts in his own behalf and his positive outlook will make him a much more likely candidate for release than he was before he reestablished contact with society. This same method has worked with other clients, so I do not view the results of this specific case as purely fortuitous.

In summary, the vocational rehabilitation counselor in the correctional setting must include guidance in social readjustment as a vital part of his dealings with the client. And most important, while he must aid the client in making an adequate institutional social adjustment, he must also employ whatever means he can to keep the client's gaze directed toward a successful social reentry into that "real" and inevitable world beyond the steel barred doors of what often seems like institutional oblivion.

Exercise 21

PROBLEMS CONFRONTING THE SCHOOL UNIT VOCATIONAL REHABILITATION WORKER

RATIONALE

During the last several years, there has been an increased emphasis placed on the establishment of vocational rehabilitation units within the public school systems in the United States. The underlying premise supporting these school units is quite obvious: Vocational rehabilitation can provide the necessary services to insure successful job placement at an earlier age. Initiating services while the person is young rather than after he becomes entrenched in the habits of the non-worker is the goal of this organization. The initiation of services at this age often encourages the youngster to help himself rather than to rely solely on others. Through rehabilitation the counselor attempts to develop and support the client's feelings of self-worth.

ASSIGNMENT

Part A. Discuss the following situation: A school vocational rehabilitation worker has a caseload composed primarily of mentally handicapped people. Training opportunities within the school vocational rehabilitation unit for this group are overtaxed. In order to improve this situation, what could be done regarding (1) increasing the referral sources' knowledge of vocational rehabilitation; (2) the development of vocational training in schools; (3) the involvement of community resources?

Part B. In one of the several schools to which you are assigned the number of referrals is inadequate. Assume that within this school system nearly all referrals come from guidance counselors. Recommend an approach the vocational rehabilitation counselor could take to increase the number of referrals. What other steps could be taken to remedy this situation, assuming

192

the school guidance counselor is the only one "authorized" to make referrals to your agency?

STUDENT WORK: SAMPLE 1

Part A

With regard to increasing the referral sources knowledge of vocational rehabilitation, the school vocational rehabilitation worker can employ a variety of techniques. Since the referral source from which the rehabilitation worker operates is the guidance department and since the guidance department depends upon other sources for its referrals, the rehabilitation counselor can, at faculty meetings, discuss the various methods employed by vocational rehabilitation. In addition he can describe the types of individuals which vocational rehabilitation serves and the types of disabilities to which this organization addresses its efforts. Still another technique which can be employed would be to utilize the guidance department's readiness to serve its students, by showing them firsthand the types of activities in which vocational rehabilitation engages. This might include tours, discussion groups, and lectures organized by the school unit for the benefit of referral sources within the schools. Since vocational rehabilitation constituted within a school unit has as its primary aim to provide services to the students that the school itself cannot provide, it is up to the school unit to educate and inform those referral sources (i.e. the schools) about the various types of services that can be provided by vocational rehabilitation.

The development of vocational training in schools is a need which the school easily can recognize. Vocational rehabilitation often can assist the school in recognizing this need by showing to them the number of individuals desirous of learning a trade or a vocation and explaining that the facilities available for such training simply are not present. A variety of techniques can be used to establish such training and one of these techniques is a cooperative plan between both the state department of vocational rehabilitation and the school itself. In such a plan the school pays or contributes part of its services to the general unit, and likewise the state contributes part of its resources to the unit. The general outcome of such a plan is vocational training in a cooperative joint effort between the school and vocational rehabilitation. The end result would be of considerable benefit in additional training sources for the student. Since not all areas of training can be provided by the school unit of the department of vocational rehabilitation, general catagories of training can be instituted for boys and girls. Such high demand catagories could include such things as cosmetology, food service training, nurse's aide, practical nursing, shoe repair, service station mechanics, woodworking and furniture repair, and other related training areas. Since the training must be geared toward mentally handicapped people, the level of training cannot be too advanced and yet must be sufficiently well grounded in order to allow these individuals who undergo training to become employable.

The involvement of community resources enters the picture particularly where the school and the department of vocational rehabilitation cannot provide services. Where the school cannot call upon its knowledge to provide services to a student and where the department of vocational rehabilitation does not operate facilities for training individuals or for diagnosing problems, the involvement of community resources should be utilized. Through the cooperative agreement between the school and vocational rehabilitation, funds become available to tap the resources within the community and engage their services in such activities as diagnostic services, rehabilitation training, on-the-job training, medical and surgical repair, professional consultation, and the most final result, employment. Because the school does not always have time to establish and work on its relations with the community, the vocational rehabilitation agency can help to tie together the many loose ends which come to light when a person is trying to learn a trade and become employed. In summary, community resources are very often the final touch to a well-rounded vocational rehabilitation program. Because the school is not always prepared to call upon its community for help and because the department of vocational rehabilitation makes that its business, the cooperative agreement very often creates an excellent marriage of individuals needing services with the services that can be provided.

Part B

Assuming the number of referrals from a school system is inadequate and further assuming that all referrals come from the guidance department, several steps could be taken to remedy this situation. First, an in-depth process of education sometimes is necessary for guidance people. It is the function of the guidance counselor to call upon the various resources available to the school to aid the student. If the source of referral is not sufficiently familiar with the services of vocational rehabilitation it is the responsibility of either the school unit or the vocational rehabilitation counselor to educate and inform the guidance counselor within the school of his function as a rehabilitation counselor. Secondly, since the department of guidance often depends on teacher feedback for its information, it is of great assistance for the vocational rehabilitation counselor to speak to the faculty as a group during the faculty meeting, explaining his function in addition to the various services provided by the agency. Often teachers are amazed that such services actually are available within the school system, and upon learning this information they immediately call upon their funded knowledge and relate such knowledge to the guidance department for further referral. Still another technique is an in-depth conference with school administrators within the school itself. The principal, the assistant principals, the attendance workers, and even the secretaries are aware of problems that do not come to the attention of the guidance department. These administrative and staff personnel need information regarding the function of vocational rehabilitation and the types of service provided so that they can relay this on to students in their school.

Another technique is going to the student body itself during an assembly or student rally. Students themselves are uninformed as to the resources available to them in the schools. Speaking at an assembly recently, vocational rehabilitation counselors were amazed to find that most students have no knowledge of the training available to them within the school system let alone through the sponsorship of rehabilitation. At such an assembly it might be explained to them that various types of services are available to individuals who are experiencing difficulty or thinking of dropping out of school for one reason or another and that these individuals need only contact their guidance counselor for further information.

Another excellent resource for the guidance counselor to call upon is the PTA. Parents know their children far better than teachers, counselors, or ministers; but parents very often are equally as uninformed as to the resources available in the community and within the school situation as are these other people. The counselor needs to make the parent aware of the various functions of vocational rehabilitation and the services that can be provided to students. In addition, the parent needs to know how his child can take advantage of these services and through whom he must go in order to be referred.

A final aid in increasing referral sources is the community itself. The vocational counselor needs to speak with various commercial institutions in the community so that they may call upon the school through its guidance counselors as well as the rehabilitation counselors for individuals who might need training. Various other service groups such as the YMCA or the Red Cross should be informed about the school unit of vocational rehabilitation so that they too may get in contact with the guidance counselor in order to refer a specific individual. Churches, commercial institutions, and service agencies all need to be informed within the community as to the services provided by the vocational rehabilitation school unit. They need to understand the rationale through which referrals are made. The more advertising (public relations work) and explanation that can be provided, the greater the probability of increasing the number of referrals from various resources becomes.

Summary

The following are recommendations for improving the working relationships with the school staff and field program.

In attempting to develop or improve working relationships with school personnel, the vocational rehabilitation counselor should be first of all a professional. The term *professional* implies here that the counselor must keep abreast with the latest changes in philosophy and expansion of services within his agency. He then has the responsibility of educating his referral sources as to the services he can provide prospective clients. This type of education can take many forms, from the informal discussion after lunch in the teachers' lounge to a rather formal presentation at faculty meetings within schools. By developing a clear understanding of the services that you as a counselor can provide and the role you thus play within the educational system, the foundations for good working relationships have been laid.

By taking quick action on referrals from the school personnel and by reporting back to them the results of your action you have further strengthened your working relationships. In situations where a single counselor services several schools it is advisable that he maintain a schedule and make this schedule known to all school personnel so that they can depend upon his presence at a particular place and time to discuss referrals or problems with clients he is serving.

STUDENT WORK: SAMPLE 2

This educable mentally retarded white male was referred to the agency by a local junior high school in December of 1968. At the time of referral he was in the ninth grade and 15 years old. He lived with his family which consisted of seven other members. Neither the mother nor father completed high school and only one sister was finishing high school that year. The rest of the children were either younger and in grade school or older and also did not finish high school.

The client's previous work experience consisted of work as a carpentry assistant with a home building contractor and work with a fence-erecting company. His only listed vocational choice was carpentry. His only hospital admission was for a tonsillectomy in 1961. His general medical examination of September 1969 showed no abnormalities.

The counselor who accepted the referral processed it to the folder stage, and then another counselor had the psychological testing done but did no case progress recording before he left the agency.

The WAIS was administered in May of 1969 along with the

MFD, HTP, and the reading section of the WRAT. The client was sixteen years and five months old at that time and still in junior high. According to the observations of the psychologist, the client was eager and somewhat excited about the testing. The client said he wanted to be a carpenter or fence erector. The examiner asked him what three wishes he wanted and the client said, "Money, a good job, and a wife." He was also asked what animal he would like to be if he could become one and he said, "An elephant—because they never forget."

During the performance subtest of the WAIS he worked enthusiastically and fairly efficiently. He even expressed at one point he thought it was fun. He showed no signs of unusual stress. The examiner felt rapport was good.

IQ scores from the WAIS were VSIQ 75; PSIQ 95; FSIQ, 83. These scores found him to be functioning near the top of the borderline category of intellectual ability. The significant difference in the verbal and performance IQ indicated he was deficient in "common sense" and concentration on auditory stimuli but had above-average ability in visual-motor skill. He also appeared to have slightly above-average ability in visual-spatial skill.

His reading level was third grade according to the WRAT reading section. The HTP indicated a weak self-concept, a tendency to be passive-aggressive and that he probably reacted to frustration by regressing to childlike behavior.

Recommendations were that he be considered in need of vocational rehabilitation services; his goal of being a carpenter's helper be encouraged; and he be given as much help as possible with his reading deficiency.

My first contact concerning this client was July of 1969. I went by the home and talked with his mother, as he was working at the time. I made arrangements for the general medical to be done and explained our agency's function which the mother seemed to understand. I left my name and number with her. After several contacts with the mother, the general medical was finally done on September 25, 1969. At this time the boy was enrolled in the tenth grade of a local high school.

A very unfortunate thing happened in relation to the medical examination. The doctor with whom the family made the appointment used a stamp which read "mental retardation" and stamped this several places on the medical form. After the examination was finished the form was handed to the boy himself (either by the doctor or the secretary) instead of being mailed to this authorizing office. When the boy saw this, it of course had a very traumatic effect on him. His mother called me to tell me about it and said her son threatened to quit school. Fortunately the mother realized our office was not at fault. She said she would mail the form to me and I assured her I would see her son the next day and try to take care of the situation.

My supervisor was informed of the incident and a letter was sent to the doctor involved explaining what had happened. It was requested that he please not hand the form to the clients but give it to the counselor, if present or else mail it to our office. Evidently this particular doctor automatically assumed our clients were all mental retardates.

The day after the boy's mother informed me of the incident I went to the school and saw him. He said he was upset with the doctor. I explained to him a mistake was made by the doctor's office in handing him the form instead of mailing it to us. I told him his test scores were too high for him to be placed into special education (he had the impression that special education was only for mental retardates and undoubtedly thought of mental retardation as the low level; and also some of his family members had told him that vocational rehabilitation worked only with mental retardates). I explained that we work with problems other than mental retardates and we were working with him because he did have academic problems and his frustration with school seemed to be upsetting him. (He had always hated school, and a great deal of this was due to his reading deficiency.)

The client spoke of joining the service, which he had been considering for some time, but I told him to think hard about such a decision and to remember that several people cared about him and were willing and trying to help him. He said he needed work to help with expenses at home, but he had not bothered to look. I told him if he wanted work he had to go after it. He then responded by saying he didn't know if he could work and keep up his school work too and had no transportation anyway. He said he would think about it. Based on the psychological testing, he was "running true to form" in the opinion of this counselor. He mentioned an interest in wrestling and I encouraged him to talk with the coach about trying out, in hopes that an active extracurricular activity might improve his attitude about school.

I spoke to his school counselor on the same day. She had been continuously confronted with his wanting to talk to her, using any excuse to see her as well as missing classes. She said she would investigate the possibility of getting him into a special reading class.

The next day I called his mother. She said her son was in much better spirits and that he liked me. The family was trying to keep him from quitting school, especially an older brother who had quit. I related to her the basis of my talk with him and that I felt the incident concerning the medical form was straightened out. She said he did not need to work to help out with finances in the home. She was very nice and cooperative.

I saw the client two weeks later. He said he was failing but would stick with school a bit longer. He appeared quite dejected. Three days later I called his school counselor. Standardized tests had been given and she said he didn't even try. I told her his reading deficiency was the real hang-up, and if she could not get reading help to investigate the possibility of special education as a last resort.

Three weeks later, November 4, I again saw the client. He was absolutely miserable in school and was determined to quit. He said his mother held him back from quitting because she told him he could not quit. It is my opinion that this was an excuse, or he would have quit long before. I asked him why he didn't go ahead and quit if he felt that strongly about it. He gave no answer to this except to "fall" back on his mother again. I told him I would talk to his mother the next day about the situation but whatever he finally decided would be his own doing. He said his mother said he would have to leave home if he quit, but that he could manage fine on his own. He said he had friends he could live with, could get a job on his own, and did not need my help. I told him quitting might be the best thing, but it would be his decision. He told me not to "plot" with his mother to keep him in school. I told him I would merely inform her of his plans and feelings. He then proceeded to tell me he could easily get kicked out of school (obvious avoidance of the responsibility of quitting being his). I told him to do that would be a double blow to his mother, and this would not make sense in relation to his being concerned about her feelings. I discussed with him the fact that being on his own was not as simple as he thought, but he insisted he could make it and was going to quit.

I talked with his counselor at school after seeing him. She seemed to think he might need special help such as psychiatric. I told her I felt it was the build-up of frustration from school all these years. She had made arrangements for him to be in a special reading class, and he was all for it but then backed out. I determined this to be due to the fact that he did not want this as a reason for him to stay in school and felt special help would take away his reason for failing. He told his counselor he just did not want the course. His counselor also informed me that the client's gym teacher had hit him in the head with a roll book and refused to let him try out for wrestling. He did assist one teacher in adding numerical grades for her and did a good job but his overall attitude had gotten progressively worse.

The next day I went to the home and talked with his mother. She said her son had been a problem at home and school all along, that he would not look for work, and that he ran around at night with a group of boys who were potential trouble. She said they had tried to do all they knew how to in guiding him properly, and this included me and the school. His attitude was poor, and he had skipped school a lot and had been suspended for three days for this in one instance. I related my conversation with him on the previous day and she verified much of what he had said. I also told her my general conclusions. She told me his school counselor had called her the previous day and also just before I had arrived. Our final decision was to let him quit and go into the service. She said they would sign for him because his interest in this had been so strong that it seemed the only alternative.

I called his school counselor upon returning to my office, and she informed me the client had just completed filling out his drop-out forms. She said she had talked with the principal and assistant principal and they said the client was on the verge of being kicked out anyway so he was doing himself a favor to quit on his own. I called his mother to tell her he had dropped, and I told her I would call her in two days to find out what the final decision was within the family.

I called the home two days later. His mother said his whole attitude had changed for the better. They had given him a time limit to find work. He evidently dropped the idea of joining the service as he no longer needed it as an excuse to quit school, and he got a job with a home construction contractor he had worked with one summer. His mother said this contractor knew and understood her son, and her son really liked him. The type of work was an excellent outlet for the boy's carpentry interest. I activated the case at this point.

I checked with his mother four days later and she reported all was well. Shortly after this I had to leave for Fishersville. Upon returning, I called and spoke with the client. He was still on the same job, liked it and felt he was learning a trade. He said he did not plan to join the service.

I followed up by contacting his employer. He said the client was still with him and did well for what he knew at this stage. The client did "goof off" at times but the employer said he would reprimand him when needed and that he felt the boy really wanted this type of work enough that he would stick with it and continue to learn. The client had been on the job for three months, and was progressing at a successful pace of effort and satisfaction.

Final Comment

If only these children with reading problems could be diagnosed and treated earlier, so many of these problems could be avoided. Rehabilitation is flooded with clients with high borderline up to above-average IQ's who dropped out of school because

of reading problems. Even most vocational schools require text
work in the better paying courses, so they fail often even in rehabilitation. How could rehabilitation counselors influence elementary schools to cope with this problem more adequately is
a question that should be investigated if we ever hope to solve
some of the social issues confronting our society.

Exercise 22

THE UTILIZATION OF PSYCHOLOGICAL TESTS AND INFORMATION IN VOCATIONAL REHABILITATION

RATIONALE

The employment of psychological tests in rehabilitation has definite advantages to which the counselor should avail himself. For the counselor utilizing psychometric devices it is important he understand why such tests were administered and by whom; the interpretation of the test results; and how this information will help the counselor work more effectively for the client's welfare in vocational planning.

ASSIGNMENT

Analyze three cases which have a complete test battery. Look at the psychological report and relate data from test scores to the vocational objective. Show specifically the role individual test scores played in the selection of a vocational objective. Discuss the meaning of each score and the relationships between these scores.

STUDENT WORK: SAMPLE 1

Thomas H

Thomas H is an 18-year-old white male referred to vocational rehabilitation by the guidance department of a comprehensive high school. Last year he was absent forty-six days and failed because of it. In the second month of the current scholastic year his attendance has deteriorated to the point where the school administration, feeling that to maintain him on the roles would be meaningless, is forcing his withdrawal.

In the initial interview Thomas was highly verbal and aggressive, directing the conversation to a detailed review of his medi-

204

cal, scholastic, and social problems. In 1964 Thomas was struck by an automobile resulting in a three-month hospitalization, during which he was unconscious for twenty-seven consecutive days.

Thomas feels that his real problems date back to the year after the accident when he suffered a "nervous breakdown" and was committed to a state mental hospital. This admission was a result of his constant running away from home, frequent skipping of school, and his inability to get along with his teachers. When released after four months the diagnosis was "adjustment reaction to adolescence" and the prognosis was "good."

Thomas states that his home situation is good and that his father is a most understanding man. Thomas has been taking drugs recently in an effort to become more acceptable to his peers and to make friends, which he desperately desires. He wants to work in a situation where he will be with people his own age and establish positive relationships with the "right kind of people."

The general medical examination notes a slight right strabismus which has been corrected surgically, a nervous tremor, and possible brain damage as a result of the auto accident.

Needing additional information to determine eligibility for services and to gain insight into the vocational implications of Thomas' apparent adjustment difficulties, the vocational rehabilitation counselor obtained a full psychological evaluation. The psychologist was instructed to test for organic brain damage, current level of intellectual functioning, manual dexterity, and personality adjustment.

To obtain the requested information the psychologist selected the following test instruments: Bender Visual Motor Gestalt Test, Wechsler Adult Intelligence Scale, Non-Language Learning Test, Pennsylvania Bi-Manual Work Sample, Crawford Small Parts Dexterity Test (Screwdriver Section), and the Thematic Apperception Test. Recent wide-range achievement scores were available through the referral source.

The psychologist rated motivation throughout the testing session as high. There were no overt manifestations of bizarre behavior or psychosis during the three-hour session. Rapport was established easily and the subject was most cooperative. This is of interest in that Thomas' school record shows evidence of his refusal to perform the nonverbal sections of group intelligence tests on two separate occasions. Thus, individual testing under the above conditions will provide the most accurate measure of his ability yet obtained.

The *Bender Visual Motor Gestalt Test* is one of a number of instruments based upon the premise that the ability to establish spatial relations is one area most sensitive to organic pathologies. The task is for the subject to reproduce nine simple figures as they are separately presented on individual cards. At all times the subject has the model before him to duplicate as accurately as possible.

The test is good for screening the most serious organic disturbances. Retest reliabilities are around .70 in normal samples and much higher in abnormal ones. Performance is unrelated to drawing ability, but is significantly affected by level of general intelligence and amount of education.

The *Wechsler Adult Intelligence Scale (WAIS)* is the most widely used instrument by psychologists in the determination of general learning ability. It is composed of eleven subtests. Six of these form the verbal scale while the remaining five form the performance scale. Together they yield a full scale intelligence score which is most reliable. Even short forms of this test yield reliable full scale scores. However, these abbreviated versions should not be accepted because the formulation of profiles from the subtest scores requires the administration of the complete WAIS.

The WAIS measure of general intelligence is no more valid than those obtainable from many group tests. The advantages of this test are found in the additional information available through careful analysis of the subtest scores to establish the existence of deterioration due to organic brain damage, psychotic conditions, and other pathological disorders. It is necessary to keep in mind that when taken separately or in small groups, these subtests are not as reliable as is the full scale measure of intelligence, ranging from reliability coefficients in the .60's for Digit Span, Picture Arrangement, and Object Assembly to coefficients such as .96 for Vocabulary. The interpreter must also take into consideration the standard error of measurement for the three IQ scores and each of the subtest scores. Obviously there are great risks involved when WAIS profiles are accepted as face value without supporting data from other instruments.

Finally, an accurate interpretation of Wechsler's profiles must consider language handicaps, socioeconomic situations, urban-rural differences, as well as occupational and educational factors. Much of the value of the WAIS is found in the qualitative interpretations made by the examiner, as can be said for most tests which seek to produce more than mere IQ scores.

The *Non-Language Learning Test (NLL)* is a concrete problem-solving performance test involving the fitting together of certain geometric shapes under timed conditions. It is used often in the psychological evaluation of the totally blind to determine ability to apply learned procedures, degree of manual dexterity, and tactile sensitivity, as well as anxiety.

The *Pennsylvania Bi-Manual Work Sample* is a timed performance test of gross motor function which compares subject production to those of an established normative sample. Unlike the NLL there is no learning involved.

The *Crawford Small Parts Dexterity Test* is used to determine the degree of fine motor coordination through time tasks involving the tightening of small bolts with a screwdriver (the section used specifically in this evaluation).

The *Thematic Apperception Test (TAT)* is a constructive-type projective test calling for the subject to construct complete stories based upon certain vague pictures and in one case a blank piece of white cardboard. Through content analysis the examiner determines who the subject identifies with in the story, what needs are expressed by the subject in the story and what environmental factors the subject sees as affecting the satisfaction of the needs.

Most clinicians interpret this test based upon their experience in using it. There is much evidence to support the contention that such factors as hunger, sleep deprivation, social frustration, and the experience of failure have a significant effect upon TAT responses. The relationship between clinician and subject is obviously an important factor in the qualitative interpretation of responses. Many practitioners feel that the content analysis of such tests as the TAT provides more data than the formal scoring used on such tests as the Rorschach, and there has been some movement toward this type of test over those based upon associative techniques.

Wide-range achievements tests such as the IOWA Test of Educational Development are used to determine amounts of

REPORT OF TEST SCORES FOR THOMAS H

1. Bender Motor Visual Gestalt Test: Negative

2. WAIS

Verbal Scale IQ	116
Performance Scale IQ	112
Full Scale IQ	114

Subtest Scaled Scores:

Verbal		*Performance*	
Information	8	Digit Symbol	7
Comprehension	12	Picture Completion	9
Arithmetic	12	Block Design	8
Similaries	10	Picture Arrangement	11
Digit Span	11	Object Assembly	9
Vocabulary	12		

3. Non-Language Learning Test

Trial I	1' 29"
Trial II	1' 55"
Trial III	2' 06"

4. Pennsylvania Bi-Manual Work Sample

Assembly	8' 41"	15th percentile
Disassembly	5' 11"	8th percentile

5. Crawford Small Parts Dexterity Test

Screwdriver Section	8' 26"	85th percentile

6. Thematic Apperception Test: No Scores

7. IOWA Test of Educational Development

Science	47th percentile
Literature	41st percentile
Vocabulary	54th percentile
Source Information	46th percentile

academic knowledge in various areas. Scores are reported as grade levels or in percentiles. They are used in most education systems in class placement.

Discussion and Interpretation of Test Results

There were no indications of organic involvement in the Bender Gestalt drawings. This finding is further substantiated by an analysis of the WAIS subtests employing the development of a deterioration index. In deriving this comparison, the sum of "Hold" tests (Vocabulary, Information, Object Assembly, and Picture Completion) is subtracted from the sum of "Don't Hold" tests (Digit Span, Block Design, Digit Symbol, and Similarities) and divided by the sum of "Hold Tests." The larger the number thus obtained, the greater is the evidence of brain damage. This construction is based upon the observation that tests requiring the use of past learnings decline less than those involving speed, new learning, and the perception of new verbal and spatial relations. We must therefore conclude that Thomas H suffered no significant brain damage as a result of the 1964 accident, and that his problems are the result of nonorganic factors.

Examination of the Wechsler profiles reveals that Thomas is, at present, functioning within the average classification of adult intelligence. Thomas' verbal IQ approaches the above-average range, and his ability to grasp the meanings of problems and their solutions, his understanding of the basic arithmetic processes, his understanding and use of words and vocabulary, and his short-term memory are well above the norm.

In view of the Bender Gestalt and WAIS deterioration index analysis, his lower scoring on the performance subtests is attributed to a severe anxiety neurosis. Further evidence of the existence of an almost incapacitating anxiety is found in his performance on the Non-Language Learning Test where his scores deteriorated with each trial of the same task under timed stress conditions as his anxiety increased.

Observation of Thomas' performance on the WAIS performance tasks and the NLL reveals that his approach to new problems is characterized by the employment of an illogical trial and error technique.

The Pennsylvania Bi-Manual Work Sample and Crawford Small Parts Dexterity Test profiles point to poor gross and fine motor coordination. In part, these results suggest that Thomas may not be a competitive individual.

Support for Thomas' emotional problems come from the TAT profile and his personal history. Many of his problems are related to his home environment and adolescent conflict between him and his parents. It is strongly suggested that school has been a very threatening experience for Thomas. This is interesting because the WAIS shows clearly that he possesses the verbal skills to succeed in school without difficulty. The ITED achievement show him to be slightly below the norm in all but vocabulary. These scores may underestimate his achievement. There is strong indication that Thomas is much concerned about failure and has decided to withdraw rather than to compete.

Thomas' past difficulties have resulted from the pronounced insecurity he feels and his inappropriate means of coping with the stresses of life. The TAT profiles clearly show that he uses the childlike defenses of withdrawal and regression. He also uses excessive verbalization and intellectualization. Thomas internalizes his hostilities which leads him into periods of acute depression.

There are no indications that Thomas H is at present a psychotic, nor were there clues of a totally incapacitating neurosis although severe anxiety is evident. He can best be described as experiencing a serious adjustment reaction to adolescence.

Formation of the Counseling Plan

With regard to eligibility it is obvious that Thomas' anxiety and adjustment problems constitute a disability which is a definite handicap to employment. There is also strong indication, based upon his general ability, lack of organic involvement, and desire to seek assistance in the solution of his problems, that rehabilitation services will result in substantial gainful employment. The client will be accepted.

Too often when dealing with emotional disorders the rehabilitation counselor decides to ignore the disability as much as possible and to work around it. In view of the client's age, and to prevent further serious disturbances, the counselor has decided to work with the handicap.

Since the client is highly verbal and manifests enough anxiety regarding his current life situation to experience considerable growth through psychotherapy, this will be provided for a short term on a weekly basis through the local mental health clinic. Concurrent to this, the family will be directed and encouraged to make use of family therapy services available from the same psychiatrist at the clinic.

In view of the defenses used by the client, the counselor will be directive in his counseling approach and gradually force the client to face reality. This, of course, will be closely coordinated with the work of the psychiatrist. The family, especially the father, will be included in all planning decisions made by the counselor and the client to tie the family therapy and the rehabilitation program more closely together in their minds. The client will be encouraged to recognize his real abilities and see himself more positively. Because school has been such a threatening experience for him, and he is not of a competitive nature, he will not be placed in a formal training institution.

However, there is a place for work in the rehabilitation program. Certainly the client has expressed a definite preference for direct placement. The situation should satisfy his expressed desire to work with people in his age group. So as not to reinforce his insecurity, the work must be rather simple and routine in nature, far below the level on which we would hope to eventually see him.

Thomas' needs in the early stages of the rehabilitation effort are those of success and self-appreciation. These can be met in the form of a part-time twenty hours per week placement at a convenience food retail outlet during setting-up hours in the morning or clean-up time in the evening. There he will be working with and serving his peers in a period of minimum stress and pressure. This placement will serve also as a period of evaluation of Thomas' motivation to work. It is hoped as successes build, the motivation will develop and increase.

If the psychotherapy proves successful and Thomas is able

to make better adjustments, he will be encouraged to take advantage of the high school review program run by the county school system leading to the GED examination and certificate. The program lasts only eight weeks and meets but twice a week. Thomas will be directed to see the long-term advantages to be gained by conscientious participation in this short-term program.

It would be meaningless for the counselor to envision a program beyond the already ambitious one outlined. In this case the psychological report diagnosed the disability and provided a positive prognosis and information vital to the development of the rehabilitation plan and occupational objective.

Martin J

Martin J, who is 49 years old, was referred to vocational rehabilitation through the personnel office of his previous employer, a large national insurance company. Last year, suffering with severe headaches and occasional dizziness, he sought medical assistance through the company physician. It was determined that Mr. J had developed a brain tumor and that surgery was required.

After several months of convalescent leave, Mr. J returned to his position as a distrct manager. It soon became evident to all, including Mr. J, that for some reason he could no longer function as he had before the surgery. The employer released him, recommending that vocational rehabilitation provide diagnostic and evaluative services. Upon specific recommendation of vocational rehabilitation, the employer would rehire him in the capacity decided upon by the counselor.

Mrs. J, who now accompanies her husband wherever he goes, began to notice subtle behavioral changes in Martin J after he returned from the hospital. These changes she attributed to the reaction of an active person such as her husband to a lengthy period of inactivity. She noticed that loud noises easily irritated him. It soon became apparent that he was now most uncomfortable in groups larger than three or four. She stated that she was proud of her husband because he "holds it in so well," displaying few outward signs of his emotions to others.

Mrs. J reveals considerable understanding of her husband's

problems and though she said many things diametrically opposed to statements made by her husband, he would look at her, though near tears, and make no attempt to argue the point. The only difficulty he will admit to is that he forgets recent happenings easily. He denies physical fatigue, any speech slurring, or paralysis.

The Martin J's are financially secure, owning their own home and having no outstanding debts. Mr. J is a high school graduate with one year of college training. Considering this background, he did well becoming an $18,000 per year salaried employee.

The Need for Psychological Testing

Before the rehabilitation process can proceed, there are many questions about Martin J that must be answered. Psychological testing will be the main diagnostic tool in this evaluation. The counselor must determine the existence and extent of organic brain damage resulting from the destructive surgery. He must know what specific areas of performances are diminished.

It is reasonable to assume from the initial interview that the applicant is aware of his difficulties, but voluntarily provides little information to the counselor. It is necessary to determine exactly the nature of his reaction to the disability. Finally, it must be decided whether the personality changes noticed by his wife are a direct result of the surgery, or of his personality adjustment to the disability.

The counselor was most selective in the choice of the psychologist to perform this evaluation. A clinical psychologist was selected with many years of experience in Veteran's Administration hospitals working with organically involved patients. The psychologist was also in the applicant's age group. The counselor reasoned that the selection of a middle-aged clinician would help to lower Mr. J's anxiety and reluctance to communicate.

The psychologist, after reviewing all of the case information with the counselor, selected the following test instruments: The Benton Visual Retention Test, The Wechsler-Bellevue Intelligence Scale Form 1, The Purdue Pegboard, the Rorschach Inkblots.

Review of Tests

The Benton Visual Retention Test presents ten designs of increasing complexity on individual cards in the same manner as the Bender-Gestalt test. Like the Bender-Gestalt this instrument seeks to measure intellectual impairment through the comparison of the subject's task completion performance to the performance of a representative sample of the general population.

All tests of intellectual impairment are based upon the belief that memory, spatial relations, perception, and abstract or concept formation are the areas of performance most subject to deterioration. This test adds to the perceptual task of the Bender-Gestalt the task of memory.

After each design is presented it is removed and the subject asked to reproduce it as accurately as possible. Performance is scored in terms of correct reproductions and number of errors. The scores are then interpreted in relation to the subject's measured IQ.

The Purdue Pegboard is a dexterity test designed to aid in the selection of employees for manual positions. It measures two types of activity: one involving gross movements of hands, fingers, and arms, and the other involving fingertip dexterity. Tasks involving the manipulation of parts, collars, and washers are timed. Performance then can be measured against several norm groups.

The Wechsler-Bellevue Intelligence Scale (Form 1) is an outdated, less reliable forerunner of the WAIS. This lower reliability is traced to fewer number of tasks in many of the subtests. Because of this, many feel that the diagnostic profiles obtained from the Wechsler-Bellevue subtests are of little value. However, many clinicians feel the validity of the subtests and the number of other tests brought into the configurational relations which one seeks to establish are of equal importance.

It also is noted that older subjects obtain higher IQ scores on the Wechsler-Bellevue than on other intelligence scales. However, in that no instrument has perfect retest reliability, we can accept W-B-1 scores as general indicators. The real purpose for using intelligence scales is not to obtain one IQ score, but to measure special intellectual abilities and weaknesses and to indicate how these influence the global functioning of the subject.

To obtain a deterioration index using the Wechsler-Bellvue Form 1 the sum of scaled scores for the "Hold" tests, Information or Vocabulary, Comprehension, Object Assembly, and Picture Completion, are compared with the sum of the scaled scores of the "Don't Hold" tests, Digit Span, Arithmetic, Digit Symbol, and Block Design. This comparison is then expressed as a ratio or as a difference between the two sums in the form of a percentage of difference.

The Rorschach Inkblots is the least structured projective personality assessment in general use. The Rorschach utilizes ten bilaterally symmetrical inkblots, each on an individual card. Five of the blots are in black and shades of gray. Two contain touches of bright red while the remaining three are pastel shades. As each card is presented, the subject is asked to describe what he sees. After the ten cards are presented, the examiner questions the subject in detail as to what portions or aspects of the card brought about the association. During this discussion the subject clarifies and elaborates upon his initial responses. During the presentation the examiner considers all manifestations of behavior, positions in which cards are held, incidental remarks, emotional expressions, etc.

The most often used scoring categories for the Rorschach rely upon location, which refers to the particular section of the blot used in the association, and determinants such as color, form, shading, and impression of movement, as well as content, which usually includes human figures, parts of human figures, animal figures, and related parts. Popularity scores also are used based upon the frequency of certain responses obtained in general practice.

There are several factors which must be considered in the interpretation of Rorschach responses. Research shows that color has limited influence upon response. Verbal aptitude also affects several Rorschach scores which are indicators of personality traits.

Another factor to be considered is the number of responses, which appears to be related to age, intellectual level, and amount of education and not to the basic personality variables upon which much Rorschach interpretation depends. The Rorschach was found to have little or no predictive value or validity when checked against other diagnostic procedures.

Because of these basic weaknesses of the Rorschach, many clinicians have turned to content analysis of the responses and use them as an adjunct to interviewing. As with the Thematic Apperception Test, a great deal of the Rorschach's value lies in the skill of the clinician and the relationship he develops with the subject.

REPORT OF TEST SCORES

Wechsler-Bellevue Intelligence Scale Form 1

Verbal IQ	116
Performance IQ	112
Full scale IQ	114

Subtest Scaled Scores

Verbal		*Performance*	
Information	13	Picture Arrangement	9
Comprehension	12	Picture Completion	13
Digit Span	10	Block Design	8
Arithmetic	9	Object Assembly	9
Similarities	14	Digit Symbol	8
Vocabulary			

Deterioration Index −10 or .22 or 22% (.15+ significant)

Benton Visual Retention Test: Positive for Organicity

Purdue Pegboard; Norms for Veterans and College Students

Right Hand	60th percentile
Left Hand	60th percentile
Both Hands	55th percentile
Right and Left and Both Hands	55th percentile
Assembly	45th percentile

Rorschach: No scores reported

Discussion and Interpretation of Tests and Interviews

On the Information subtest, which seeks to determine the subject's general range of knowledge, Martin J did well in recalling past and present events, tending to be quite concrete in his answers to factual questions. As the questions became less concrete and more abstract, he experienced difficulty with recall.

On the Comprehension subtest, which measures practical judgment and common sense, the subject did well. However, some of the questions had to be repeated two and three times before an adequate response was obtained, especially where the first responses were vague.

The subject's performance on the Digit Span subtest is of interest in that he recalled nine digits forward (which is rather unusual) but could recall only one backwards. He was unable to reverse the series in his mind.

On the Arithmetic subtest he answered the first seven questions correctly, indicating that he can effectively use all of the basic mathematical principles. He was unable to answer correctly any of the word problems and experienced difficulty with fractions. The examiner allowed Mr. J to read the questions, but this proved to be of no advantage to him.

On the Similarities subtest, which measures processes fundamental to verbal concept formation and logical thinking, the subject's performance deteriorated as the relationships became more abstract. Many times he responded, "They cannot be the same." However, when the words were simplified, he was able to produce more correct responses.

Mr. J did well on the visual motor tests with the exceptions of Block Design and Object Assembly. He experienced difficulty in getting the *gestalten* of these two tasks. There appears to exist some difficulty in overall organization, which increases with stress or pressure. The subject also tended to forget the directions, but tried to hide this from the clinician.

On the Benton Visual Retention Test there was evidence of definite deterioration when the designs became more complex. Although the problems are quite apparent, they are not major.

Performance on the Purdue Pegboard was in the average range; however, the scores declined when the tasks called for organization. Mr. J could work in many production line situations, if his performance would not deteriorate under stress.

The client tended to perseverate in his responses to the Rorschach Inkblots, which is to say that his response would be the same to several inkblots, regardless of size, shape, or color.

Many of his associations were to crabs: "I don't see the feelers and the claws are missing." These responses indicate an underlying feeling of castration, of not being a complete person. Such responses are typical of paraplegics and quadraplegics—men who have been reduced from intellectual and physical activity to passivity and dependence.

On the cards introducing the color red which is taken as emotional stress, the subject blocked. He would respond that they did not remind him of anything. Under questioning when all of the cards were carefully discussed, he was, however, able to make appropriate responses. From these cards the impression is gained of a person not wishing to appear hostile to others, fearing that he cannot cope with the hostility which, in turn, would be directed at him.

On the fifth card, that of self-image, he again blocked and could not make an association. With encouragement he could only respond, "It looks like an inkblot to me." This type of response is borne of pure anxiety in that the subject is responding only to texture. There is evidence of some ego destruction, loss of self-confidence, and anxiety about his self-image.

Developing the Rehabilitation Plan

The psychological testing leaves little doubt that Mr. J has suffered brain damage as a result of the destructive surgery removing his tumor. The positive results of the Benton Visual Retention Test and the deterioration index developed from the Wechsler-Bellevue subtests clearly point to it. The counselor will obtain a neurological evaluation to provide medical conformation of these findings to satisfy legal requirements for eligibility.

Taking an anatomical viewpoint we are forced to conclude that Martin J will never regain the level of performance that made him a district manager. His powers of reading comprehension are severely limited as demonstrated by his inability to comprehend the word problems in the Wechsler-Bellevue arithmetic subtest when given the advantage of reading the problem. His ability to consider abstractions and to organize his thinking is also diminished. This conclusion is warranted by Mr. J's performance on the Information, Digit Span, Similarities, Block Design, and Object Assembly subtests.

There is considerable evidence to confirm performance deterioration under stress. Block Design and Object Assembly performance was observed to decline under timed conditions. Mr. J's responses to the Rorschach Inkblots speak of his anxiety. Even though the IQ scores point to a bright normal intelligence, it is clear that in most vocational situations his performance will fall far below those we might expect from a person with such scores. The Purdue Pegboard performance scores are more representative of what we might expect.

A more useful approach to the rehabilitation of Martin J would be to consider what assets Mr. J brings to the job market. He possesses a good speaking vocabulary, a well-modulated voice, a gentle manner, and a cooperative nature and approach to life. Mr. J demonstrated an ability to persist in tasks which were difficult and obviously frustrating during the testing session. His tendency to withdraw from traumatic situations is a good defense which he uses to maintain himself under stress. There is evidence to believe that he will never act out and will always behave as a gentleman, even in difficult situations.

Martin J requires assistance in making a better adjustment to his disability and accepting his dependent role. The counselor will provide family counseling service to Mr. and Mrs. J, as well as their two college-age children. Mr. J needs to accept the fact he cannot return to his old job, but must see that there are many jobs, paying lower salaries, in which he could perform well and be a most productive person. His family needs to develop an awareness of the effect of condescension upon Mr. J.

There is no question that Martin J should obtain employment on a limited scale. He needs evidence of personal worthiness to see himself again as a whole person. The work situation will be one where he will not work with figures or experience undue stress or a sudden shifting in job requirements.

His tolerance for work must be redeveloped. He will begin working a two- or three-day week and gradually build up to his limit. The position will be near his home because he no longer should drive, as his ability to make swift decisions is impaired.

In view of the information obtained through psychological testing and discussion with the client, it is decided that Mr. J will not return in any capacity to his previous employer. The effect of going back to a much lower position would be traumatic to the client in his present adjustment stage.

The client will be placed in the position of guard at the community hospital near his home. His duties will consist of making regular rounds through the hospital and its grounds, providing general information to people during visiting hours, and assisting hospital personnel in the general performance of their duties. His hours will be increased over a period of months at the discretion of his immediate supervisor. In this position Mr. J will be able to see himself as providing a useful service to others, having some responsibility, and being physically active. The activity will allow him to work off some of his anxiety.

The results of psychological testing provided a description of the parameters of the disabilities presenting a substantial handicap to the employment of Martin J. While brain damage must be confirmed through a neurological examination, the vocational implications of the disability were clearly defined. The counselor was presented with a discussion of the client's vocational assets and liabilities. This information provided the basis of the rehabilitation plan and was a valuable aid in selecting the vocational objective.

Nicholas E

Nicholas E is a self-referral to the Division of Vocational Rehabilitation who was recently released from the state children's detention center where he was placed for three months by the juvenile services division of the juvenile court following the arson of a drive-in theater.

He is 17 years old and the second of five children born to parents who married at an early age. All of the children are on record in the files of the special services department of the public school system. As behavior problems the three boys all have arrest records. No family member completed the ninth grade.

Nicholas first came to the attention of the authorities during his first year in school when he failed to cooperate in any way with his teachers or classmates. He would do only what he wanted in his own way. To force compliance to his demands, he often resorted to physical force, throwing stones at teacher and other students. His temper was described as violent, uncontrollable, and explosive.

Concerned school administrators obtained a full psychological evaluation to gain greater insights into his problems. The psychologist administered the Stanford Binet Form L-M, Rorschach Inkblots, and the House-Tree-Person Test.

Description of Tests

The Stanford Binet is primarily a measure of scholastic aptitude and as such is heavily weighted toward verbal performance. Because of this characteristic the test should not be used with language deficient subjects or people whose strengths are best measured in terms of nonverbal performance; such people are penalized by this measurement device.

The Stanford Binet has long been favored in academic circles. The content of the instrument is interesting to children, while boring to many adults. Intelligence is measured in terms of a ratio of mental age to chronological age. By correctly responding to a specified number of tasks in each subsection, additional units of age are added to the subject's basal mental age score. For subjects over the age of 14 this method requires certain manipulations which some researchers feel are detrimental to an accurate measurement of intelligence.

This test is not well suited for use by the vocational rehabilitation counselor because it does not report measurement of differential aptitudes as do the Wechsler Scales. The instrument yields one composite IQ score.

Many clinicians use the Stanford Binet as yet another adjunct to the interview. Due to the constructive nature of the test, many opportunities exist for clinician-subject interaction and for observance of such personality characteristics as confidence, approach to problem solving, and willingness to work.

The House-Tree-Person (H-T-P) is a projective test of an

expressive nature which considers methods and styles as well as production. In the administration of the H-T-P the subject is asked to draw in succession a house, which is believed to arouse associations related to home and family; a tree, which evokes associations concerned with the subject's role in life and his ability to derive satisfaction from the environment; and a person, which calls forth associations pertaining to interpersonal relations. Many clinicians use this as the first test in a complete battery. Because of its nonthreatening nature, it often serves to alleviate subject anxiety.

While the subject prepares the drawings, the examiner notes the sequence in which the parts are drawn, spontaneous comments of the subject; and any overt manifestations of emotion. As a clinical instrument, the H-T-P is of questionable value, at best weakly substantiating insights into personality gained through other diagnostic procedures.

Test Report and Interpretation (From School Records)

> Nicholas is a talkative 16-year-old of average intelligence or better, obtaining a Stanford Binet IQ of 96, who is unable to function at his expected level because of emotional problems. He has considerable difficulty in forming lasting relationships. In normal situations he is verbally hostile and uses inappropriate language. Under stress he loses control, acting out in an immature manner. He has a lively fantasy life and experiences considerable difficulty distinguishing between what is real and what he imagines. There are strong suggestions of rejection.

It is interesting to note that the psychologist reports a possible above-average intelligence. This is possible with the Stanford Binet in that the subject may have failed to gain points in several subsections by a single question.

As a result of this evaluation, a conference was held with the parents where the findings were discussed and recommendations made to seek the services of the Family and Children's Society and the mental health clinic.

During this conference, the psychologist observed Mrs. E to be an extremely tense, anxious, and hostile young woman who could not listen to others, but who under the pressure of her own interpretations and ideas passed from one subject to another with superficial excuses for her behavior and for the behavior of her children. The psychologist concluded that the mother was trapped in her own tremendous need to deny responsibility for her own involvement in the family situation and that she was incapable of relating to her own husband, school authorities, or her own children.

The father was working two jobs at the time, at the insistence of his wife, who maintained that the extra income would be the key in the solution of their problems. He appeared to be interested and willing to cooperate, but helplessly overwhelmed by his wife.

The parents did not follow any of the recommendations of the school, maintaining that there was no need for outside assistance in managing the business of the family.

Nicholas failed the first grade, and made below-average progress scholastically until he withdrew after failing the eighth grade twice. Soon after his withdrawal he was arrested for setting fire to lawns in a residential area. However, this charge was never pressed. Three weeks before his arson arrest he was found guilty of breaking and entering and larceny. He was released into the custody of his parents who again failed to provide any supervision.

While in detention at the children's center his actions were closely observed and reported. Nicholas remained relatively quiet and reserved while at the center. He was cooperative and often volunteered to help other students and workers. He established normal peer relations, becoming an accepted member of the group.

He demonstrated great respect for authority and responded well to direct and indirect supervision, although the staff believed that he might not be so responsive in other situations. He did not participate in competitive sports and declined any position of leadership in recreational activities. Academically he could read on an eighth grade level and use mathematical concepts on a seventh grade level.

The counselor needed to resolve this apparent reversal of what records indicated to be a chronically maladaptive behavior pattern. To gain some insight into the dynamics of Nicholas' personality the counselor obtained a complete personality assessment. The psychologist reflected this emphasis in the selection of a purely projective test battery composed of the Rorschach Inkblots, Bender Visual Motor Gestalt Test, Machover Draw-a-Person, and the Blacky Pictures.

Description of Test Instruments

The Blacky Pictures are used to evaluate certain areas of psychosexual development. The test consists of twelve cartoon-like pictures, each on an individual card, about a dog named "Blacky," his parents, and a sibling. As with the TAT, another constructive procedure, the subject is asked to create stories based upon each picture. Unlike the TAT, which is completely unstructured, the clinician makes certain preliminary remarks to structure the response to each card. After the subject relates the story the examiner asks a standard series of questions.

The great problem encountered when utilizing the Blacky Pictures is the absence of any scoring criteria for children. The authors of the test recommend that the clinician construct his own set of norms as to what is a weak and a strong response in terms of psychosexual analysis. Many researchers feel that the logic behind this test's construction is valid, but that the difficulties associated with scoring and interpretation all but eliminate it from consideration as a clinical instrument at this time.

The Machover Draw-a-Person is an expressive-type projective test. Its administration requires that the subject draw a person on a full-sized piece of paper. After this is accomplished he is asked to draw another person of the opposite sex of that originally drawn.

The scoring of this instrument is qualitative in nature. Through analysis of the various features of the drawing such as relative and absolute size of the figures, quality of lines, position upon the page, sequence of parts drawn, stance, profile, and many other features, the psychologist constructs an interpretation of the subject's composite personality.

There is some evidence to indicate that the Machover Draw-a-person may be of greater value when administered to children than to adults. There is also great question as to the validity of this test. While some psychologists feel that it can discriminate between normal and seriously disturbed personalities, that data at this time is inconclusive.

Interpretation of Test Results

The test results indicate that we are dealing with a personality which is extremely impulsive and has weak controls. There are indications of a personality that will act out its frustrations in stress situations. Additionally, there are indications that the subject has strong aggressive impulses which are under only limited restraint. There is a strong probability that he maintains some of his integration by fantasizing aggressive actions, but that these fantasies are not sufficient to drain off much of his unconscious aggressive feelings.

There is question concerning this individual's psychosexual adjustment, and also some evidence that there may be some underlying homosexual drives of which he is unaware. He sees no possibility of satisfying interpersonal relationships in that people are perceived to be in constant combat with one another, a projection of his own interpersonal conflicts. He unconsciously sees himself as rejected, particularly by the female figure which he sees as possessing many masculine characteristics.

The subject exhibits many of the hallmarks of a sociopathic personality. He displays no evidence of organic brain pathology nor any evidence of poor visual motor coordination. He does display hostility, a feeling of emptiness, and a feeling of unworthiness. He is not psychotic at this time.

Formation of the Counseling Plan

While the counselor could use much of the evidence in the client's history and psychological testing record to support the contention that rehabilitation services are infeasible, the counselor also can find in these records reason to believe that Nicholas could become a productive member of society.

The counselor accepted Nicholas, remembering that the client was able to make a more than adequate adjustment in his relations to peers and adults while in the detention center. The client did come voluntarily to vocational rehabilitation. He is suppressing, however, tenuously, his aggressive impulses. He is a young man with potentially many years of productive work ahead of him.

All available psychological information confirms the belief that Nicholas' problems are an extension of those of his parents. He reflects his father's weakness in his failure to develop an adequate male self-image. He fears that women will usurp his desired masculine position as his mother did in his family. He is unable to react in an acceptable fashion in social situations, because his primary models are incapable of setting a positive example.

Rehabilitation services should be extended to this client as rapidly as possible. If allowed to remain inactive in his present home situation any positive carry-over from his experiences in the detention home would be lost. For this reason the counselor will enter Nicholas in an outdoor exploration program similar to the Outward Bound Program which has been so successful in the modification of the behavior of delinquent youths. In such a program the client will be forced to work effectively with others in order to survive in some measure of comfort. It will be necessary for him to depend upon others and to recognize the fact that others are depending upon him. The counselor feels certain that Nicholas will react as positively to this opportunity as he did in the detention center.

There can be no question that in this program he will be surrounded by masculine figures engaged in masculine activities. In this situation, where he will not have the security of his mother's protection, he will be able to develop his own senses of identity and security based upon his experiences.

The counselor will make explicitly clear to Nicholas that he will be on his own in this program, that he will not be able to withdraw or return home before it is completed. Hopefully, he will not want to return home but will enter into a period of work evaluation and work adjustment in one of the many Job Corps centers throughout the country.

Concurrent to Nicholas' behavioral modification program, the parents will be required by the juvenile court to attend weekly or biweekly counseling sessions available through any one of several human service agencies. To support his effort and to emphasize the role of vocational rehabilitation in the program, the counselor will make regular visits with the juvenile service worker to the home to evaluate the results of the family counseling sessions. If the family fails to make progress and continues to refuse to accept reality, the counselor will not hesitate to recommend that Nicholas be made a ward of the state.

Summary

In the case of Nicholas E, the focus of the rehabilitation program is not involved with vocational training. It is involved with the alleviation or elimination of an emotional disability in the same way that physical therapy is concerned with the alleviation or elimination of pain resulting from a physical handicap.

While in the Job Corp Center, Nicholas may be encouraged to refine his academic skills. In that school records indicate that he reads on an eighth grade level and uses mathematical concepts on the seventh, this should not be difficult for him. Hopefully, the rehabilitation program will allow Nicholas to use the abilities which he could not use while engaged in fantasy and hostility.

If the program, as outlined, is successful, Nicholas will become independent to the point where he will wish to sever ties with vocational rehabilitation and proceed on his own. If the program fails, Nicholas will become an even greater problem for society.

Psychological information from many sources again provided the counselor with a description of the many facets of a near sociopathic personality. Insights into the development of his personality became the backbone of the therapeutic program. Without the added support gleaned through a careful analysis of the psychological information available, it is most probable that Nicholas E would never have become a client of vocational rehabilitation and most certainly would not have had the opportunity to find himself and become something more than a confused, dangerous member of a society already tiring of the burden of support for its less productive members.

Bibliography

Anastasi, Anne: *Psychological Testing,* second edition. Macmillan Company, New York, 1966.

Buros, O. K.: *The Fifth Mental Measurements Yearbook.* Gryphon Press, Highland Park, New Jersey, 1959.

Cronbach, L. J.: *Essentials of Psychological Testing,* third edition. Harper & Row, New York, 1970.

Rapaport, David: *Diagnostic Psychological Testing,* Vols. I and II. Yearbook Publishers, Chicago, 1950.

Wechsler, David: *The Measurement and Appraisal of Adult Intelligence,* fourth edition. Williams & Wilkins Company, Baltimore, 1958.

Exercise 23

SELECTING A VOCATION

RATIONALE

Vocational selection often can be a difficult process if the counselor does not take time to plan *with* his clients. More thought should go into helping the client plan for a chosen vocation (rather than just sending him out to knock on doors or answer want-ads in the local newspaper). The vocational selection process should begin as soon as the client walks into your office the first time; not after he has undergone extensive physical restoration and/or training.

ASSIGNMENT

The purpose of this exercise is to have the counselor trainee make an in-depth study of at least one vocation. It is recommended that the counselor utilize a multitude of resources including contacts with personnel managers, the state employment service, and books such as the *Dictionary of Occupational Titles* and *Occupational Outlook Handbook*.

Step 1. Interview a client who has not selected a vocation. Determine his interest and extent of his knowledge about a selected vocational field such as mechanical, scientific, computational, selling, social services, art, literary, music, etc.

Step 2. Make a detailed study of the client's field of interest (e.g. selling) and be prepared to give the client information which may assist him to make a vocational choice. In preparing for the second and subsequent interviews, develop your preparation along the following guidelines:

A. What is the nature of the vocation the client selected? Give duties; advantages; disadvantages; and present outlook.

B. What education is necessary? How much? What would

it cost? Where can it be obtained? Are any special licenses, examinations, and certificates necessary?

C. What qualifications should the individual have (mental ability, personality, talents and special abilities, union sponsorship, age, sex, height, and physical requirements)?

D. Compensation expected (pay scale, opportunity for advancement, possibility for transferring to other vocations and civil service jobs).

E. How can one enter the field (where to apply, apprenticeship necessary, and where to obtain more information)?

F. What are the possibilities of expansion in the near future and long range?

G. What specific training can one get for the job?

Step 3. Subsequent interviews; use the outline in Step 2 to discuss with the client the vocational information you have collected.

Step 4. Write a brief summary on how you and the client may have benefited from the exercise. Evaluate the method used here to give clients information on vocations.

STUDENT WORK: SAMPLE 1

Intended below is the process used in determining a vocation for one Mr. John Doe.

Step 1

Mr. Doe, during the initial interview, made a detailed vocational report of various positions he had held. His main interest always has been working with people of all levels. He relates easily and maintained a very objective outlook toward his alcoholism. Mr. Doe graduated from a university where he had majored in English and physical education. He was certified to teach secondary grades of education. Since he was also qualified in physical education, Mr. Doe became the coach of his local high school basketball and baseball teams. During his career, this gentleman eventually became the high school principal of 1500 students. He also served in the military (Army) for a period of six years. During this time he reached the rank of captain. Naturally, being the commanding officer of two separate companies, he had the responsibility of guiding and counseling several hundred men. Upon returning to civilian life Mr. Doe returned to the teaching profession. Eventually, he applied for and became a notary public.

Now, for the past ten years Mr. Doe has been quite successful leasing oil rights in this state for the Standard Oil Company. This profession calls for constant contact with both the rural peoples as well as contact with administrative and executive personnel. He is well-rounded in all areas of communication, e.g. letter writing, oral projections and written documentaries.

Lastly, Mr. John Doe carries several recommendations regarding his work, attitude, and leadership.

As the interview continued Mr. Doe presented a new ambition; i.e. to enter the social services. He expressed a desire to be a field worker. Specifically, Mr. Doe wants to work with families who have alcoholic members. Mr. Doe has talked with several social workers in the field as well as in the hospital setting. He has also held several meetings with two alcoholic coordinators, one in the hospital and the other in his home community.

Step 2

In studying Mr. Doe's field of interest this counselor held meetings with the following persons:

1. The hospital alcoholic coordinator.

2. The director of social services in the hospital and two of his workers.

3. The social service department in the mental health centers; i.e. Owensboro, Henderson, and Hopkinsville.

4. The alcoholic coordinator in the Bowling Green Mental Health Center.

5. The educational evaluator in our rehabilitation unit.

Lastly, information was gathered from the *Dictionary of Occupational Titles (D.O.T.)*.

Step 3

In preparing for subsequent interviews the following guidelines were used.

What is the nature of the vocation the client selected? (Duties, advantages, disadvantages, and present outlook.) Social work is a service profession which works for and with people. A social worker performs social service functions in a public or voluntary (private) social welfare agency, organization, or department. Workers help people who have individual or family problems which interfere with healthful and useful living. They arrange for counseling services, job guidance, money grants, medical care, or other types of aid. Some social workers conduct leisure-time programs and informal educational activities to help people improve their social relationships. Other workers are engaged by communities to help plan and develop health, welfare, and recreation services on a broad scale for a neighborhood or larger area.

A caseworker may arrange for financial assistance, homemaking services, vocational guidance for job placement or improvement, faster family or institutional care, and health services. Through interviews with their clients, caseworkers try to modify feelings, attitudes, and behavior which are detrimental to normal adjustment and development. More specifically, psychiatric social workers who are employed in mental hospitals and mental health clinics assist patients in their return to the community. These workers inform the families as to the nature of mental illness, encourage the patients to use the various kinds of help available, and guide patients in their social adjustments to their homes and communities.

The working conditions of most social workers are quite good. Usually, the centers of operation are offices provided by the agency for whom they work. Most offices are comfortable and are equipped with the essentials necessary for efficiency. Records must be maintained of all home visits, interviews, and assistance provided.

Reports must be made to supervisors, and all correspondence must be noted, written, or dictated. Much of a worker's time is spent in the field; visiting clients, leading group activities, speaking before civic groups, and consulting other professional people. At times, it may be necessary to serve clients during evening hours, weekends, or even holidays. The predominant scheduled work week is 35 to 40 hours. Those who work evenings or on weekends usually receive compensatory time off.

Presently, there are over 125,000 employed social workers in this county. Since a large percentage of these are women, there is considerable turnover because many leave for marriage or to care for families. In addition, new opportunities become available each year due to expanding present programs, the development of new projects, and the expanding population. In such a career field hundreds retire and leave for other jobs each year. All these conditions result in an acute need for many new social workers. The Bureau of Labor Statistics estimates as many as 15,000 new social workers will be needed *annually* up to 1975.

During subsequent interviews with the client the above vocational information shall be discussed by means of these key questions:

1. You, Mr. Doe, have been an alcoholic. Presently, you feel that you can maintain your sobriety, but as the stress mounts in working with other alcoholics and their families how do you know you won't break? What would you do being a professional man in the above situation?

2. Even social workers socialize together and with friends. How would you handle the office parties and conventions?

3. The duties of a social worker require a tremendous amount of both mental and physical energy and vitality. How could you prove to your prospective supervisor that you have the energy needed? What concrete procedures could you identify in convincing him?

4. Mr. Doe, can you present examples as to how you have separated your personal problems from those of other people you have worked with? (For example, in being a coach, teacher, principal, captain, or athletic director).

5. Lastly, Mr. Doe, the success rate in working with alcoholics is small and terribly frustrating. Let us discuss some of these frustrations and disadvantages.

What education is necessary? How much? What kind? What would it cost? Where can it be obtained? Are any special licenses, examinations, and certificates necessary? Social work education is virtually the same for all types of professional social work. Full professional status requires the completion of a two-year program of graduate study in an accredited school of social work. The National Association of Social Workers (NASW) has established requirements for certification of professional social workers. To be eligible, social workers must have two years of paid employment in social work and two years membership in NASW (open only to graduates of accredited schools of social work). Those found qualified are identified as members of Academy of Certified Social Workers (ACSW). For admission to a graduate school of social work, a student must have a bachelor's degree, perferably with a background in liberal arts. (Undergraduate work should include courses in economics, history, political science, psychology, sociology, social anthropology, biology, and statistics. Courses in journalism and public speaking may be helpful to social workers in interviewing, writing reports and case histories, and participating in conferences. Graduation from a graduate school of social work is required for employment in voluntary family and children's agencies, in social group work, community organization work, research, and many administrative positions. For teaching positions, a master's degree in social work is required, but a doctorate is preferred. In research work, training in social science research methods is required in addition to social work education and experience. Most entrance jobs in public assistance and public child welfare agencies require a bachelor's degree as a minimum. In all states, beginners must pass a written examination in social work for work with a government agency. Total cost figures in Kentucky universities run anywhere from $740 per semester to $1800 per semester.

The above information will be discussed with Mr. John Doe by means of the following questions:

1. Mr. Doe, your graduation from the university took place approximately thirty years ago. We have discussed the necessary qualifications. How exactly do you measure up? What courses have you had that would enable you to counsel effectively with your clients?

2. As you can see, a bachelor's degree is a minimum. Can you picture yourself in today's graduate program? Why or why not?

3. Schooling costs have risen sharply. What funds do you have available to secure a master's degree in social work?

4. Earlier we discussed the fact that you took a qualifying examination eighteen months ago. Why did you not follow through? Why have you changed your mind now?

5. Mr. Doe, how do you feel your age (53) will affect your schooling and future in social work?

What qualifications should the individual have? (Mental ability, personality, talents and special abilities, union sponsorship, age, sex, height, and physical requirements.)

SPECIAL KNOWLEDGES AND ABILITIES. Every social worker must have a basic knowledge of supervisory principles, methods, and functions. He must have a working knowledge of the philosophy, history, and development of social welfare programs as well as a knowledge of the operation of state and local government. A general knowledge must be held regarding the programs of community agencies and of social programs as well as a knowledge of the principles and methods of social work and their application to mental health and mental retardation. A social worker must also be aware of human behavior patterns and the dynamics of group and interpersonal relations and social interaction. Social problems such as family disorganization, discrimination, disability, poverty, unemployment, and aging, and their effect on the individual must be known to the worker at all times. He must demonstrate his knowledge daily of living conditions, values, and behaviors of the ethnic and subcultural groups served by his facility. Lastly, each worker must show ability to speak and write clearly and effectively; to establish and maintain working relationships; and to lead, exercise authority, and provide supervision.

PERSONAL CHARACTERISTICS. As a social worker, the person must respect individual differences, show adaptability, and be physically and emotionally stable. He must have a keen interest in people and their problems, respect for the dignity and worth of the individual, and the ability and desire to get along with all kinds of people. Tolerance, flexibility, and a better than average intellectual ability also are valuable assets.

The above qualifications shall be presented to Mr. Doe in the following manner:

1. Mr. Doe, in considering a career as a social worker what personal characteristics and special knowledges and abilities do you think are absolutely necessary?

2. How would you rate yourself in relation to the qualifications you have just presented?

3. At this point the counselor will say, "I disagree with you, Mr. Doe." Watch for reaction; i.e. change in behavior pattern, eye contact, any stress or flow of conversation.

4. Evaluate Mr. Doe's response in regard to verbalizations, change of inflection pattern, mood swings.

Compensation expected (pay scale, opportunity for advancement, possibility for transferring to other vocations, and civil service jobs). Earnings of social workers employed full time in direct service positions such as casework vary by geographical location and type of employing organization. Both the Family Service Association of America and the National Association of Social Workers recommend a beginning salary of $7,000 to $7,500 for social workers with a master's degree and no previous experience. Actual salaries for this group are several hundred dollars less than this recommended figure. A Social Worker I (B.A. only and no experience) now begins in the south with a salary of approximately $6,050.

Opportunities for advancement are limited for those persons without a graduate education. For those with graduate training, opportunities for promotion to supervisory jobs are better, particularly for those workers who are willing to move from one job location to another. Promotion opportunities are good for both men and women, but men are more often found in top administrative positions.

Nearly 60 percent of the approximately 125,000 social workers are employed by state, county, or municipal government agencies. About 3 percent were in federal government organizations. However, recent federal emphasis on social work activities is increasing the demand for qualified workers. These state, county, and federal workers are employed in public assistance, child welfare, and various other welfare programs. The remaining social work-ers are employed primarily by voluntary (private) agencies, which are supported by contributions, by endowments, and occasionally by fees paid by the people served.

Transfer is always good.

The above information shall simply be relayed to Mr. Doe. Any comments will be welcomed.

How can one enter the field? (Where to apply; apprentice-ship necessary; and where to obtain more information.) There are several ways that interested parties may participate in social work activities. Volunteer work with the YMCA, YWCA, Red Cross, and other social agencies would prove an excellent means of measuring one's interest. Part-time or full-time paid positions often are available in counseling and in clerical work in a so-cial agency office. Aspirants to this career field should also talk with social workers in their communities about their work and visit schools of social work. Applications and interviews should be made in the following manner:

1. The applicant may present his applications and hold his initial interview with the supervisor in the work locale in which he is interested.

2. The applicant may apply directly through the department of personnel in the state capitol and obtain an interview with the department director.

3. Usually before the interview (s) is scheduled the applicant must take an examination and pass. His name is then placed on a register (he must rank among the top three) .

This information will be explained to the client in full. Then it will be arranged for Mr. Doe to apply through the department of personnel and take the qualifying examination. Interviews will be scheduled with the mental health centers in Bowling Green, Kentucky; Hopkinsville, Kentucky; and Owensboro, Kentucky. A final interview will be scheduled with the department director.

The following are sources of further information:

1. Social Welfare as a Career
   National Social Welfare Assembly
   345 East 46th Street
   New York, New York

   2. Fields of Social Work
      National Commission for Social Work Careers
      345 East 46th Street
      New York, New York
   3. Kent School of Social Work
      University of Louisville
      Louisville, Kentucky 40208
   4. Louisville and Western Kentucky Chapter
      National Association of Social Workers
      Kent School of Social Work
      University of Louisville
      Louisville, Kentucky 40208
   5. American Association of Psychiatric Social Workers
      1860 Broadway
      New York, New York 10023
   6. Council on Social Work Education
      345 East 46th Street
      New York, New York 10017
   7. Kentucky Mental Health Manpower Commission
      7320 LaGrange Road
      Louisville, Kentucky 40222

What are the possibilities of expansion? More and more the social service department is moving into school programs. More mental health centers are being planned and built. More workers are needed to help the alcoholics; thus, several alcoholic coordinators are being hired. Rehabilitation centers are being planned now. Upon completion a large number of social workers will be needed as well as counselors. Movement is toward working with and in the penal institutions and other correctional facilities. Recreation programs are expanding in both the public and institutional programs. Again, workers will be needed.

The counselor will relay the information and await discussion.

What specific training can you get for the job? If a social worker does not have an undergraduate degree in social work, he should participate in an orientation and on-the-job social work training program to acquaint him with and prepare him for the responsibilities of this position. This position should be supervised by a social worker in a more advanced social work classification at the discretion of the director of social work.

The two years of graduate work consists of intensive concentration in personality growth and development, social problems of both the individual and groups, abnormal behavior, supervision, consultation, and research methods. In addition, the social worker has extended training in interviewing techniques, as well as highly focused instruction in developing and making use of the therapeutic relationship with the individual and groups. An important part of the social worker's training is the field work experience during which he is gaining actual practice, thereby sharpening and developing his skills in working with people.

The above information shall be conveyed by means of open discussion.

Questions:

1. How do you feel about on-the-job training and constant supervision?

2. Are you prepared to take instruction from a younger worker?

Step 4

Both the client and counselor benefited from the exercise in that both became more aware of the detailed qualifications needed. Mr. John Doe realizes that preparation for this career will be detailed and prolonged. He realizes that it won't be a "snap" to really develop into a good social worker. He also realizes that his education meets only the bare minimum and that educationally he has a long way to go. The counselor also realizes that to acquire such a position Mr. Doe will have to prove his sobriety to his supervisor. The task surely will not be an easy one; Mr. Doe has been demotivated but yet he remains constant in goal. He realizes his limitations more clearly but has retained the desire to succeed.

Exercise 24

THE INVOLVEMENT OF REHABILITATION WORKERS IN THE COMPREHENSIVE REHABILITATION FACILITY

RATIONALE

Functioning within a rehabilitation center often creates situations unlike those existing within a general field office. As a rehabilitation counselor or work evaluator, you are required to gather information in a slightly different manner than that usually obtained by other vocational rehabilitation workers. It is imperative that you have all the appropriate diagnostic information on your client. This is either provided by the field counselor prior to admitting his client to the center or gathered by the center counselor and/or evaluator after the client has arrived at the facility.

ASSIGNMENT

Follow up a former client to determine the accuracy of prediction. With the aid of your training supervisor, select an appropriate case which is representative of the clients coming to you for service (s) .

    A. Describe the evaluation process used in your facility. Include the following in your report:
        1. Type of tests given, scores, interpretation.
        2. Medical evaluation.
        3. Work tryouts administered.
        4. Counseling.

    B. Describe the training given to this client. Include the following:
        1. The chosen objective; why this objective was chosen.
        2. Problems encountered (as predicted) .

240

    3. Identifiable skills (as predicted).
    4. Rate of progress.
    5. Grades.
C. Placement. Include the following:
    1. Description of job.
    2. Suitability of job to client's needs; suitability of client to job demands.
    3. Client satisfaction. Employer satisfaction.
    4. Length of time on job in which he was trained.
D. Counselor's or work evaluator's recommendation for future programs based on the information derived in this case.

STUDENT WORK: SAMPLE 1

Client X is a 20-year-old male from a small town; he has nocturnal seizures and a speech defect. The father is a retired miner and the mother a homemaker; there are eight siblings ranging in age from 17 to 35.

Part A: The Evaluation Process

1. TYPES OF TESTS GIVEN, SCORES, INTERPRETATION. The Wechsler Adult Intelligence Scale revealed a Verbal IQ of 86, a Performance of 78 and a Full Scale of 81; the Wide Range Achievement Test (WRAT) indicated a reading score of 2.6, spelling of 3.3, and arithmetic of 7.7; on the Nelson Reading Test, a measure of silent reading comprehension, the client scored a total of 4.4; on the Peabody Picture Vocabulary Test, an IQ of 83 was determined; the Bender Gestalt Drawings by this man were below average. Functioning in the dull normal classification is suggested by the test results indicated above. There is no significant difference indicated between verbal and performance spheres. The word recognition score on the WRAT, falling at the mid-second grade level, may not be a valid appraisal of his ability in this area due to his speech defect.

2. MEDICAL EVALUATION. The physician found this client to have been cyanotic at birth with residual speech defect and seizure disorder. His last seizure was in June 1968 (two and a half years prior to the writing of this report). The seizures always are nocturnal and he never has injured himself. He is on

medications of Dilantin ® and phenobarbital, which offer him good seizure control; therefore, seizure precautions were not indicated. His speech clinician recommended speech therapy to improve articulatory skills.

3. WORK TRYOUTS ADMINISTERED. After the screening processes of psychological testing and medical evaluation, a discussion of vocational considerations were perused; the client indicated a primary interest in drafting. With his low scores in both scholastic and performance areas, it was not felt by the evaluator that this was realistic to attempt (the client was counseled regarding this by the evaluator and the counselor assigned to the facility). In a work sample laboratory the client was administered tryouts in watch repair, general mechanics, and food service. Upholstering and health and domestic related occupations tryouts were suggested but rejected by the client. He was recommended by the evaluators for a trial enrollment in general mechanics or for enrollment in the lower level food service training. In the watch repair tryout he did not remember too well how the watch parts fit together but learned readily when shown. Additionally, his hands shook badly, thereby causing a problem working with delicate mechanisms. With this in mind he was not recommended for this training.

4. COUNSELING. Counseling during his evaluation involved initial orientation, advice regarding personal hygiene, demotivation concerning unrealistic tryout areas, and final discussion of vocational possibilities. There was a coordination of effort by both the evaluation team and the vocational rehabilitation counselor responsible for the client's welfare.

Part B: Training

1. THE CHOSEN OBJECTIVE: WHY THIS OBJECTIVE WAS CHOSEN. The client was enrolled in training as a cook and baker's helper on the fifth of January. This was justified by the results of the evaluation and the client's interest and willingness to relocate in a metropolitan area where jobs would be more available. He would not have to communicate directly with the public in this trade; therefore, the speech problem would interfere only

minimally; however, speech therapy was an adjunct to his training.

2. PROBLEMS ENCOUNTERED (AS PREDICTED). There were no severe problems; the client showed interest and initiative and was a conscientious worker, according to his instructor. While in training he needed and received clothing, orthopedic shoes, medications, glasses, and dental work. His overall intelligibility improved somewhat, but it was determined by the speech clinician that he should not be placed in a situation where continuous verbal communication was required.

3. IDENTIFIABLE SKILLS (AS PREDICTED). During evaluation, the client accepted authority rather well, seemed emotionally stable, and exhibited good work quality and habits. These qualities carried over into training and contributed greatly to his success.

4. RATE OF PROGRESS. He remained on schedule in spite of the fact that he was not considered a fast worker. This was felt to be due to his good initiative, application, and motivation.

5. GRADES. His first progress report indicated ratings of *good* on grooming and reliability, and ratings of *fair* in all other areas. At the time of graduation, his final report revealed *fair* in speed and handling of equipment and a *good* in all other areas.

Part C: Placement

1. DESCRIPTION OF JOB. The client was hired as a baker's helper at $1.75 per hour for a catering service at a small university.

2. SUITABILITY OF JOB TO CLIENT'S NEEDS; SUITABILITY OF CLIENT TO JOB'S DEMANDS. The job obtained was consistent with the client's evaluation and recommendations and subsequent training results. His performance on the job has borne out the appropriateness of the job choice.

3. CLIENT AND EMPLOYER SATISFACTION. Both client and employer state that each is pleased with the other's performance in relation to the job situation. Client's employer feels that adequate vocational preparation has enabled the young man to adapt to the world of work with no apparent difficulty.

4. LENGTH OF TIME ON THE JOB IN WHICH HE WAS TRAINED.

Client has been employed in this job for two months. Thus far client has progressed beyond the predicted expectations of the evaluation team.

Part D: Recommendations for Future Programs

1. A client with multiple disabilities obviously is best evaluated and trained in a comprehensive rehabilitation facility if such is available.

2. Psychological and medical evaluation, work tryouts, and counseling all are essential as they contribute toward matching the client's abilities to an appropriate job objective, thereby eliminating the guesswork from choosing a vocation.

3. The medical evaluation in this case was most important as it indicated that the seizures need not be considered as contraindicating food service training.

4. Speech evaluation and subsequent therapy also added to the client's readiness for the particular job. An awareness of the speech disability prevented the psychologist from assuming a low word recognition score as indicated on his low reading ability.

The following Evaluation Laboratory Report has been included as an example of a form utilized by our comprehensive rehabilitation center. This report is placed in the client's folder so that the evaluator can make appropriate comments as he progresses through the evaluation process. Upon completion of this process, the material gleaned on this report is transferred to the client's counselor so that training plans can be formulated.

STATE COMPREHENSIVE REHABILITATION CENTER
EVALUATION LABORATORY REPORT

Name   Date

Summary of evaluation in:

PERSONAL   (appearance, grooming, personal habits, manners,
      etc.)

INTERPERSONAL (peer relations, acceptance of authority, awareness of environment, etc.)

EMOTIONAL (stability, dependency, potential for independence, attitudes, etc.)

VOCATIONAL CONSIDERATIONS (work quality, habits, quantity, tolerance; judgment, comprehension of directions; motivation; safety consciousness; physical condition, etc.)

RECOMMENDATIONS (acceptance for training, special abilities, special considerations for training or work environment, etc.)

Evaluator

Exercise 25

THE DEVELOPMENT OF A WORK SAMPLE

RATIONALE

The role of a work evaluator is vital if the rehabilitation process is to benefit a client. One of the most important aspects of the evaluator's job is the development of work samples.

ASSIGNMENT

Develop and describe a work sample which you have not used before (you may wish to refer to the *Journal of Rehabilitation,* January-February 1970, Vol. 36, No. 1; "Basic Assumptions Underlying Work Sample Theory" by Walter A. Pruett).

A. State why a work sample is needed by you and your facility.

B. Record an analysis of the job to which the sample is related.

C. Set up a procedure for administering the sample.
   1. Plan for the presentation of the task (use a standardized method and at the same time maintain flexibility in relation to the client's handicap).
   2. Comment on the client's skill(s) in relation to his ability to function in this area; his work personality; his reactions relative to supervision.
   3. Describe reporting techniques employed by you and the evaluation staff in your facility.

D. Plan for follow-up and discuss your approach to evaluate this work sample's predictive value.

STUDENT WORK: SAMPLE 1

Part A

Within the comprehensive rehabilitation center where I work, the vocational evaluation team plays a major role in the provision of services to handicapped clients. Probably one of the most important functions in which our unit is involved is the development of work samples.

Our facility has approximately 500 clients enrolled on any given day and they are involved in 35 different vocational trade courses. These range in difficulty from low-level food service training to the more complex business education curricula. Since 38 percent of our total population (fiscal year 1969-70) is classified mentally or functionally retarded, trades with a favorable occupational outlook are needed, especially those requiring less than a high school education.

Many clients who do not have high enough IQ's and an educational background commensurate to succeed in business training areas such as accounting or bookkeeping have expressed interest in the "family" of jobs related to business. For these reasons, the training department of this facility added stockroom clerk training to its curricula. This training involves roughly one quarter of business education courses integrated with complementary courses in filing and typing. Actual practice in a storeroom situation comprises almost one-half of the client's time since it has been determined that such an experience can enhance his employability in the labor market upon the termination of training.

The addition of this training area necessitated that a work sample be set up in the evaluation laboratory of our comprehensive rehabilitation facility for use in giving tryouts for this training.

Part B

An analysis of the job to which the sample is related has been derived by examining the following listing in the *D.O.T.*:*

Stock Clerk (clerical) 223.387. Receives, stores, and issues equipment, material, supplies, merchandise, foodstuffs, or tools, and compiles stock records in stock room, warehouse, or storage yard. Counts, sorts, or weighs incoming articles to verify receipt of items on requisition or invoices. Examines stock to verify conformance to specifications.

Dictionary of Occupational Titles. Vol. 1, *Definition of Titles,* third edition. U.S. Dept. of Labor, Washington, D.C., 1965.

Stores articles in bins, on floor, or on shelves, according to identifying information, such as style, size or type of material. Fills orders or issues supplies from stock. Prepares periodic, special, or perpetual inventory of stock. Requisitions articles to fill incoming orders. Compiles reports of use of stock handling equipment, adjustments of inventory counts and stock records, spoilage of or damage to stock, location of changes, and refusal of shipments. May mark identifying codes, figures, or letters on articles. May distribute stock among production workers, keeping records of material issued. May make adjustments or repairs to articles carried in stock. May determine methods of storage, identification, and stock location, considering temperature, humidity, height and weight limits, turnover, full loading capacities, and required space. May cut stock to size to fill order.

According to the *1966 Supplement to the Dictionary of Occupational Titles,* third edition, a stock clerk could perform tasks requiring light to heavy lifting with some stooping, kneeling, crouching, and/or crawling as well as reaching, handling, fingering, and/or feeling.

Part C

1. A plan for the presentation of the task is as follows:
   A. The Minnesota Clerical Test is administered according to standardized directions. This reveals abilities in checking names, addresses, and prices.
   B. Fifty letters are given to the client to be filed in an alphabetical file according to the correspondent's name.
   C. Sample merchandise is to be stocked on shelves according to directions given orally and/or in writing by the evaluator.
   D. A sample purchase order is to be filled out, extended, and totaled using costs found in the inventory file.

Approximately 75 percent of each of the above steps in this evaluation training area should be accomplished correctly for probable success to be predicted before the client can be considered a candidate for the full course in stockroom clerk training. As indicated below, prescription courses can be somewhat tailored to individual needs if placement is assured in the client's home area.

2. Concerning the client's skills in relation to his ability to

function in this training area, his work personality, and his attitude toward supervision, one must examine these components if a successful outcome is anticipated.

To complete the full course in stockroom clerk, the client should be able to lift and to climb a ladder. The client should have been screened thoroughly by psychological tests with a measured educational level of approximately seventh to ninth grade (for an adult this would correspond to the dull normal to average intelligence range) .

He must have revealed potential for developing acceptable habits of punctuality, honesty, neatness, and industriousness as well as for being able to work harmoniously with others. Prescription courses can be arranged for wheelchair clients to accomplish only the inventory portion of the training or for epileptic clients who cannot climb a ladder to accomplish only the portion of stocking on the lower shelves as well as the inventory work. On the lower academic levels the client could stock shelves without accomplishing the inventory work other than simply being able to locate the items on the proper shelf.

3. Reporting is accomplished by brief narratives from each staff member, evaluating the client's potential for the training. The narrative report is considered superior to the checklist method as it is less ambiguous. Regarding the reporting of the client's work sample accomplishment, the evaluator notes personal and interpersonal characteristics, emotional stability, and vocational considerations; he then determines whether or not to recommend the client for the particular training in which he has been evaluated.

Part D

The evaluator using this work sample is required to keep a record of all clients evaluated, noting client potential and recommendations for job success. The home counselor (located in the field) ultimately responsible for training and placement is asked to report back to the evaluator on a designated form as to the client's success or failure within the work setting. Appropriate statistics are then compiled to aid in determining success in evaluation.

Remembering the important role that evaluation can play in the total rehabilitation process, it is imperative the evaluator as well as the counselor utilize every available resource within the comprehensive center in order to maximize or insure client success.

Exercise 26

THE REHABILITATION WORKER'S INVOLVEMENT WITH THE VISUALLY HANDICAPPED

RATIONALE

Working with the visually handicapped often poses problems different from the problems of working with other disability groups. As a professional person providing services to this population, one must be aware of specific needs not considered when working with sighted individuals.

ASSIGNMENT

A. List several elements of caseload management necessary when working with the visually handicapped that may be different from the management of sighted cases. Substantiate your answer with discussion and examples.

B. Using an active case, evaluate the following:

   1. Counselor's understanding of visual problems as evidenced by available client progress reports used in relation to the ophthalmologist's report.

   2. Need for and use of consultation with an ophthalmologist.

   3. Quality of the medical report(s) and the counselor's concern with secondary physical and/or mental disabilities.

   4. Relationship of visual and other physical limitations to employment objectives.

STUDENT WORK: SAMPLE 1

Part A

Work with the visually handicapped poses a problem of an inherent and unique nature distinctively different from the oper-

251

ational procedures of the general rehabilitation agency. This is not to insinuate in any manner that work with general rehabilitation agencies does not involve operational procedures and problems which are similar to those of the agencies for the visually handicapped, especially if the general rehabilitation counselor is working with special categories of clients such as the mentally retarded, the quadriplegic or paraplegic, psychiatric patients, and correctional inmates. The extreme nature of these problems necessitates case management which is somewhat different from the case management incurred in lesser cases of disability. Since the great majority of states either have separate agencies for the visually handicapped or specialized divisions within departments of vocational rehabilitation for the visually handicapped, it may be assumed there is a general recognition that work with the visually handicapped is substantially different from work involving other types of disabilities.

This recognition of the visually handicapped as a separate entity is not necessarily an emotional recognition, although there is some basis for belief that blindness and visual impairment is heavily laden with emotion, but is a recognition based on cognitive perceptions of the differing needs of the blind and visually handicapped. Therefore, to meet these needs, the case management within an agency for the visually handicapped must reflect these contextual particularities inherent in the visually handicapped.

The initial and immediately most obvious difference is the documentation required during the referral process prior to the acceptance of the client as an active case. The files of the general rehabilitation agency must include only the general medical examination, with the occasional inclusion of a special examination where deemed desirable or upon the recommendation of the examining or consulting physicians. During the referral process, it is extremely important for the counselor to obtain as complete a diagnostic work-up of the client as is feasible and/or possible. The diagnostic material must include a general medical examination, an optical examination, often an otological or auditory examination, and preferably a psychological examination and a work evaluation. The greater the visual impairment of the client, the greater the need for these latter two diagnostic examinations. There is some question concerning the relevancy of psychological examinations in regards to the visually handicapped. At this time there are no psychological examinations for the visually handicapped which have a sufficient population sampling to adequately supply statistics concerning validity and reliability of the tests. However, even though it is difficult to obtain a valid intelligence quotient for the visually handicapped individual, it is still extremely important that some type of psychiatric or psychological interview be conducted to ascertain the client's at-titudnal set and to obtain some prognosis concerning the client's success during the rehabilitation process. Work evaluation is often necessary and desirable in order to diagnose the client's work habits, his work skills, his ability or inability to socially interact with his co-workers, his frustration level, and his work attitudes. The work evaluation is of paramount importance if the client has no work history or if his visual limitations have necessitated the cessation of previous work skills.

This counselor recalls a case of one client, Phillip, who had no previous work history at the time his vision was lost. To further complicate matters, at the time Phillip lost his vision he also suffered severe brain damage which caused organic mental retardation. As the client had no known work skills from which to work, the counselor considered it desirable to have the client attend a two-week work evaluation at the Charlottesville work-shop. During the time the client was in the Charlottesville workshop, a psychological examination was also conducted to determine the client's mental capabilities and his attitudinal set. During the course of both evaluations, it was learned that Phillip was a definitely mentally retarded boy, but cooperative, willing to learn, capable of learning simple tasks, polite and receptive, socially naive, and somewhat shy and withdrawn. Furthermore, the work evaluation showed that Phillip had the ability and interest to do small craft work, such as making small wood articles not requiring great skill or precision. Without the psychological and work evaluation, the counselor would have had hardly more than intuition with which to work. Now, however, the counselor does have some basis from which to operate and is more knowledgeable of the total person or the client. In this particular case, even with the assistance of the psychological examination and the work evaluation, it has still been extremely difficult to place this client in gainful employment. The problem lies not with Phillip, but with the overprotective attitude of Phillip's parents.

The medical reports are used by an agency for the visually handicapped as diagnostic tools for determining both the eligibility of the applicant and the physical capabilities and/or the limitations of the client as regards the rehabilitation process. The ophthalmological examination is used in determining the disability and vocational handicap of the client. To be considered eligible for services from the Virginia Commission for the Visually Handicapped, a person must meet one of four criteria: (1) a visual acuity of 20/200 in the better eye with best correction, or his visual field must subtend an angle of no greater than 20 degrees, (2) a visual acuity of 20/100 in the better eye with best correction and a deteriorating condition, (3) a visual acuity of 20/70 in the better eye with best correction and an emotional inability to adjust to the loss of vision, or (4) any condition which requires immediate surgery as recommended by the examining ophthalmologist. If the applicant meets one of the above four criteria, he is considered to be disabled. This disability determination is made by the examining physician; however, the handicap to employment determination is made by the counselor. The third selection criteria, also made by the counselor, is the determination of a reasonable expectation that vocational rehabilitation services will eventually lead to gainful activity. If one of the four disability determinations is indicated by the examining ophthalmologist and the other two selection criteria are determined by the counselor, the applicant is then accepted in 02 status or in 04 or 06 status.

Statuses 04 and 06 provide for an extended evaluation of the client by the counselor and other personnel. Status 04 provides for a six-month extended evaluation, and 06 status provides for an eighteen-month extended evaluation. The 04 status can be and is used by the general rehabilitation counselor for those individuals who need further evaluation but are not so seriously disabled as to necessitate an eighteen-month extended evaluation. The eighteen-month extended evaluation is reserved exclusively for those individuals who are so severely handicapped as to necessitate a lengthy period of extended evaluation to determine the client's limitations, capabilities, medical prognosis, psychological stability, adjustment potential, and vocational capacity. The extended evaluation is a useful and often utilized tool of agencies for the visually handicapped. Any service provided for a client on active status can be provided for a client in 06 status with the exception of vocational training. Therefore, a client suffering from severe psychological or emotional disorders pertaining to his visual limitation may be placed in status 06 to determine what course of action is necessary and advisable to effect rehabilitation of the client. After diagnostic services have been rendered and the eligibility determination has been made by the counselor, the client is then placed in active status. In a process of writing the vocational rehabilitation plan, the counselor must take into consideration the vocational objective and the services necessary for attainment of his objective. Services necessary for rehabilitation of the client may include counseling and guidance, adjustment training, pre-vocational or vocational training, physical restoration, maintenance, transportation, books and materials, goods and equipment, placement and follow-up, and other more specialized services depending upon the nature of the vocational objective. The extent and nature of the services provided during the rehabilitation process depend upon the relationship of the client and the nature of the vocational objective itself. In some cases, guidance and counseling is both an integral and necessary part of the rehabilitation process, especially in cases where adjustment to the handicap is a problem in the client's attainment of the vocational objective. Visual impairment or total loss of vision often results in the necessity for the client to alter or change his life style in some manner or form. If the client is unable to alter his life style so as to meet his new needs, then various adjustment problems are experienced. However, adjustment problems are not limited to the client alone. The family of the client often experiences the same problems of adjustment as the client. Members of the client's family are often unaware of what their role in this new situation should be. Many family members become overprotective of the client, encouraging dependency and non-active behavior. It is important, therefore, that the members of the family be included in the counseling process as well as the client. In many respects, the counseling process is similar to the educative process in that the client and the clients's family must learn new techniques for accomplishing old goals. Often the counseling process is one of redefinition of roles for the client and his family members. The case of Phillip, already mentioned, has involved extensive amounts of counseling with the client and with the parents. The success of this particular case rests almost entirely with the attitudes of the parents. Due to Phillip's double handicap, mental retardation and blindness, the parents have become extremely overprotective and rather than to encourage independence of the client have provided a nurturant atmosphere of almost total dependence. In Phillip's case, lengthy counseling sessions with the parents will be necessary before the rehabilitation of the client can become a reality.

Another service provided during the rehabilitation process is physical restoration. However, in relatively few cases can physical restoration be effected with 100 percent accuracy in cases of visual impairment. There are, of course, exceptions to this. Cataracts, refracted errors, corneal scarring, many traumatic conditions, and many infections of the eye can be treated so as to restore full or almost full use of vision. However, degenerative cases such as optic atrophy, macular or retinal degeneration, glaucoma, retinitis pigmentosa, and diabetic retinopathy, while conducive to arrest, are not subject to full restoration. Often the client, while noticing the loss of visual acuity or a progressive restriction of the visual field, assumes there is no great cause for alarm and will procrastinate in having an eye examination conducted with the thought that there is no great urgency involved. The result of this procrastination often leads to severe visual loss which is not capable of being fully restored. As a result, many cases referred to a counselor are of an emergency nature by the time the counselor first contacts the client. Just as procrastination of the client can lead to further visual loss or total blindness, procrastination on the part of the counselor in scheduling physical restoration can have the same tragic results. This counselor has been involved in two cases within the past three months which required immediate emergency surgery. In both cases, the ophthalmological examination required during the referral process lead to the discovery of severe funduscopic ailments which would have resulted in retinal detachment and total loss of vision. In both cases, emergency surgery was recommended and conducted with favorable postoperative prognosis.

Transportation can and does often prove to be a problem when working with the visually handicapped. Obviously, if the client is visually handicapped to the extent that services can be provided from the Virginia Commission for the Visually Handicapped, he is also too handicapped to operate a vehicle. Since the client is not capable of driving an automobile, he must rely on public transportation or on transportation provided by friends and relatives. In urban areas, the transportation problem is minimized by a mass transit systems; however, in rural areas it is magnified in relation to the distances which must be traveled and the lack of public transportation. It is not unusual for transportation of the client to an examining physician or to the hospital to become a problem of major proportions. One manner in which this problem can be alleviated to some degree is for the client to have a third party drive him to his destination and the third party will be reimbursed for his mileage at the extent of nine cents per mile. However, in the scheduling of any services the counselor must always take into consideration the transportation available and the client's ability to utilize that transportation which is available.

If training is required as a part of the rehabilitation plan, the counselor must consider the types of facilities available for training the visually handicapped. Some states do not have comprehensive rehabilitation centers for the blind and training must be sought outside the state. Since the adjustment problems of the blind are often unique, it is desirable to send the client to a center which is geared toward the blind and the visually handicapped. Training of the visually handicapped can be one or more of three basic types: (1) Adjustment Training, (2) Pre-vocational Training, and (3) Vocational Training. Often all three types of training are utilized during the rehabilitation process in a sequence from adjustment training to vocational training. In cases where the client is experiencing difficulty in adjusting to his loss of sight and visual limitations, it is desirable to have the client attend an adjustment center for the learning of skills necessary for psychological and social adjustment of the client. If and when the client becomes emotionally and cognitively adjusted to his visual condition, it is then advisable to send the client to a facility offering pre-vocational and/or vocational training. In cases where the client still retains the use of vocational skills, the latter two types of training are usually superfluous to the rehabilitation process. Such a case involves the rehabilitation of a school principal in southwest Virginia whom we shall call Mr. K. Mr. K was suffering from diabetic retinopathy and glaucoma in the left eye. Because of this condition, Mr. K was experiencing an increasing loss of vision. Mr. K was becoming greatly concerned and alarmed over this loss of vision, as he expected that job proficiency would concomitantly be lost. Therefore, Mr. K sought help from the Commission for the Visually Handicapped for retraining in some other vocation. Mr. K's preference was to become a rehabilitation teacher or rehabilitation counselor with the commission; however, after evaluation by a Home Teaching Department supervisor, the recommendation was made that Mr. K remain in his present position and attend a period of adjustment training at a specialized facility for the visually handicapped. Mr. K agreed to this and in the summer months of 1968, he attended a two-month period of adjustment training at the Arkansas Enterprises for the Blind. While attending AEB, Mr. K underwent instructions in communicative skills, including braille, typewriting, the use of the slate and stylus, and the use of the Perkins brailler. In addition to training in communication skills, Mr. K also received instructions in recreation, shop and craft work, orientation and mobility, social skills, and activities of daily living. Mr. K's progress after the period of adjustment training had terminated was so apparent that the school board offered to retain him in his position as elementary school principal for another year. That was two years ago and Mr. K is still employed as an elementary school principal in the same school.

In the instance of Mr. K, it was obvious that pre-vocational and vocational training were totally unnecessary, as Mr. K still retained vocational skills which were useable and were in demand. It was necessary, however, for Mr. K to learn to adjust to his visual limitations and to relearn orientation to his work environment.

Severe loss of sight necessitates the need for substitution of sight; therefore, the counselor must be continually aware of the types of substitutions which particular clients require. Quite often, orientation and mobility instruction is an essential part of the rehabilitation process as are substitutions for printed matter. As in the case of Mr. K, it was necessary for him to learn braille and braille notetaking, as his occupation required daily use of both verbal and written communications. In addition to the desire to learn braille, many visually handicapped persons, as well as persons suffering from a variety of other types of handicaps, desire the use of the talking book machine. Talking book machines are now in wide use by the visually handicapped and are meant to supplement rather than to compensate for other types of communications and use by the visually handicapped. If the client has a visual impairment, but still retains useable vision, it is sometimes desirable to provide low vision aids or large printed materials; especially if the client is in vocational training or is attending an educational institution. Often, a low vision aid is all the client requires in order to read a regular size textbook. When, however, a low vision aid does not prove sufficient and large print textbooks cannot be obtained, the agency may provide reader services for the blind.

Agencies for the visually handicapped have at least one option which is not open to the general rehabilitation agency, this option being the vending stand program. The visually handicapped can be trained in the operation of vending stands and upon completion of training, the client can be placed in an operational vending stand within a government facility or some other desirable location. The only requirements for such a program are that the client be neat and presentable, have a better than average aptitude for business, possess social skills conducive to good business transactions, be willing to relocate, have no other physical limitations which would preclude standing for long periods of time, and be willing to work long hours. One such client has recently been closed from this district office in status 26. Mr. J underwent five months training in vending stand operations at the Charlottesville workshop and then completed two months additional training at an operational vending stand in northern Virginia. The initial process involved referral to the Business Opportunities for the Blind Department of the VCVH, evaluation of the client from a supervisor of that department, a scheduling of the training period, and close cooperation and communication between members of the Rehabilitation Department and the Business Opportunities for the Blind Department. Not all clients qualify for vending stand training; however, the counselor must be aware of this option when dealing with the client and be ready to refer any promising client to BOB for their evaluation.

Placement is a very real problem with the visually handicapped. Part of the problem results in the discrepancy between general public concept of blindness and the legal definition of blindness. Another problem is a lack of awareness of the general public as to what a visually handicapped or even totally blind individual can accomplish with training and experience. An even more real problem is simply the location of jobs within a given area which is suitable for blind labor. A visually handicapped individual with a good education can often learn to readjust to his present work environment, if it is one which requires skills other than the use of his hands. However, a person with a poor educational background who is accustomed to working with his hands is often no longer able to function at the same job with the same proficiency as he was prior to his loss of vision. In practically all such cases, extensive retraining is required before placement in a vocational environment can succeed. The greatest problem in placement is a simple matching of job opportunities with skills available in a client. This concern becomes greatly magnified in rural areas where employment opportunities are minimal under the best of conditions. In such cases, the counselor must make every effort to locate suitable employment for the client and to insure that the vocational training received by the client is compatable with the employment possibilities within this specified geographical location. While the general rehabilitation counselor may become actively involved in the placing of approximately 10 percent of his clients, a counselor for the visually handicapped must assume every client will require placement assistance.

Part B

NAME: Mr. H
AGE: 36
SEX: Male
RACE: Caucasian
PRIMARY DISABILITY: Congenital Nystagmus
SECONDARY DISABILITY: Macular Scar with Exotropia, O. S.
VISUAL ACUITY: O. D., 20/300; O. S., Light Perception
DATE OF REFERRAL: 1960
MEDICAL HISTORY: Mr. H has medical and ophthalmological reports in our files dating back to March 4, 1960. According to these medical reports, Mr. H suffers no systemic or metabolic diseases, but has complained of chest pains at various times. There is no evidence of angina, and the medical diagnosis was excess acidity resulting from nervousness. Mr. H's chief complaint is poor vision, and the various ophthalmological reports indicate nystagmus, left exotropia, and amblyopia, O.D., as well as macular scarring and a history of cataracts and retinal detachment. The etiology has been diagnosed as congenital toxoplasmosis, and no treatment other than corrective lenses has been advised.

PSYCHOLOGICAL REPORT: A psychological testing interview conducted in 1960 shows a man of clean and neat appearance who is alert and friendly with a pleasant smile. The results of the interview also indicate the client is probably a slow learner, but has an intelligence quotient well within normal range. Although a verbal IQ on the Wechsler was scored at 81, the examining psychologist felt the IQ score was somewhat lowered by Mr. H's lack of formal education and his inability to relax in the testing situation. Mr. H scored high normal to superior on manipulative skills and the arithmetic subtest of the WAIS. The general conclusion reached by the examining psychologist was that Mr. H functioned in most situations requiring some judgment and involving some complexity in challenge so long as his limited academic background was not a prominent factor. Another intelligence test, the Stanford-Kohs Block Design Test, administered in the summer of 1969, shows the client with an IQ of 111.

WORK HISTORY: Mr. H has no work experience other than that associated with the mines. Mr. H had worked in the mines for ten years until his visual limitations forced him to quit such activities in 1960. A one-month work evaluation conducted at the Virginia Workshop for the Blind in 1969 shows Mr. H ranking good to very good in all categories evaluated. All work attitude scores were ranked four on a four-point scale with exceptions of Enthusiasm and Interest which were ranked three; Social and Interpersonal Relationship scores were all ranked four; Learning Ability and Intellectual Performance were ranked four; Emotional Characteristics ranked four, and Physical Function and Work Performance subscores were four with the exception of Endurance which had a rank of three. The recommendations of the work evaluation were that Mr. H is ready for competitive employment, he has particular skill in the use of his hands, he learns quickly, has good judgment and a mature outlook. Mr. H could work very well under work conditions requiring accuracy and precision and the manipulation of small work materials and he also made very good use of his residual vision.

Since Mr. H's retirement from the coal mines, he has been drawing social security disability benefits in a present amount of $354 per month.

Even though this case has been known to the Commission for

the Visually Handicapped for approximately eleven years, this is the first contact which this counselor has had with this client. It apparently has been extremely difficult to obtain competitive employment for Mr. H due to the large amount of his social security disability benefits which he has been receiving for the past ten years. Mr. H has five young children and has been understandably reluctant to accept employment which will pay less than the disability benefits which he is now receiving. However, Mr. H now has been offered the opportunity to purchase a tract of land for strip mining. It is now this counselor's responsibility to determine the degree of probability of success of such a venture and to determine in what ways the Commission for the Visually Handicapped may be able to assist Mr. H in the purchase of the land and the operation of the business.

As evidenced by Mr. H's ophthalmological reports, the visual condition suffered by the client is not one which is capable of restoration. Therefore, it must be assumed that Mr. H's visual limitations are either stable or possibly deteriorating. At present, Mr. H's best correctable vision in the right eye is 20/300 and in the left eye is light perception. This indicates that Mr. H retains useable vision in his right eye, and according to the work evaluation report of 1969, Mr. H continues to use his remaining vision to its best advantage. In this counselor's estimation, Mr. H, while having enough remaining vision to supervise and coordinate the activities of a strip mining operation, would be unable to perform most of the labor required. While Mr. H may theoretically be capable of operating the heavy equipment involved in strip mining, it is this counselor's conclusion that it would be unduly dangerous and unwise for the client to attempt such an undertaking. Therefore, the client would have to hire suitable assistance for the operation of the heavy equipment. The same visual limitations also insure the necessity of the client hiring personnel to haul the coal.

Mr. H's file contains unusually voluminous and complete medical diagnostic work-up. The volume of the medical material can probably be attributed to the length of time this individual has been a client of the commission. Medical and ophthalmological reports indicate Mr. H to be a normal, healthy individual with no medical complications other than his visual limitations. The latest medical examination, dated 1969, specifically indicates there are no physical limitations to job training or employment other than visual disability.

This case has been discussed with the consulting ophthalmologist and his only recommendation was that a more complete medical evaluation be conducted to rule out any possibilities of a peptic ulcer or gall bladder disease. This examination was conducted in 1969, and no physical or medical abnormalities were found. In view of this, the consulting ophthalmologist recommended the continuance of rehabilitation efforts from the standpoint of the client's visual impairment and a minimizing of the client's other complaints.

There seem to be no medical or physical limitations which would preclude the success of the rehabilitation process of this client other than the visual limitations which have previously been discussed. Mr. H will therefore continue to be evaluated in areas regarding his management capability, his psychological maturity, and the success probability factor of the strip mining operation. If reports from representatives of the Small Business Administration regarding these factors are favorable, there is no reason this agency will not be able to assist Mr. H in this business venture.

Exercise 27

AN OPEN-ENDED EXERCISE TO DEMONSTRATE THE PROFESSIONAL WORKER'S KNOWLEDGE OF REHABILITATION

RATIONALE

As a newly employed worker you have probably thought of several areas of concern in rehabilitation which you would like to investigate further. The exercise described below should afford you the opportunity to pursue your interests in a specific area of vocational rehabilitation. This assignment has several purposes: (1) It should create an awareness that there is room for individual initiative in rehabilitation even though one has been employed for a relatively short period; (2) the formulation of personal concepts relevant to rehabilitation philosophy is a necessary component of personal and professional growth; (3) this approach furnishes the occasion to express one's self in a style indicative of a professional and, in turn, can clearly be understood by other professionals.

ASSIGNMENT

Ask yourself a question and answer this question in such a way that it is demonstrated you have a comprehensive grasp and a working knowledge of some area of vocational rehabilitation of particular interest to you. In writing this report, the title will be the question which you are asking. The body of the paper will be your solution to that question. Since this exercise might involve a great deal of your time, you may substitute this exercise in place of two other exercises; but before so doing, you *must* have this approved by your training coordinator or the faculty supervisor.

265

STUDENT WORK: SAMPLE 1

The purpose of this exercise is to demonstrate a comprehensive grasp and a working knowledge of some area of vocational rehabilitation which is of particular interest to the counselor. This is to be accomplished by asking a question and then answering it.

The question I would like to ask is, *How can the rehabilitation counselor assigned to a residential school for the blind on a part-time basis best carry out his assignment?*

This is a large and complex question which leaves much room for generalization, and almost demands it. The main reason for this question is because of one important aspect of this counselor's duties: that of working with the Virginia School for the Deaf and Blind one day of each week. This counselor has the responsibility of working with the ninety or more visually handicapped students of the school who are fourteen years of age or older. He must act as the representative of the Virginia Commission for the Visually Handicapped to the school, parents, students, and individuals and agencies associated with the school. He also must act as the representative to the commission from the school, parents, and students. In doing this he must share information with any one of fourteen field counselors throughout the state, as well as his supervisors. This type of responsibility demands flexibility in working with persons on all levels; the mentally retarded or very slow student, as well as the school administration; the parents who are overly protective of their child, as well as those parents who have no interest at all in the future of their son or daughter.

This counselor is new in the field of rehabilitation, and even newer in the field of working with a residential school for the blind. There is much to be learned, and by trial and error, and time and experience, this will be accomplished. But there are certain basic areas of responsibility in which this counselor must work, and perhaps these can be divided into five main headings: the counselor's relationship with the school, with his agency, with the parents of the students, with the students, and with individuals, groups, or agencies who can aid the counselor in his work.

The Counselor and the School

The counselor has to convince himself that his purpose for being at the school is worthwhile, and once this is done he must do the same thing for the school administration. The counselor will find that the success of his work will depend largely upon his being able to work smoothly and in cooperation with school authorities, whether they be teachers, office staff, principals, or other counselors at the school. He must realize that he is a guest of the school, and yet should not be apologetic regarding his presence there. The counselor's work should be done as professionally as possible, and yet he should not succumb to stuffiness or artificiality in his relationships.

The school will see the Virginia Commission for the Visually Handicapped through the counselor; therefore, as well as presenting a proper demeanor, the counselor also must be ready and able to answer questions regarding his agency. He must be well informed about agency policy and procedures, and if questions are asked that he cannot answer he should know where or to whom to go to find out the answer. A possible solution to this problem would be to investigate the cooperative agreement with an associate of the school.

The counselor should take the initiative in making himself known to the school, and not hesitate to meet the various teachers and let them know of his work and his interest in the students he will be working with. When conferences with the teachers can be arranged with the school, these can be very helpful in dealing with certain students, especially those having academic, behavioral, or emotional difficulties.

The Counselor and His Agency

Students at the school come from all over the state and therefore have counselors in their home area. While they are in school, which is for about nine months out of the year, they have little or no contact with their home counselors. The home counselor, with his large caseload, is not able to keep in touch with his clients who are students at the residential school, and must depend upon the counselor assigned to the school to feed information to him concerning the students. This counselor must decide what information is important enough to share with the home counselor, and also when to seek the advice or help of the home counselor.

This counselor also has the responsibility of sharing information with his supervisors concerning school policies and activities.

The Counselor and the Parents

On occasion this counselor has to meet with parents of a student. In this situation he is again the representative of the commission, and not of the school. If the parents are displeased about something at the school, the counselor must be careful not to take sides with them against the school, and yet he must listen sincerely to the problem and do all that he can to help.

The counselor may have the responsibility at times of seeking the presence of a teacher or school official in a meeting with parents, or he may also have to request the presence of the student. These activities must be coordinated with the school administration.

Sometimes the parents will express dissatisfaction with the home counselor, and again this counselor must not take sides, either with the parents or the home counselor. Often, when the situation of a home counselor's caseload is explained, and the fact that this counselor is giving information to the home counselor, the parents are more understanding and feel less that their son or daughter is being neglected.

The Counselor and the Student

Herein is the main part of the counselor's work and responsibility—with the student himself. The counselor will be confronted with a myriad of questions, problems, and comments from students who are often sincere and seeking, but who are just as often merely looking for attention or a means of escaping a class session. In this setting is where the counselor will have to determine what approach to counseling he will use; whether directive, nondirective, or eclectic. At times he will use none of these, but will fill the role of an information-giving source, answering questions concerning his agency, or speaking for the home counselor.

It almost goes without saying that the counselor must gain the confidence of the student. This is not easy, for the student will be looking often for an ally against the school, the home counselor, or his parents. When the student finds that the counselor is not going to reinforce him in his gripes, he may become hostile toward him. Sincerity and patience are the key factors in this situation. When the student discovers that the counselor is truly concerned about him, and wants to help in a constructive way, he will begin, hopefully, to trust the counselor and have confidence in him.

One problem in this area is confidentiality of information. In order for the student to trust the counselor and have confidence in him, the student must know that the counselor is not telling all that he hears to the school and to the home counselor. In order for the counselor to be effective, the student must feel free in talking with him and know that he can be completely open. On the other hand, the counselor has responsibilities to the school and to his agency. When a student shares something with the counselor which the counselor feels should be shared with the school or the home counselor, he should say so, and state why. The important criterion in this situation seems to be what course of action best will serve the student, for this is why the school exists and is why the counselor is present.

The Counselor and Others

This counselor sometimes will have to deal with persons, groups, or other agencies outside of the school or his own agency. Examples of this are welfare departments or even police departments. Various relatives of a student may seek information from the counselor or seek to give him information. The counselor may have to work in the community of the residential school seeking qualified ophthalmologists, audiologists, general practitioners, psychologists, and others to provide services to the students. The counselor may also help the student who is able and qualified to find part-time work in the area of the school. He may also go into schools and colleges in the area of the residential

school seeking volunteers to serve as readers for his visually handicapped clients.

Summary

As was stated in the beginning, the question asked left room
for many generalities. Working as a part-time counselor with a
residential school for the blind will expose a counselor to many
situations he never imagined could confront him; thence each
situation demands a response by the counselor. With certain
basic guidelines established and at his disposal, the counselor
hopefully will respond correctly a majority of the time. It is a
challenge which is unique to most field counselors.

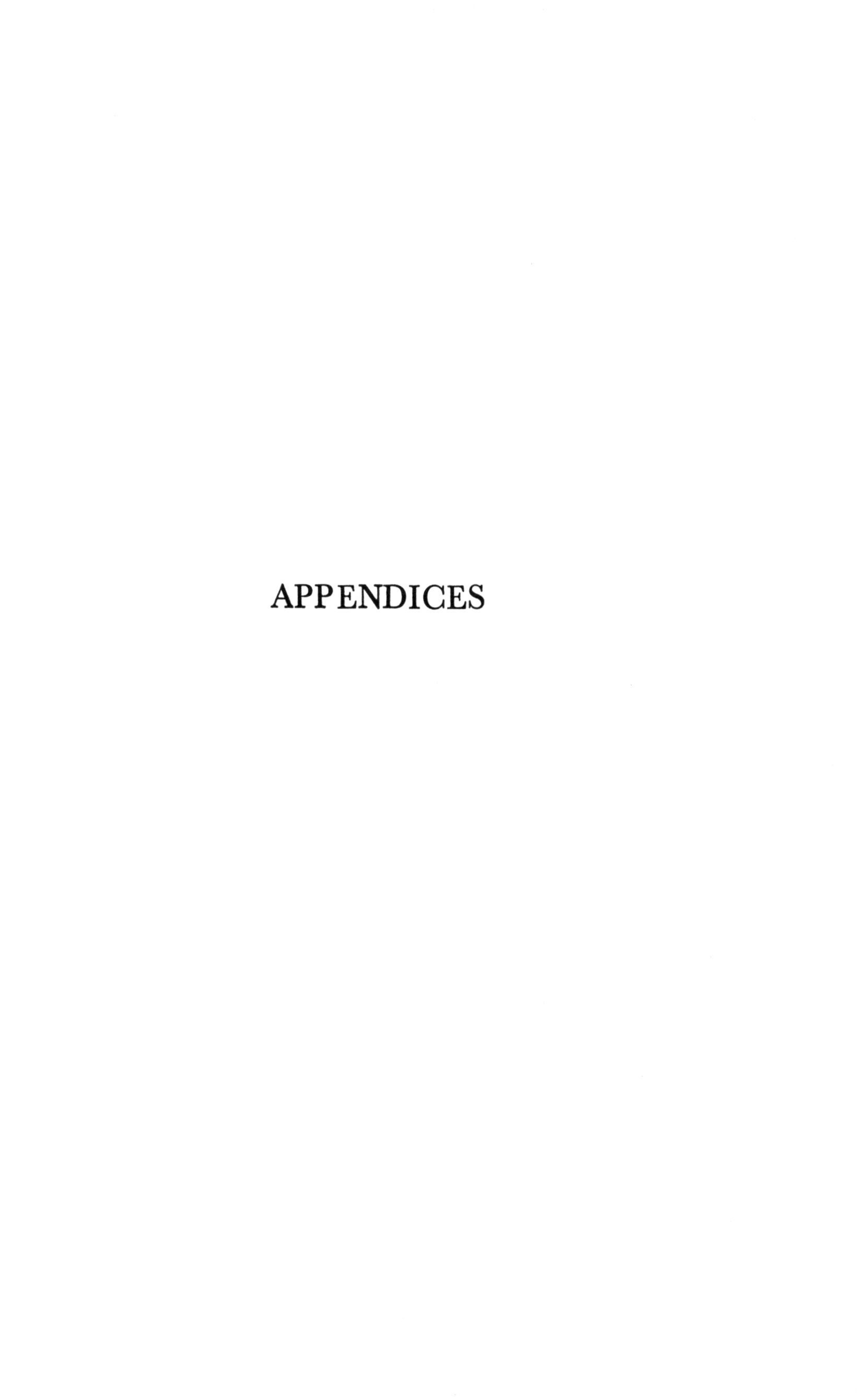

APPENDICES

Several appendices have been included in this manual for specific reasons: (1) some of them are useful in guiding the trainee and his coordinator toward a better understanding of the evaluation process in relation to the trainee's professional growth in vocational rehabilitation; (2) several of the appendices serve as models from which the trainee will pattern his exercises; (3) six supervisor evaluation report forms are included in an effort to provide the training coordinator a form which best approximates his evaluation of the trainee's work performance; (4) the remaining appendices serve as checklists and worksheets for the trainee's own information.

A suggestion is made that the training coordinator as well as the trainee review each appendix thoroughly, especially the description justifying the inclusion of it in this manual. Notice the comment signifying which appendices are to be turned in with appropriate exercises and which appendices are included for information purposes only.

Appendix A

INDIVIDUAL PLAN FOR SIX WEEKS FIELD WORK ASSIGNMENTS

The inclusion of this appendix is intended only as a guide for the training coordinator's development of the trainee's first six-week field work plan. For the university intern this individual plan will serve as a guide for *only* the first six weeks of field work; the remaining nine to twelve weeks of the semester will follow the same format as directed by your supervisor.

The final plan will denote the specific exercises chosen for the trainee by his training coordinator and faculty supervisor. This plan is to be completed and returned to the faculty supervisor within two weeks (the interim period) after completion of the academic program.

INDIVIDUAL PLAN FOR SIX WEEKS FIELD WORK ASSIGNMENTS (EXAMPLE)

MONDAY	TUESDAY	WEDNESDAY	THURSDAY	FRIDAY
Routine Professional Activities	Routine Professional Activities	Exercise 18 Business Survey	Routine Professional Activities	Routine Professional Activities
Routine Professional Activities	Routine Professional Activities	Routine Professional Activities	Exercise 1 Evaluation of Computer Print-Out	Exercise 7 Evaluation of Closed Case Conference with Supervisor
Routine Professional Activities	Routine Professional Activities	Exercise 18 Business Survey	Routine Professional Activities	Routine Professional Activities
Routine Professional Activities	Routine Professional Activities	Routine Professional Activities	Exercise 2 Frequency Distribution of Referral Sources	Exercise 3 Primary & Secondary Disabilities-Conference with Supervisor
Routine Professional Activities	Routine Professional Activities	Exercise 18 Business Survey	Routine Professional Activities	In-Service Training Conference with Supervisor
Exercise 13 A. Selecting a Vocation	Routine Professional Activities	Routine Professional Activities	Exercise 13 B. Community Resources	Routine Professional Activities
Routine Professional Activities	Routine Professional Activities	Exercise 18 Business Survey	Routine Professional Activities	Routine Professional Activities
Routine Professional Activities	Routine Professional Activities	Routine Professional Activities	Exercise 27 Open-Ended Exercise	Exercise 23, step 1 Selecting a Vocation Conference with Supervisor
Routine Professional Activities	Routine Professional Activities	Exercise 18 Labor Market Analysis	Exercise 23, step 3,4 Selecting a Vocation	Routine Professional Activities
Exercise 23, step 2 Selecting a Vocation	Routine Professional Activities	Routine Professional Activities	Routine Professional Activities	Exercise 27 Open-Ended Exercise Conference with Supervisor
Routine Professional Activities	Routine Professional Activities	Exercise 18 Labor Market Analysis	Routine Professional Activities	Completion of Field Work
Routine Professional Activities	Routine Professional Activities	Routine Professional Activities	Completion of Field Work	Conference with Supervisor

COUNSELOR TRAINEE PLACEMENT SURVEY

This survey form will be used in conjunction with Exercise 18. It is to be duplicated in sufficient number to provide worksheets for the trainee when he does surveys in the field and for the final typed copies. After the completion of this exercise it is recommended the trainee duplicate additional copies of these surveys and place them in a file accessible to all professional staff in your territory. The accumulation of an impressive occupational information file, utilizing these survey sheets, will come about in a relatively short period of time (there are many supervisors now requiring their professional staff make one new business survey per month).

COUNSELOR TRAINEE BUSINESS AND INDUSTRY SURVEY

Establishment____City_____________________________

Industry and Major Product (s) ________________________________Street___________________________

Employing Officer____Phone________________Date of Contact___________________

Union Requirements: Yes______No______ Insurance Requirements: Yes______No______ Medical Requirements: Yes______No______

VR Explained? Yes______No______ No. Employed in Plant________________________ No. Disabled Employed______________________

Is there a systematic training program? Yes______No______ Will they train? Yes______No________________________

Is employment seasonal? Yes______No______ If so, peak__________________________ Slack______________________________

Distance to transportation line? Blocks/miles_______________________ Ramps? Yes______No______ Elevators? Yes______No______

Parking facilities? Yes______No______ How far from office?__________________ How far from work area?__________________

Architectural barriers?__________________________ Describe____

Type of reception received from business establishments: High receptive______ Receptive____ Indifferent____ Antagonistic______

Job Titles (D.O.T.)	Number in Position	Percent Standing	Age Requirements Min. Age	Max. Age	Physical Demands (D.O.T.)	Primary Function of Job (D.O.T.)	D.O.T. G.E.D.	S.V.P.

Additional Comments:

Appendix C

SAMPLE *D.O.T.* LISTING

Appendix C has been included as representative of a *Dictionary of Occupational Titles* survey relative to the needs of vocational rehabilitation professionals; it serves only as a guide for the trainee in his completion of Exercise 12. All of the information contained in this appendix has been extracted from the three volumes of the *D.O.T.* The different vocations should be studied using this appendix as a standardized format.

SAMPLE D.O.T. LISTING
BOTTLING-LINE ATTENDANT (Distilled Liquors)
D.O.T. 920.887

Alternate Titles:

Line Operator; Bottle-Label Inspector; Stamp Presser; Strip-Stamp Straightener

Definition:

Prepares filled whisky bottles for packing and shipping, performing any combination of the following duties: Pastes labels and tax stamps on filled whisky bottles as they pass on conveyor. Examines bottles to ascertain that labels and stamps have been correctly applied. Straightens labels and stamps on bottles. Presses stamps on necks of bottles. Wipes excess glue and moisture from bottles. Packs whisky bottles into cartons. Pastes identification labels on cartons. May be known according to task performed.

Physical Demands: Sedentary, Reaching, Handling, Fingering, and/or Feeling, Seeing.

Working Conditions: Inside, Noise, and Vibration.

Training Time:

General Educational Development:

1 (Approximately Less Than 8th Grade Education)

Specific Vocational Preparation:

1 (Short Demonstration only)

Work Performed:

Work activities in this group primarily involve performing routine, non-machine tasks involving little or no latitude for judgment. Adherence to rigid standards or specifications is not involved.

Worker Requirements:

An occupationally significant combination of: Physical stamina; an inclination toward routine, repetitive activities; some dexterity with the fingers and hands; eye-hand coordination; form perception; and the ability and willingness to follow instructions.

Worker Trait Group:

Handling

Related Classifications:

Manipulating (.884), Tending (.885), Feeding-Offbearing (.886)

Appendix D

OUTLINE FOR EVALUATION OF PROFESSIONAL WORKER'S LEARNING OF SUPERVISED FIELD WORK

This appendix analyzes various aspects of counselor proficiency in an effort to offer bases for judging his growth in vocational rehabilitation as well as for graduate credit. This material is included only for the supervisor or training coordinator's information. The trainee may also use it as a guide regarding the evaluation his supervisor will be making at the completion of the field work period.

Evaluation of Professional Worker's
Learning of Supervised Field Work*

I. SUCCESS IN FORMING MEANINGFUL AND EFFECTIVE RELATIONSHIPS
    A. With Clients in Caseload
        1. Evidence reflecting a genuine desire to be helpful
        2. Evidence of ability to help client assess and use own strengths
        3. Evidence of capacity to be at ease with usual client with problems referred to the agency
        4. Evidence of sensitivity to client's feeling and needs
        5. Evidence of acceptance of individual differences in clients
        6. Evidence of little or no stereotype behavior in relations with clients with physical, mental, or emotional defects, or racial, creedal or ethnic differences
        7. Evidence of a listening and observing approach rather than advising and doing approach in relationships
    B. With Agency Staff
        1. Evidence of meeting routine personnel requirements
        2. Evidence of personal responsibility an being a staff team member

---

*This evaluation outline has been included in this manual from the original appearing in the Joint Liaison Committee Report, *Guidelines for Supervised Clinical Practice*, No. 1, 1963.

278

3. Evidence of acceptance of staff and student acceptance by staff
4. Evidence of "we" feeling rather than "they" by counselor
5. Evidence of willingness to perform the "extra" assignments which do not appear to be imposition upon student but designed for better learning

C. With Immediate Supervisor
1. Evidence of efforts to use supervision for learning and growth
2. Evidence of "relaxed" relationship with supervisor, no undue anxieties from wrong use of relationship
3. Evidence of normal freedom from gross self pre-occupation over supervisor-student relationships with adequate insight
4. Evidence of willingness to share case material with supervisor without reservation
5. Evidence of initiative to prepare and plan for student-supervisors conference
1. Evidence of adequate rapport with referral representatives
2. Evidence of acceptance by persons in "collateral" agencies
3. Evidence of acceptance by others in community groups
4. Evidence of freedom from undue anxiety in working with the above personalities

II. DEVELOPING SKILLS IN THE HELPING PROCESS
A. Evidence of Growth in Knowledge of Rehabilitation Concepts, Goals, and Methods
B. Evidence of Growth in Knowledge and Understanding of Human Behavior
1. Recognition of complexity of behavior
2. Recognition that there are causes, not a cause to be sought
3. Recognition that persons vary in capacity to accept help
C. Evidence of Growth in Ability to Recognize and Obtain Pertinent Information
1. Through use of client interview
2. Through use of interview with others
3. Through study of case records
4. Through participation in case or other conferences
5. Through readings and other techniques
D. Evidence of Deliberateness and Discriminate Consideration of all Facts in Diagnosing Client Needs and Problems
E. Evidence of Comprehensive Rehabilitation Diagnosis and Realistic Formulation of Rehabilitation Plan
1. Making maximum use of agency policy and services for helping
2. Making maximum effort to discover and use other helping facilities and services with sensitivity in using them
3. Making discerning use of client assets, physical, psychological, vocational, financial, and relational

III. GROWTH IN ABILITY TO FUNCTION WITHIN LIMITATIONS
    A. Evidence of Ability to Work Within Agency Policy and Physical Limitations
        1. Appreciation that scope of agency program limits counselor role
        2. Ability to interpret policy and practice realistically
        3. Acceptance of limitations in policy and practice
        4. Imagination in reaching from agency base into the community in implementing planning and services permissible within agency policy and practice.
    B. Evidence of Ability to Distinguish Between Responsibilities in Counseling, Planning, Executing Plans, and Community Organization
    C. Evidence of Ability to Use Agency Setting for Integration of Client Services and Coordination of Sequences of Services
    D. Evidence of Ability to Organize and Participate in Workload
        1. Capacity for consistent effort (rather than spasmodic effort)
        2. Ability to schedule and work to schedule with consideration for necessary interruptions
        3. Capacity for adequate tempo in performance without undue physical or mental fatigue
        4. Capacity for promptness in meeting deadlines within limits of good administrative requirements
        5. Ability to gear agency activities to clients' needs
        6. Capacity to reflect dependability as to details in agency administrative requirements
        7. Capacity for enlarging knowledge of community needs and community assets in participating in expanding agency vision in meeting the needs of the handicapped
        8. Ability to develop skill in understanding use of case recording
            a. As a diagnostic tool
            b. As a planning and service tool
            c. As an aid to counselor growth under supervision
            d. As a device for agency or other research purposes
        9. Capacity for improved oral and written expression
            a. In counseling and casework support
            b. In case recording
            c. In public and client relations
            d. In professional writing

IV. GROWTH IN CAPACITY FOR SELF-EVALUATION
    A. Evidence of Recognition of Own Strengths and Weaknesses as a Helping Person
    B. Evidence of Awareness of Self as Contrasted to Awareness of that Perceived as Outside of Self
    C. Evidence of Ability to Face Life Realistically

1. Satisfactory philosophy of living fairly free from anxiety over conflict in personal values
2. Acceptance of clients, peers, and others as they are rather than as counselor wants them to be
3. Ability to maintain perspective and objectivity in appreciation of another's feelings in relation to counselor's own personal reactions
4. Demonstration of sense of personal obligation in counseling, casework, professional and other relations
5. Ability to recognize the involvement of one's own feelings in counseling and rehabilitation casework practice
6. Recognition of anxiety stemming from imagined or real criticism during evaluations of field work performance

D. Evidence of Awareness of Personal Appearance Appropriate for the Work Setting as Usually Judged by the Cultural Standards
E. Evidence of Identification with Goal and Values in Rehabilitation Counseling as a Professional Practice

V. STUDY OF CASE RECORDS
A. As Source or Lack of Verifying Evidence in Appropriate Areas Above
B. As Support or Lack of It to Kind, Quality, and Degree of Counselor Supervision in Comparison to Agency Standards as Reflected in Policy Statements, Policy Manuals, Casework Manuals, Evaluative Standards, and Administrative Climate, Community Recognition, etc.
C. As Source for Directing Faculty Representation to Areas of Need for Counselor Learning, Motivation, Counselor Behavior as a Helping Person, and Counselor Supervisor Sensitivity

EVALUATION REPORTS

There are six evaluation forms in this appendix. The training coordinator or supervisor will select *one* most appropriate for reporting his trainee's progress to the faculty supervisor. This final report will accompany the field work turned in to the university. It is recommended the completed evaluation form be duplicated and a copy be placed in the trainee's personal file since it is representative of agency standards.

Form 1
EVALUATION FORM FOR COUNSELOR TRAINEES*

Name of Counselor

Period Covered by Report: From   To

Please rate the counselor on the following scale by circling the appropriate number for each category for each of the statements listed below.

?	5	4	3	2	1
No	Above		Below		
Evaluation	Excellent	Average	Average	Average	Poor

Please circle "?" for any statement on which you feel there has not been sufficient opportunity to make an evaluation of where that statement is not relevant in the counselor's program.

KNOWLEDGE, PROPER INTERPRETATION AND APPLICATION OF:

Medical information (diagnostic categories, prognoses, surgical procedures, etc.)   ?   5   4   3   2   1

Psychological information (personality theory, motivation, human growth and development, etc.)   ?   5   4   3   2   1

---

*This evaluation form was adapted to meet the needs of this supervised field-work experience from an experimental form developed by Dr. John Stout of the University of Scranton.

Social information (family situation, values, attitudes, interfamily structure, etc.)	?	5	4	3	2	1
Education information (educational record and program, training facilities and programs)	?	5	4	3	2	1
Occupational information (world of work, job, qualification and skills, availability of jobs)	?	5	4	3	2	1
Background information (in general, relation of past performance with present and future performance)	?	5	4	3	2	1
Community resources (availability of, methods of referral, cooperation, with, etc.)	?	5	4	3	2	1
Information from consultants (medical, speech, psychiatrist, instructors, OT, PT, social workers)	?	5	4	3	2	1

KNOWLEDGE, PROPER INTERPRETATION AND APPLICATION OF:

Information from other evaluative devices (work samples, observations, job tryouts)	?	5	4	3	2	1
Counseling theory and techniques	?	5	4	3	2	1
Agency organization, functions, and procedures	?	5	4	3	2	1

WORK HABITS, PERSONAL AND PERSONALITY CHARACTERISTICS

General Appearance	?	5	4	3	2	1
Attendance and punctuality	?	5	4	3	2	1
Dependability	?	5	4	3	2	1
Cooperation	?	5	4	3	2	1
Interest and Motivation	?	5	4	3	2	1
Taking and following directions	?	5	4	3	2	1
Attitude of inquiry, seeking of further knowledge	?	5	4	3	2	1
Initiative and assumption of responsibility	?	5	4	3	2	1

Creativity and imagination in problem solving	?	5	4	3	2	1
Independent judgment, decision making	?	5	4	3	2	1
Learning and assimilitation of new ideas	?	5	4	3	2	1
Acceptance and use of supervision	?	5	4	3	2	1
Tolerance of daily routine	?	5	4	3	2	1
Meeting deadlines	?	5	4	3	2	1
Coping with new and/or ambiguous situations	?	5	4	3	2	1
Functioning relatively autonomously	?	5	4	3	2	1
Maintaining reasonably objective relationships with clients and colleagues	?	5	4	3	2	1
Withstanding frustrating situations	?	5	4	3	2	1
Redirecting thinking and/or behavior when met with obstacles	?	5	4	3	2	1
Personal adjustment, stability, maturity	?	5	4	3	2	1

WORK HABITS, PERSONAL AND PERSONALITY CHARACTERISTICS

Relatively well-defined personal goals	?	5	4	3	2	1
Work under pressure	?	5	4	3	2	1
Self-understanding, knowing own strengths and weaknesses	?	5	4	3	2	1
Oral expression and communication skills	?	5	4	3	2	1
Perceptiveness	?	5	4	3	2	1

UNDERSTANDING OF RELATIONSHIPS WITH CLIENTS

Understanding and acceptance of clients' different social class orientation, attitudes, and values	?	5	4	3	2	1
Acceptance of individual differences in clients	?	5	4	3	2	1
Sensitive to clients' feelings and needs	?	5	4	3	2	1
Avoidance of overgeneralization and the forming of stereotyped attitudes and behavior toward clients	?	5	4	3	2	1

	?	5	4	3	2	1
Establishment and maintenance of good and productive relationships with clients	?	5	4	3	2	1
Ability to diagnose the clients' significant problems	?	5	4	3	2	1
Ability to plan with the client to overcome the clients' problems	?	5	4	3	2	1
Understanding the relationship of physical disability to personal, social, and vocational adjustment	?	5	4	3	2	1
Understanding of the relationship of emotional disability to personal, social and vocational adjustment	?	5	4	3	2	1
Understanding the relationship of mental retardation to personal, social and vocational adjustment	?	5	4	3	2	1
Ability to relate to and work with physically disabled clients	?	5	4	3	2	1

UNDERSTANDING OF AND RELATIONSHIPS WITH CLIENTS

	?	5	4	3	2	1
Ability to relate to and work with emotionally disturbed clients	?	5	4	3	2	1
Ability to relate to and work with mentally retarded clients	?	5	4	3	2	1

CASE RECORDING AND/OR REPORT WRITING

	?	5	4	3	2	1
Reports concise, pertinent information included	?	5	4	3	2	1
Generalized appropriately and accurately from basic information	?	5	4	3	2	1
Well constructed and integrated	?	5	4	3	2	1
Understandable and readable	?	5	4	3	2	1
Grammatically correct	?	5	4	3	2	1
Punctual	?	5	4	3	2	1
Overall quality	?	5	4	3	2	1

INTERPERSONAL RELATIONS

	?	5	4	3	2	1
With clients	?	5	4	3	2	1
With agency staff	?	5	4	3	2	1
With outside agency staff	?	5	4	3	2	1

With fellow counselors	?	5	4	3	2	1
With agency supervisor (s)	?	5	4	3	2	1

PROFESSIONAL CHARACTERISTICS

Professional and ethical conduct	?	5	4	3	2	1
Sense of personal obligation and commitment to work and to clients	?	5	4	3	2	1
Development of an overall philosophy of and attitude toward rehabilitation	?	5	4	3	2	1
Understanding of relationship between rehabilitation and other social welfare programs	?	5	4	3	2	1
Recognition of his professional role	?	5	4	3	2	1

1. Additional comments regarding counselor's need for further training and supervision.

2. Comment on your overall impressions of counselor in relation to his performance on these exercises.

Signature of Reporting Supervisor Title Date

Signature of Trainee Title Date

Form 2

COUNSELOR TRAINEE EVALUATION REPORT ON FIELD WORK EXPERIENCE

Counselor Trainee's Name: _________________ Date _____________

Return Form To: ____

This form has been devised solely to indicate the Counselor Trainee's progress during his field training.

Make check mark (X) in the column which best describes his level of performance.

Performance Factors	Above Average	Average	Below Average	Does Not Apply*
1. Organizing, planning and carrying out work				
2. General industry and attention to duties				
3. Cooperative relationship with staff				
4. Motivation and enthusiasm for work				
5. Knowledge and concepts of agency goals				
6. Knowledge and growth of human behavior				
7. Skills in interviewing				
8. Use and interpretation of psychological tests				
9. Attitude toward Agency supervision				
10. Professional/ethical standards				
11. Evidence of ability to assign relative values				
12. Recognition of own strengths and weaknesses in a helping role				
13. Ability to record accurately client/counselor relationships				
14. Ability to write/speak concisely				
15. Ability to establish and maintain a satisfactory counseling relationship				
16. Ability to be objective without emotional involvement				
17. Ability to use imagination and initiate new ideas				
18. Ability to formulate a rehabilitation plan				
19. Ability to accept increasing responsibility				
20. Personal appearance/dress				

*Did not have an opportunity to observe Counselor Trainee on this factor.

Comments:

(1) Statement regarding over-all impressions:

(2) Statement on potential of Counselor Trainee:

(3) Statement on needs for additional training and supervision:

Signature of Reporting Supervisor	Title	Date

Signature of Trainee	Title	Date

Form 3

EVALUATION SCALES FOR
REHABILITATION COUNSELOR TRAINEES*

The following rating scales represent an attempt to evaluate the progress and potentialities of counselors in the rehabilitation counselor training program. The first ten scales are designed to evaluate the more objective aspects of training on a short-term basis and apply to abilities and knowledges which may be appraised during the period of supervised field work. The last ten scales in general attempt to evaluate the long range potentialities of the counselor which may be appraised only after an extended period in the area of rehabilitation counseling. In regard to these scales, an opinion from the supervisor regarding the counselor's potentials is desired.

Counselor's Name _______________________________________

Position _______________________ Date _______________________

Place an "X" at some point along the line where you feel the trainee is functioning.

1. Ability to separate the significant from the trivial and to make a rehabilitation diagnosis based on an analysis of client's needs including the ability to utilize common sense or maturity of judgment, and to be flexible and versatile.

Does not meet basic requirements	Meets basic requirements	Meets average requirements	Meets maximum requirements

---

*Adapted for inclusion in this book from scales developed at the University of Florida.

2. Ability to organize work and to utilize time effectively including ability to make decisions, to keep cases moving, and to put first things first.

Does not   Meets basic   Meets average   Meets maximum
meet basic   requirements   requirements   requirements
requirements

3. Ability to express oneself concisely and effectively, both orally and in writing, including ability to record and report results and implications of work.

Does not   Meets basic   Meets average   Meets maximum
meet basic   requirements   requirements   requirements
requirements

4. Ability to establish and maintain a satisfactory counseling relationship.

Does not   Meets basic   Meets average   Meets maximum
meet basic   requirements   requirements   requirements
requirements

5. Ability to maintain enthusiasm for work, to be curious about things, especially new and unfamiliar things, and to be resourceful.

Does not   Meets basic   Meets average   Meets maximum
meet basic   requirements   requirements   requirements
requirements

6. Ability to maintain objectivity in casework situations, involving ability to act as a helping person without personal, emotional involvement.

Does not   Meets basic   Meets average   Meets maximum
meet basic   requirements   requirements   requirements
requirements

7. Ability to recognize when and where to seek help, including ability to make use of available community services and resources in meeting problems of disabled persons and to maintain effective relationships with such sources.

Does not   Meets basic   Meets average   Meets maximum
meet basic   requirements   requirements   requirements
requirements

8. Ability to follow instructions.

Does not   Meets basic   Meets average   Meets maximum
meet basic   requirements   requirements   requirements
requirements

9. Ability to maintain a professional attitude and outlook.

Does not   Meets basic   Meets average   Meets maximum
meet basic   requirements   requirements   requirements
requirements

10. General understanding of the rehabilitation program, its purpose, general philosophy, and social significance.

| Does not meet basic requirements | Meets basic requirements | Meets average requirements | Meets maximum requirements |

11. Ability to use imagination or to visualize possibilities in seemingly impossible situations.

| Does not meet basic requirements | Meets basic requirements | Meets average requirements | Meets maximum requirements |

12. Ablity to detect and identify the manifestations of disability, mental or physical, and to understand their relationships to vocational and social adjustment.

| Does not meet basic requirements | Meets basic requirements | Meets average requirements | Meets maximum requirements |

13. Ability to work under pressure.

| Does not meet basic requirements | Meets basic requirements | Meets average requirements | Meets maximum requirements |

14. Ability to be tolerant and understanding of the behavior of others.

| Does not meet basic requirements | Meets basic requirements | Meets average requirements | Meets maximum requirements |

15. Relative freedom from insecurity in personality structure including a wholesome self-confidence and overall emotional maturity.

| Does not meet basic requirements | Meets basic requirements | Meets average requirements | Meets maximum requirements |

16. Ability to develop technical competence in psychometrics, counseling, occupational analysis, placement, and other technical skills needed by a rehabilitation counselor.

| Does not meet basic requirements | Meets basic requirements | Meets average requirements | Meets maximum requirements |

17. Ability to utilize total rehabilitation processes rather than segmented portions.

| Does not meet basic requirements | Meets basic requirements | Meets average requirements | Meets maximum requirements |

18. A person with a well-rounded background with more than just a technical education.

| Does not meet basic requirements | Meets basic requirements | Meets average requirements | Meets maximum requirements |

19. An understanding of mental and emotional conditions affecting social
and vocational adjustment, their nature, course, and probable cause.

Does not   Meets basic   Meets average   Meets maximum
meet basic   requirements   requirements   requirements
requirements

20. An understanding of federal, state, and local laws pertaining to rehabilitation and of related social legislation, including an understanding
of agency policies and standards as they apply to the counselor's work.

Does not   Meets basic   Meets average   Meets maximum
meet basic   requirements   requirements   requirements
requirements

Statement of supervisor regarding general overall impressions of counselor's
skills, ability, knowledge, attitude, and understanding of rehabilitation processes. (Please give a statement in narrative form regarding your impressions
and opinions of the counselor trainee's competency and professional future
in rehabilitation.)

____

Signature of reporting supervisor

____

Signature of trainee

Form 4

PERFORMANCE EVALUATION FOR VOCATIONAL REHABILITATION WORKERS*

Name _________________________ Date _________________________

Position ____

Place a Check Mark (X) in Column Which Best Describes Trainee's Level of Performance.

---

*This evaluation form was adapted for use in this book from and acknowl-
edgment is given to The Colorado Division of Vocational Rehabilitation.

	Unsatisfactory	Fair	Good	Very Good	Outstanding	Does Not Apply
Work Habits						
1. Notifies his own or state office as to his intentions of itinerary when out of office so that he may be reached.						
2. There is evidence of extra duty beyond the 8-hour day, such as speaking to groups, working on committees within community and handling urgent situations that come up after hours.						
3. Office visits and field contacts are scheduled in such a way as to conserve or make most efficient use of time and expenditures of travel funds.						
4. Billings from vendors are current.						
5. Training agencies are well informed as to their responsibility to trainees and reporting system to our office.						
6. Schedules his work to make the most effective utilization of his time.						
7. Counselor keeps appointments as set up.						
8. Statistical records each month are prompt.						
9. Keeps regular hours as job demands.						
10. Maintains wholesome attitude toward his job and responsibilities.						
11. Keeps his casework up to date.						
12. Responds promptly to new referrals and their contact.						
13. Keeps flow of cases moving.						
14. Cancellations are up to date.						
15. Case recording is sufficient for good case review and evaluation.						

Relationship With People	Unsatis-factory	Fair	Good	Very Good	Out-standing	Does Not Apply
1. There are few or no justifiable complaints of an adverse nature brought to mind because of improper action on the counselor's part.						
2. Referral agencies are kept properly informed of client's status at proper intervals of rehabilitation process.						
3. Outside agencies are utilized adequately in working out the needs of the rehabilitant.						
4. Counselor conducts and presents himself in the way of dress, mannerisms, speech, tact, behavior, etc., which reflects a credit to the department.						
5. Has good working relations with medical consultant.						
6. Is considerate of his fellow worker.						
7. Displays tact, courtesy and diplomacy in dealing with clients and the public.						
8. Displays an attitude of cooperativeness within as well as outside the department of rehabilitation.						

Dependability	Unsatis-factory	Fair	Good	Very Good	Out-standing	Does Not Apply
1. Individual can be relied upon to carry out assigned duties.						
2. Counselor can work well without close supervision.						
3. Shows discretion in confidential matters.						
4. Shows enthusiasm and confidence in his work as a rehabilitation counselor.						
5. Counselor directs his work energy in a logical and productive sequence.						

Quantity	Unsatis-factory	Fair	Good	Very Good	Out-standing	Does Not Apply
1. New referrals are in keeping with requirements to perpetuate an adequate caseload within the area served.						
2. There is evidence of a substantial active caseload with services resulting in flow from status 10 through 22.						
3. Closed cases in status 26 indicates adequate production.						
4. Develops the number of resources necessary to meet the various requirements of the client's rehabilitation.						
5. Correspondence and record keeping is always current.						
6. Expends funds adequately to meet the needs of his district or area covered.						
7. Shows a wide range of services to his caseload.						
8. The number of reopened cases are held to a small percentage.						

Quality of Work	Unsatis-factory	Fair	Good	Very Good	Out-standing	Does Not Apply
1. Bills are covered by authorizations, accurate and current.						
2. Authorizations are accurate and specific with reference to services which are to be provided.						
3. The plan in the case folder reflects proper case evaluation and good case planning.						
4. The case record shows adequate supervision of the client and services to meet the rehabilitation goal.						
5. Case recording is adequate to document the services provided.						

6. Employed closures reflect a quality job and within the maximum potential of the client.

7. The case record reflects good evaluation which may result in closed "08" cases, closed employed, as well as closed from active load as "not employed."

8. Status changes within caseload shows good flow of cases.

9. Decisions tend to raise rather than lower quality of services.

10. Plans developed for client show sound judgment in expenditure of funds.

11. Counselor uses good counseling technique.

12. Counselor uses good judgment on decisions necessary in borderline cases.

13. Counselor gives thorough consideration to the medical, social, economic, educational, vocational and psychological aspects of the client's situation.

14. Counselor follows the proper sequence of steps necessary in providing vocational rehabilitation services.

Willingness and Interest	*Unsatis-factory*	*Fair*	*Good*	*Very Good*	*Out-standing*	*Does Not Apply*
1. Counselor endeavors to increase efficiency through review of literature, workshops, clinics, particular vocational meetings and other media.						
2. Counselor is receptive to constructive analysis and guidance aimed toward bettering his professional competence.						

3. Employee relates well the philosophy of vocational rehabilitation to clients and community.

4. Counselor shows willingness of acceptance of responsibility of providing the necessary services to rehabilitate the client.

5. There is evidence of actively participating in community and professional organizations to further the objective of vocational rehabilitation.

6. Shows a desire to serve the more difficult cases as well as the ordinary case.

7. Counselor is continuously seeking new and stimulating solutions to his client's problems.

8. Counselor displays an attitude of continuing self-analysis within his overall job.

9. Counselor displays sensitivity, understanding and sympathy toward client's problems.

Adaptability	Unsatisfactory	Fair	Good	Very Good	Outstanding	Does Not Apply
1. Responds adequately to situations requiring tactful handling.						
2. Accepts and adjusts to new administrative requirements such as new forms, different procedures, lack of funds.						
3. Shows adaptability in working with all types of disabilities as well as different personalities and economic segments of the population.						
4. Counselor is able to reorganize when necessary and make adjustments to a client's rehabilitation plan.						

5. Counselor does not allow prejudice to interfere with the counseling process.
6. Counselor adapts readily to community pressures or resistance in the rehabilitation process of individuals.
7. Counselor is able to say "No" when the situation requires it.
8. Counselor adapts his thinking to the need of his client rather than the easiest route for himself.

Job Intelligence

	Unsatisfactory	Fair	Good	Very Good	Outstanding	Does Not Apply
1. Knows how to utilize the medical consultant in the rehabilitation process.						
2. Is able to assess the situation of his disabled client.						
3. Has a good knowledge of the resources available in the community.						
4. Has a good working knowledge of all forms and methods of utilization.						
5. Maintains facts and figures necessary in the everyday casework procedures, such as hospital per diem rates, fee schedules, tuition rates, type of supplies, tools, etc.						
6. Follows the proper steps and procedures necessary to carry a client from "00" status through "Closed" status.						
7. Employee has a good working knowledge of State Plan and federal regulations.						
8. Counselor has an understanding of the mechanics related to the statistical procedures.						

9. Counselor understands the necessary steps and procedures to facilitate authorizations and expenditures.

10. Counselor has the ability to make decisions based on the analytical appraisal of various factors influencing the vocational objective.

Administrative or Supervisory Ability	Unsatisfactory	Fair	Good	Very Good	Outstanding	Does Not Apply
1. Is able to assign work to his secretary and other office staff in an efficient manner.						
2. Is able to appraise the work of his secretary, resulting in smooth, efficient and effective operation.						
3. Participates in meetings and activities of the community which bear a relation to the interests of vocational rehabilitation.						
4. Possesses the quality of self-assurance and enthusiasm towards the objectives of vocational rehabilitation and transmits this to those in his office.						
5. With the aid of his secretary, reports are accurate, meaningful, thorough and submitted on schedule.						
6. Actively supports and participates in professional organizations directly or indirectly associated with the course of vocational rehabilitation.						
7. Establishes standards that present a challenge to the job performance of the other counselors and secretaries.						

8. Displays a willingness to assist each of his workers to develop their maximum potential as a counselor or other staff worker.

9. Has the ability to constructively discuss differences without bringing into the conversation such things as personal dislikes, prejudices, personalities, and tones of hostility.

10. Functions for the overall objectives of vocational rehabilitation rather than concentrates on selected areas of the service.

11. Creates an air of confidence in his own judgment and the feeling of freedom to consult when the need arises.

12. There is evidence of overall growth and status of the department within the district served.

A. Other comments in relation to counselor's training needs.

B. Training Coordinator's overall impressions of trainee.

_______________________   _______________________
Signature   Title

_______________________   _______________________
Signature   Title

Form 5

FIELD AGENCY REPORT ON SUPERVISED FIELD WORK*
(A recommended outline)

In order to facilitate the final reporting on the work of the rehabilitation counselor trainee, the following suggested evaluation form has been devised. The agency may use this form in any way most convenient to its own policies or standards.

1. Name of the Agency
2. Name of Title of Supervisor
3. Type of Work Performed by Trainee
4. Total Number of Hours Completed in Field Work (Approximately)
5. Evaluation of Supervised Field Work
    a. Quality of work
    b. Ability to adjust to work schedule
    c. Amount of supervision needed by trainee
    d. Attendance at staff meetings and other professional conferences.
    e. Reliability
    f. Interpersonal relationships
        1. With staff
        2. With clients
        3. With other professional organizations
    g. Personal stability
6. What Type of Recommendation Would Agency Give Trainee
7. Additional Comments

8. Recommended Grade for Course
    a. Outstanding performance in all activities of work
    b. Average to good performance in most activities of work
    c. Below average performance in most activities of work, but shows ability for professional growth
    d. Poor in most activities with little promise for improvement

Form 6

OUTLINE FOR SUPERVISORY EVALUATION OF A TRAINEE'S PERFORMANCE IN SUPERVISED FIELD WORK

I. Basic Information Regarding the Supervised Field Work
    A. Identifying Data

---

*This and the following evaluation form have been amended from the *Manual for Supervised Clinical Practice in Rehabilitation Counseling*, Bureau of School Service, University of Kentucky, 1969.

    1. Name of trainee

    2. Name of agency

    3. Name of supervised field work training coordinator

    4. Period of supervised field work assignment

    5. Date this final report submitted by training coordinator supervisor

B. Plan of this agency regarding trainee's supervised field work

    1. Number and kinds of cases assigned to counselor

    2. Nature and frequency of trainee conferences with training coordinator

    3. Counselor participation in case staffing by rehabilitation team members

    4. Other assignments or responsibilities given to the trainee

II. Review of Trainee Performance

    A. Competence in providing services to clients

        1. Understanding the client's personal and environmental problems

        2. Assessing the client's achievements, abilities, interests, and aptitudes

        3. Establishing and maintaining a good, productive relationship with the client

        4. Requesting and using needed information

        5. Formulating a sound rehabilitation diagnosis

        6. Developing with the client a realistic rehabilitation plan

        7. Utilizing community resources to help the client into job placement

        8. Other pertinent capabilities shown by the trainee

    B. Quality of relationship with supervisor and other staff member

    C. Quality of relationship with other specialists on the rehabilitation team, both in the agency and the community

    D. Growth in self-direction

        1. Observing agency policies and procedures

        2. Handling appointments and commitments

        3. Managing case recording and other record keeping

        4. Maintaining dress and appearance befitting a counselor

        5. Other evidence of personal growth

    E. Acceptance of professional responsibility

        1. Acting in the light of ethical standards

        2. Participating in programs of organizations representing the professional field

        3. Other evidence of contributions to the profession

III. Recommended Grade and Suggestions for Possible Additional Supervised Field Work or In-Service Training

Appendix F

SUGGESTED GUIDE FOR CASE RECORDING AND DEVELOPMENT OF THE REHABILITATION PLAN

Keeping case records is a very important responsibility of state vocational rehabilitation counselors. The case record is the only written documentation of the professional job a rehabilitation counselor is doing and should be the best exhibit of his work. Good case records and case recording should show that the rehabilitation process has been covered completely for each client. The narrative recording should be a running account of the development and progress of a case from referral to closure including the counselor's evaluation, appraisal and analysis of diagnostic materials and his recommendation. These should be in chronological order with the date of each entry recorded conspicuously in the left-hand margin.

This appendix primarily is included as a guide for the trainee in an effort to increase his awareness of the importance of adequate case recording. He may use it to evaluate a closed case as described in Exercise 7.

The following headings and minimum content to be included under each heading are suggested as a format that should appear in the narrative of the case record in addition to information on forms, correspondence, and reports.

GUIDE FOR CASE RECORDING*

REFERRAL AND SURVEY DATA
1. Circumstances that precipitated the referral.
2. Summary of significant social, psychological, economic, educational, vocational, and past medical history data based on survey information.

---

*Adopted from the Appendix Section of the HEW publication, *Development and Use of Training Materials and Aids in Vocational Rehabilitation*, 1965.

302

DIAGNOSTIC DATA
1. Arrangement for general and specialty medical examination reports.
2. Arrangement for other diagnostic reports (psychological report, high school transcript, etc.).
3. Receipt of diagnostic reports and important points in each.
4. Interviews with client and others and important points covered during these interviews.
5. Important points of consultation with the agency medical consultant.

DIAGNOSTIC EVALUATION
Counselor's appraisal and analysis of survey data, current diagnostic reports and counseling interviews and his recommendations.

JUSTIFICATION AND CERTIFICATE OF ELIGIBILITY
1. Disability.
2. Employment handicap.
3. Expectations.
4. Certification (data executed).

DETERMINATION OF ECONOMIC NEEDS
Identification of services conditioned on need and whether client meets need requirements.

REHABILITATION PLAN
1. Services to be provided based on counselor's appraisal, analysis, and recommendations.
2. Duration of the plan.
3. Vocational objective.

EXECUTION OF THE PLAN
1. Progress summaries during provision of services.
2. Interviews and important points covered during these interviews.
3. Supplemental services to original plan.
4. Revisions of rehabilitation plan including justification (if any).

PLACEMENT
1. Employer contacts by counselor and client.
2. Contacts with the selective placement counselor of the state employment service.
3. Other placement contact either by client or counselor.

FOLLOW-UP
1. Contact with client and determination of satisfactory adjustment on the job.
2. Contact with employer and determination of satisfactory performance on the job.

CLOSURE
1. Justification.
2. Summary of services provided.
3. Name of employer.
4. Description of the job.
5. Client's salary (state whether gross or take-home).
6. Notification of referral source.

Appendix G

WORKSHEET FOR CASE REVIEW

This worksheet has been included to provide the trainee assistance in evaluating his case recording methodology in relation to the minimum information rehabilitation officials look for during periodic case reviews. As an appendix it is intended only as a guide for the trainee.

Worksheet for Case Review*

Counselor ________________________ Client ________________________

Vocational Rehabilitation Number ______________ Date ____________

Key to rating: 1—excellent, 2—above average, 3—adequate, 4—below average, 5—inadequate.

	1	2	3	4	5
I. INDIVIDUAL SURVEY R-4					
1. Statistical information complete	( )	( )	( )	( )	( )
2. Comments section adequate	( )	( )	( )	( )	( )

Comments: (List deficiencies and strong points)

II. DIAGNOSIS AND PLANNING

	1	2	3	4	5
1. Medical and psychological information adequate	( )	( )	( )	( )	( )
2. Recording shows information evaluated	( )	( )	( )	( )	( )
3. Recording shows evidence of counseling and client's agreement with plan	( )	( )	( )	( )	( )
4. Adequate investigation (reputation, motivation, work habits, etc.)	( )	( )	( )	( )	( )

Comments:

III. CASE EVALUATION

	1	2	3	4	5
1. Significant information summarized	( )	( )	( )	( )	( )
2. Eligibility established	( )	( )	( )	( )	( )

*Acknowledgment is given to George Cundiff of the Oklahoma Division of Vocational Rehabilitation for the development of this worksheet.

3. Reasons for selection of objective ( ) ( ) ( ) ( ) ( )
4. How planned services will result
   in employability ( ) ( ) ( ) ( ) ( )
5. Economic need determined
   where applicable ( ) ( ) ( ) ( ) ( )
Comments:

IV. PROVISION OF SERVICES
1. Adequate supervision ( ) ( ) ( ) ( ) ( )
2. Interruptions explained and
   future plans noted ( ) ( ) ( ) ( ) ( )
Comments:

V. READINESS FOR EMPLOYMENT AND
PLACEMENT PLANNING
1. Job readiness evaluated when
   placed in status 20 ( ) ( ) ( ) ( ) ( )
2. Definite placement plan made
   and followed ( ) ( ) ( ) ( ) ( )
Comments:

VI. JOB PLACEMENT, FOLLOW-UP AND
CLOSURE
1. Method of placement shown ( ) ( ) ( ) ( ) ( )
2. Adequate follow-up to insure
   suitability of employment ( ) ( ) ( ) ( ) ( )
Comments:

VII. MISCELLANEOUS
1. Prudent use of funds ( ) ( ) ( ) ( ) ( )
2. Adequate reasons given for
   non-rehabilitation closures ( ) ( ) ( ) ( ) ( )
3. Conformance to agency policy
   (cite violations) ( ) ( ) ( ) ( ) ( )
Additional Comments:

Appendix H

ACTIVITY CHECKLIST

The following appendix was used in the original Field Manual as a checklist. Due to changes in the training plan, it is no longer required; but it is being retained as a guide for the training coordinator and the counselor trainee. The list covers significant content on *Interviewing* and *Specific Activities and Processes*. It should be studied carefully because of its relevancy to the rehabilitation process.

I. INTERVIEWING
    A. Principles and techniques
        1. Planning the interview
        2. Concluding an interview
        3. Recording pertinent information
    B. Interviewing clients
        1. Initial survey
        2. Counseling interview
        3. Interview with client in:
            a. School training
            b. Employment training
            c. Correspondence course
            d. Physical restoration program
            e. Rehabilitation employment
        4. Selecting objective
        5. Develop a plan
        6. Problem solving interview
    C. Consultation with others regarding client
        1. Doctor
            a. To authorize medical examination
            b. To secure medical information
            c. To arrange for treatment
        2. Social worker to secure case data
        3. References to investigate case
        4. Referral to another agency
        5. Employers
            a. As a prospective trainer
            b. For placement purposes

        c. Follow-up
    6. Service facility
        a. To obtain information
        b. To arrange for services
    7. Employment service
        a. To arrange for placement
    8. Preparing for use of agency medical consultant
    9. Utilization of Medical consultant
  D. Promotional contacts
    1. Prospective referral agent
    2. New service facility
    3. Cooperating agency or individual
    4. Press or publicity medium

II. SPECIFIC ACTIVITIES AND PROCESSES
  A. Use of forms
    1. For determining eligibility
        a. General
        b. Financial
    2. For registration
    3. For vocational diagnosis
    4. For case reports
    5. For writing rehabilitation plan
    6. For referring case for supervision
    7. For closure data
        a. Rejected referral
        b. Closed without services
        c. Closed—employed
        d. Closed—unemployed
    8. For reporting back to referral source
    9. For acceptance of occupational tools and equipment
   10. For statistical reports
   11. For expense accounts
  B. Use of statuses
    1. Definition
    2. Use of case recording
  C. Processes
    1. Determining general eligibility
    2. Accepting cases
    3. Writing case reports
    4. Determining financial eligibility
    5. Administering, scoring, and interpreting tests
    6. Writing the rehabilitation plan
    7. Closing a case
        a. Referral

       b. Accepted—without services
       c. Case employed
       d. Case unemployed
  D. Planning field work
     1. Selecting cases for contact
     2. Planning weekly itinerary
     3. Planning daily itinerary
     4. Scheduling appointments with clients or others
  E. Planning office day
     1. Establishing routine for secretary
     2. Preparing for efficient dictation period
     3. Handling correspondence
     4. Using office records

Appendix I

ADEQUACY OF REHABILITATION EVALUATION CHECKLIST FOR COUNSELORS AND SUPERVISORS

The inclusion of Appendix I in this book has several purposes: (1) to provide the trainee an idea of the vast amount of information required in the evaluation process; (2) to increase his awareness of the need to include more than the required medical and psychological material in his case recording; and (3) to outline an approach to case recording and caseload management which has proven to be effective by other professional in vocational rehabilitation. It can either be used solely as a guide or it may be employed in conjunction with Exercises 7, 8, 9, 10, 15, or 25.

Checklist for Counselors and Supervisors*

MEDICAL

1. Was existing medical information obtained?
2. Is medical information recent (not more than 90 days old) ?
3. Is general medical information complete?
   a. Is diagnosis shown?
   b. Are physical and mental limitations shown?
   c. Is prognosis shown?
   d. Are recommendations shown?
4. Were specialty examinations obtained?
5. Were all recommended specialty examinations obtained?
6. Were specialty examinations complete (diagnosis, prognosis, recommendations etc.) ?
7. Were specialists, board-certified or otherwise, qualified?
8. Is additional medical information indicated?

---

*From *Training Guides in Evaluation of Vocational Potential for Vocational Rehabilitation Staff*. HEW, 1965.

    a. Rehabilitation facility evaluation?
    b. Speech and hearing center?
    c. Amputee clinic?
    d. Other?

PSYCHOLOGICAL

1. Was a psychological test (or evaluation) obtained?
2. Is it indicated in this case (according to State Casework Manual or RSA Bulletin on Psychological Services) ?
3. Is sufficient information recorded to make an adequate appraisal of mental ability, aptitudes, interests, personality, motivation, etc.?

SOCIAL

1. Does counselor describe:
    a. Home conditions?
    b. Personal data?
    c. Economic factors (including Economic Need Sheet) ?
    d. Attitudes of client and family?
    e. Sources of information?

EDUCATIONAL

1. Was school transcript obtained?
2. Is school transcript indicated (according to policies set forth in State Casework Manual) ?
    a. Grades completed?
    b. Preferred subjects?
    c. Educational plans or ambitions?
    d. Other relevant data?

VOCATIONAL

1. Is work history recorded?
    a. Types of jobs?
    b. Wages?
    c. Job tenure?
    d. Reason for leaving?
2. Is sufficient information recorded to determine work habits, skills, level of aspiration, attitudes, opinions of former employers, etc.?
3. Is a work evaluation needed?
4. Does client need personal adjustment training?

TOTAL EVALUATION

1. Were all data obtained in the case study analyzed or evaluated so that proper conclusions could be drawn?
2. Was the vocational plan based on the total evaluation?

REHABILITATION QUESTIONNAIRE AND FIELD WORK EVALUATION FORM

This appendix is to be completed by the trainee after the field work assignments have been concluded. The purpose of its inclusion is to gain pertinent data relative to the role of in-service training in vocational rehabilitation.

Rehabilitation Questionnaire*

GENERAL INFORMATION

1. Name _________________________________ 2. Date _________

3. District Office _____________________________ State _________

4. Type of Caseload ____

5. Age _______________________ 6. Marital Status: ______________

           _________ Single

           _________ Separated or Divorced

           _________ Married

           _________ Widowed

7. Sex: Male _______________ Female _______________

EDUCATIONAL INFORMATION

8. Educational Level you Achieved: (Check)

           _________ Completed College

           _________ Some Postgraduate

           _________ M.A./M.S.

           _________ M.A./M.S. Plus

9. Date first degree granted (state degree)

10. Date last degree granted (state degree)

11. Undergraduate major/minor

---

*Revised from a questionnaire at the University of Iowa.

12. Major field in graduate school
13. What was your undergraduate grade point average (based on a 4-point scale) ?
14. What formal training have you taken in the past calendar year?
    _____________ 1. Classwork in a local college or university
    _____________ 2. Workshops or institutes
    _____________ 3. Correspondence course work
    _____________ 4. Formal training
    _____________ 5. Other (specify)
15. In being promoted (or getting a pay increase) in your agency, how would you rank the following items ("1" equals most important, etc.) ?
    _____________ Being in the right place at the right time
    _____________ Conforming and playing politics
    _____________ Engaging in further training
    _____________ Producing 26-closures
    _____________ Having a master's degree in rehabilitation counseling
16. The following describes the extent to which the total current in-service training program helps me in performing my job:
    _____________ 1. Rarely   _____________ 2. Sometimes   _____________ 3. Frequently
    _____________ 4. Generally   _____________ 5. Almost Always
17. Comments:

18. For each activity listed below, circle a letter to indicate how well your previous training, from different sources, has helped you in performing that activity:

    A Not Helpful
    B Of Very Limited Help
    C Usually Helpful
    D Very Helpful
    E Have had no training/experience in this

Training taken from a college person	Training taken from an agency person	Experience on the job	
A B C D E	A B C D E	A B C D E	1. Finding a specific job for a client
A B C D E	A B C D E	A B C D E	2. Dealing in face-to-face contacts with client's emotions
A B C D E	A B C D E	A B C D E	3. Using test results to guide a client
A B C D E	A B C D E	A B C D E	4. Using medical reports to guide client

A B C D E	A B C D E	A B C D E	5. Dealing in face-to-face contacts with client unrealism in job choice (s)
A B C D E	A B C D E	A B C D E	6. Being able to formulate a plan from client information
A B C D E	A B C D E	A B C D E	7. Being able to handle personal problems and prejudices in work situations
A B C D E	A B C D E	A B C D E	8. Using psychological reports to guide clients
A B C D E	A B C D E	A B C D E	9. Reading and understanding research reports
A B C D E	A B C D E	A B C D E	10. Maintaining productive contact with referral sources and other professionals

19. How many books, which you use on your job, do you have in your personal library?

EMPLOYMENT INFORMATION

20. Years of experience in all types of counseling or personal work:

21. Taking your total weekly working hours into account, please rank the following activities according to the amount of time you spend on each. (Give that activity taking the most of your time a rank of 1 and the least a rank of 4, etc.)

  ———— 1. Face-to-face contacts with clients
  ———— 2. Locating jobs, developing referral sources, and related community work
  ———— 3. Contacting other professionals (social workers, etc.)
  ———— 4. Recording, administrative meetings, etc.

22. On the average, how many hours each month do you put into in-service training activities?

23. To what extent does your supervisor help you with job-related problems:

  ———— 1. Rarely
  ———— 2. Sometimes
  ———— 3. Frequently
  ———— 4. Generally
  ———— 5. Almost Always

24. Which professional meetings did you attend during the last year? (check those which apply)

	None	APA	APGA	ARCA	NRA	NRCA	NASW	OTHER (specify)
State	____	____	____	____	____	____	____	____
Regional	____	____	____	____	____	____	____	____
National	____	____	____	____	____	____	____	____

25. In which professional groups have you held office?
26. What professional journals do you read?

    I thoroughly read _______________________________________

    I casually read ____
27. All things considered, which of these statements comes nearest to expressing the way you feel about your job?

    _________ I like it

    _________ I am indifferent to it

    _________ I dislike it
28. How much of the time do you feel satisfied with your job?

    _________ All of the time

    _________ Most of the time

    _________ A good deal of the time

    _________ About half of the time

    _________ Occasionally

    _________ Seldom

    _________ Never
29. Please describe changes or modifications you would make in the field work portion of training, specifically in relation to this book. What exercise was most appropriate to your professional needs? Least appropriate? Why? Include an exercise which was not included in this manual that should be in the next revision and defend your rationale for its inclusion.

Appendix K

REHABILITATION COUNSELOR
JOB CLASSIFICATION SAMPLE

The following appendix is a job classification sample adopted by the State of Pennsylvania defining the role of the rehabilitation counselor. It is included in this manual to serve only as a guide relative to anticipated responsibilities of the newly employed vocational rehabilitation worker.

Each state agency has incorporated a similar classification into its personnel policy specifications. This sample is not intended to be an exhaustive listing.

Rehabilitation Counselor*

Definition. This is professional work in the field of rehabilitation of the physically or mentally handicapped. Employees in this class assist disabled persons select, prepare for, and attain vocational adjustment. Counseling on problems of personal and social adjustment related to vocational rehabilitation is an important aspect of this work. Employees utilize a wide variety of medical, social, and vocational resources in achieving their objectives. Employees are expected to exercise sound judgment in evaluating potentiality for rehabilitation and in guiding individuals in their vocational selection. The work is performed under supervision and is reviewed through case records, reports, and conferences.

Examples of Work Performed. Obtains information concerning the applicant's social and economic situation, educational background, work experience, physical and mental condition, personality traits and attitudes.

Arranges for medical, psychological, and psychiatric examinations as a part of determining feasibility for rehabilitation.

Works with medical resources and other agencies in securing information and arranging related services.

Evaluates in conjunction with a medical consultant the information secured to ascertain the person's potentiality for rehabilitation and to recommend a plan of treatment.

---

*This classification sample was adopted from the Rehabilitation Counselor Education Academic Program and Field Work Manual of The Pennsylvania State University.

Arranges for services needed to prepare the disabled person for employment, including medical and psychiatric services, vocational training, and financial aid for transportation and maintenance.

Provides counseling services designed to encourage and support the disabled person in his efforts and aids him in his personal and social adjustment.

Aids in securing employment and procuring tools or equipment, if necessary, and helps him with his problems of adjustment in his work.

Makes use of available community resources and secures information concerning employment opportunities.

Prepares case records and reports.

Required Knowledge, Skills, Abilities. Knowledge of individual and group behavior with special emphasis on the problems and attitudes of the physically or mentally disabled.

Knowledge of current social, economic, and health problems and resources with special emphasis on factors related to vocational rehabilitation.

Some knowledge of the principles and practices of rehabilitation.

Some knowledge of the principles and practices of casework relating to rehabilitation counseling.

Some knowledge of the more common physical and mental illnesses and handicaps and their social implications.

Some knowledge of employment practices and the skills, abilities, and physical demands of the more common occupations.

Ability to counsel persons who are maladjusted and physically or mentally disabled.

Ability to establish and maintain effective working relationships.

Ability to make clear and pertinent statements orally and in writing.

Appendix L

REHABILITATION ETHICS

A code of ethics is necessary within any organization where professional identity is a requisite. Even though vocational rehabilitation has no formalized code of ethics as of this publication date, an ethics committee was created by the National Rehabilitation Counseling Association. Every individual in rehabilitation should make it his personal as well as professional responsibility to contribute to the fomulation of this highly relevant document.

Appendix L has been included for the trainee's professional library; it should be read and understood before embarking on a career in rehabilitation. If there are sections which seem demanding and unreasonable, one should try to resolve these problems with expediency.

Ethics and Their Implication in Rehabilitation*

One phase of counselor education which is little emphasized in most programs is that of professional ethics in counseling and related activities. For the purposes of this appendix, ethical standards in counseling will be considered as they relate to the rehabilitation process. Many incidents which arise in counseling and which have ethical implications are common to a variety of settings in which counselors practice. Other incidents are peculiar to the mission of the agency, type of clients, nature of problems and information presented by the clients, and the type of decisions which the counselor has to make. Since most beginning counselors will have had a minimum of instruction in ethics as such, it seems extremely important for this topic to be included in any consideration of a supervised field work experience.

---

*This appendix has been adapted from a *Manual for Supervised Clinical Practice in Rehabilitation Counseling*, by C. D. Auvenshine, Bureau of School Services, University of Kentucky, Lexington, December, 1969.

In 1962, McGowan and Schmidt stated the following purposes which a code of ethics serves for the counselor:

1. It provides a position on standards of practice to assist each member of the profession in deciding what he should do when situations of conflict arise in his work.

2. It helps clarify the counselor's responsibilities to the client and protects the client from the counselor's violation of, or his failure to fulfill, these responsibilities.

3. It gives the profession some assurances that the practices of members will not be detrimental to its general functions and purposes.

4. It gives society some guarantee that the services of the counselor will demonstrate a sensible regard for the social codes and moral expectations of the community in which he works.

5. It offers the counselor himself some grounds for safeguarding his own privacy and integrity.

The professional rehabilitation worker whether involved in a field work experience or in his actual work activities should adhere carefully to a code of ethics. The agency and the supervisory personnel should require familiarity with a counselor's code of ethics. Agency philosophy and procedures should be compatible with such a code. Supervisors in rehabilitation settings who have responsibility for supervising counselors should observe the counseling, guidance, and rehabilitation activities carefully to insure that sound ethical practices as well as sound professional practices are being maintained. A written code of ethics will help the new professional not only by providing a set of guidelines which help to insure clientele and society of minimal standards of services but also will help the counselor internalize the ethical standards as part of his professional performance.

There are several categories of situations which have immediate and relevant implications in a supervised field work experience. These include things such as confidentiality of information, making decisions with and about clients, maintaining intellectual honesty and integrity, protecting clients, protecting life and welfare of other people, writing reports, establishing and maintaining working relationship with other professional organizations, and many others. The rehabilitation practitioner is not expected to memorize a long list to do's and don'ts with regard to ethics. Instead the ethical code should serve him in his practice, enabling him to provide services more confidently in those areas where he is trained to function. A code ethics should reduce ambiguity in certain areas where the role of the counselor may be ill-defined or where there is some confusion of priorities of responsibility among client, employer, agency, and society.

One of the most basic ethical considerations which should concern agency personnel is the compatibility between the agency and the counselor with regard to general policies and principles. "The member has a responsibility to the institution within which he serves. His acceptance of employment by the institution implies that he is in substantial agreement with the general policies and principles of the institution. Therefore, his professional activities are also in accord with the objectives of the institution . . ." (Section A, Article 2 of the American Personnel and Guidance Association Ethical Standards, 1961). So in the placement of counselors in supervised field work, the assumption is made that there is consistency of policies and principles between counselor and agency and also that both are in agreement with a counselor's code of ethics.

Another area of concern which has great ethical implications is confidentiality of information. There are two major sources of information with which the counselor has to deal. The first is that of case records which may contain information of a highly personal nature. Rehabilitation services case folders contain medical, psychological, educational, social, and vocational information. The other is content which develops by way of counseling which, in turn, is recorded routinely in the case as progress notes and contact reports. In each case the client has the right to absolute confidentiality of the information contained in his case records. Exceptions to this are (1) administrative and professional consultations which are necessary to the development of the case (2) court orders, and (3) "clear and imminent danger." Information should not be released to parties outside the agency unless requested by the client in writing. Most agencies, both private and governmental, have prepared statements to be signed by the client for obtaining medical and related information from other agencies. This is a rather common and acceptable means of releasing and transmitting records which are highly confidential in nature. The counselor in releasing information from his records should be careful to insure that persons who will be receiving the information are qualified and authorized and that the use to which the information is put is in the best interest of the client. Again this is done only on written consent from the client.

Another set of ethical issues which sometimes confronts the beginning counselor has to do with him making decisions or being requested to make decisions which he is unprepared to make. Frequently, he will not be authorized to make certain kinds of decisions about a client and yet find himself in a position of having to make some decisions. Generally speaking he will not be required to make decisions which he is not authorized to make, and in those instances where he is, he can merely hold up proceedings in the case until such time as he has the appropriate information and authority to act. Usually, the newly employed counselor has a great deal of autonomy in making professional judgments and is encouraged to make them.

Another set of issues focuses on intellectual honesty and professional integrity. The counselor should take care never to seek self-enhancement by derogating fellow professional workers. He should neither present himself dishonestly or claim or imply qualifications he does not have nor develop or continue a counseling relationship ". . . when he cannot be of professional assistance to the counselee or client because of lack of competence or personal limitation. In such instances the member shall refer his counselee or client to an appropriate specialist. In the event the counselee or client declines the suggested referral, the member is not obligated to continue the counseling relationship . . ." (Section B, Article 6, APGA Code). Above all, the beginning counselor should never feel pressured into making a decision or statement which he feels that he does not have the authority or the background to make. It is important to remember that a great deal more courage is needed to admit one's lack of information or the fact that one is unprepared to make a statement at a particular time than to intellectualize or bluff one's way through some situations.

With regard to psychological testing, it is important to note that "Different tests demand different levels of competence for administration, scoring, and interpretation. It is therefore the responsibility of the member to recognize the limits of his competence and to perform only those functions which fall within his preparation and competence" (Section C, Article 4, APGA Code). These are some tests and inventories which are simple to use and which require little or no training. However, others such as individual intelligence tests, performance aptitude tests, and projective techniques require considerably more training in order to get valid and meaningful results. Along these same lines, the counselor should be very familiar with instruments (tests, inventories, scales, etc.) he employs in his professional activities. It is important and particularly so with disabled persons that standardization groups and processes be understood by the examiner. In addition, most instruments have some unique limitations such as inadequate normative data, poor geographic or socioeconomic sampling, or unwarranted assumptions about subjects' backgrounds. These must be noted and considered in using tests with all clients but especially with disabled ones. Inference from test data must be made cautiously and in the context of all available information on the client.

These few topics have been chosen and comments offered on the basis of their apparent relevancy to the counseling process in rehabilitation services. This is not intended in any way to substitute for the official document forthcoming from the Ethical Standards Committee of NRCA.

REFERENCES

American Personnel and Guidance Association Ethical Standards. *Personnel and Guidance Journal*, 40:206-209, 1961.

Anastasi, Anne: *Psychological Testing*, second edition. Macmillian Company, New York, 1966.

A Supplement to the Dictionary of Occupational Titles; Selected Characteristics of Occupations (Physical Demands, Working Conditions, Training Time), third edition. U.S. Dept. of Labor, Washington, D.C., 1966.

Auvenshine, C. D.: *Manual for Supervised Clinical Practice in Rehabilitation Counseling*. Bureau of School Service, University of Kentucky, No. 2, December 1969.

Baker, H. J.: *Introduction to Exceptional Children*. New York, Appleton-Century-Crofts, 1956, pp. 345-351.

Buros, O. K.: *The Fifth Mental Measurements Yearbook*. Gryphon Press, Highland Park, New Jersey, 1959.

Cronbach, L. J.: *Essentials of Psychological Testing*, third edition. Harper & Row, New York, 1970.

Development and Use of Training Materials and Aids in Vocational Rehabilitation. Report No. 1, May 23-27, 1965, Norman, Oklahoma, Rehabilitation Service Series Number 66-40. Department of Health, Education and Welfare, Washington, D.C. Vocational Rehabilitation Administration.

Dictionary of Occupational Titles, Vol. 1, *Definition of Titles*, third edition. U.S. Department of Labor, Washington, D.C., 1965.

Dictionary of Occupational Titles, Vol. II, *Occupational Classification*, third edition. U.S. Department of Labor, Washington, D.C., 1965.

Goodenough, Florence, L.: *Exceptional Children*. New York, Appleton-Century-Crofts, 1956, pp. 345-351.

Hall, J. H., and Warren, S. L. (Eds.): *Rehabilitation Counselor Preparation*. Washington, National Rehabilitation Association and National Vocational Association, 1956.

Joint Liaison Committee: *Studies in Rehabilitation Counselor Training: Gudelines for Supervised Clinical Practice*, Minneapolis, Joint Liaison Committee, 1963.

McGowan, J. F., and Schmidt, L. D.: *Counseling: Readings in Theory and Practice*. New York, Holt, Rinehart and Winston, 1962.

McPhee, W.; Janse, F.; Jorgensen, G. O., and Samuelson, C. O.: Rehabilitation counseling in a dyad. *Journal of Rehabilitation*, Jan-Feb. 1969, Vol. 35, pp. 19-22.

Occupational Outlook Handbook, 1970-71 Edition. Bulletin No. 1650, U.S. Department of Labor, Bureau of Labor Statistics, Washington, D.C.

Pruett, W. A.: Basic assumptions underlying work sample theory. *Journal of Rehabilitation,* Jan-Feb 1970, Vol.36, pp. 24-26.

Rapaport, David: *Diagnostic Psychological Testing,* Vols. I and II. Yearbook Publishers, Chicago, 1950.

Sather, W. S.; Wright, G. N., and Butler, A. J.: *An Instrument for the Measurement of Counselor Orientation, Wisconsin Studies in Vocational Rehabilitation.* Madison, Wisconsin, 1968, p. 13.

The counselor: professional preparation and role: a statement of policy. *Personnel and Guidance Journal,* 42:536-541, 1964.

The professional preparation of rehabilitation counselor: a statement of policy. *Rehabilitation Counseling Bulletin,* 12:29-35, 1968.

Training Guides in Evaluation of Vocational Potential for Vocational Rehabilitation Staff. Rehabilitation Service Series Number 66-23, May 23-27, 1965, Norman, Oklahoma. Department of Health, Education and Welfare, Vocational Rehabilitation Administration, Washington, D.C.

Wechsler, David: *The Measurement and Appraisal of Adult Intelligence,* fourth edition. Williams & Wilkins Company, Baltimore, 1958.